Saving for
Economic Recovery
in Africa

Saving for Economic Recovery in Africa

Edited by

J. H. FRIMPONG-ANSAH
Fellow of the Ghana Academy
Senior Consultant, Standard Chartered Bank, London
formerly Governor of the Bank of Ghana

BARBARA INGHAM
Senior Lecturer in Economics
& Director of the Centre for Development Studies
University of Salford

ACEPOR
African Centre for
Economic Policy Research

in association with

JAMES CURREY
London

HEINEMANN
Portsmouth (N.H.)

African Centre for
Economic Policy Research

in association with

James Currey Ltd
54b Thornhill Square
Islington, London N1 1BE

Heinemann Educational Books Inc.
361 Hanover Street
New Hampshire 03801

British Library Cataloguing in Publication Data

Saving for Economic Recovery in Africa
  I. Frimpong-Ansah, J. H.
  II. Ingham, Barbara
  330.96

ISBN 0-85255-126-6   Paper (James Currey)
ISBN 0-85255-125-8   Cloth (James Currey)

ISBN 0-435-08075-X   Cloth (Heinemann Inc)

Typeset by Opus 43, Cumbria, UK
Printed in Great Britain by Villiers Publications, London N6

Contents

Notes
on Contributors

J.H.Frimpong-Ansah is Executive Secretary, African Capacity Building Foundation, Harare, Senior Consultant of the Standard Chartered Bank, London and Research Associate in the Department of Economics, University of Salford.

Barbara Ingham is Senior Lecturer in the Department of Economics, University of Salford, and Director of the Centre for Development Studies.

Robert Simmons is Lecturer in the Department of Economics, University of Salford.

Asmeron Kidane is Associate Professor of Statistics at the University of Addis Ababa.

S.O. Kwasa is Professor of Economics, Moi University, Kenya.

Germina Ssemogerere is Senior Lecturer in the Department of Economics, Makerere University, Uganda.

C. Chipeta is Professor of Economics in the Department of Economics, Chancellor College, University of Malawi.

M.L.C.Mkandawire is Senior Economist in the Economics Department of the National Bank of Malawi.

Theresa Moyo is Lecturer in the Department of Economics, University of Zimbabwe, Harare.

B.E.Mofunanya is Researcher in the Centre for Development Studies, University of Salford.

Allechi M'Bet is Assistant Professor, Department of Economics, Université National de Côte d'Ivoire.

Rosemary Nana-Fabu is Researcher in the Centre for Development Studies, University of Salford.

Acknowledgements

A number of individuals and institutions assisted the editors in the preparation of this volume. Particular thanks are due to the Rockefeller Foundation, for generously funding the project, and the African Development Bank which sponsored the Symposium at Abidjan. The staff of the Training Centre, Central Projects Department, and the Development Research and Policy Department of the African Development Bank provided the excellent reports of the proceedings of the Abidjan Symposium, which have been utilized in the Preface, and in various sections of the book. The Symposium in Nairobi was jointly sponsored by the Rockefeller Foundation and the Standard Chartered Bank.

In preparation of the final draft, the editors were greatly assisted by comments and suggestions on the various chapters, from Professor Paul Mosely, University of Manchester, Institute for Development Policy and Management, and Professor Colin Kirkpatrick of the University of Bradford, Development and Project Planning Centre. Dr Robert Simmons and Mr Robert Ward of the University of Salford greatly enlarged the scope of the discussions.

Preface

The annual meetings of the African Development Bank provide an opportunity to take stock of important topical economic issues. The theme of the 1988 Symposium, held in Abidjan, Ivory Coast was 'The Mobilization of Domestic Resources for Africa's Economic Recovery'.

It would be difficult to over-estimate the importance of the theme chosen for the Symposium. Income and income per head fell in most African countries throughout the 1980s. Together with climatic changes, poor export prospects and rapidly rising debt, events have generated a sense of crisis. Overcoming these problems is all the more urgent since the level from which income has declined is generally low. It is now widely agreed that Africa's problems are due in some combination to poor initial endowment, unfavourable external circumstances and policy weaknesses. Few would deny, however, that any set of measures to restore and sustain income growth would call for increased capital formation – on the farms, in factories and in the economic and social infrastructure needed, *inter-alia*, to make markets effective. How, the question is, can this be financed?

In an open economy, the requisite savings may come from external capital inflows (which may or may not need to be serviced), from a favourable balance of trade and from a domestic excess of income over consumption. Recent trends in capital inflows have not been encouraging, and weak balance of payments positions have been both the cause and consequence of economic decline. Efforts to increase these inflows and improve the trade balance are now properly being made.

It is to be hoped that these measures will be successful, although it has to be remembered that a substantial proportion of any such success would leak into debt servicing. Much, nevertheless, is likely to depend on domestic saving. This is, of course, related to income so that as income has fallen, not surprisingly, so also has personal and public accumulation. The challenge is to turn this vicious circle into a virtuous one, preferably in the first instance, by enabling saving to rise against the trend of declining income.

The savings-investment-income link is cumulative. An increase in saving, translated into efficient investment, leads to an increase in income. This, in turn, should boost saving and so make possible yet more investment and income growth. This process, however, is not automatic. In the interest of squeezing maximum saving from present income levels, and optimizing income growth through its efficient use, the process of generating savings has to be seen in the context of the whole economy with its particular problems and prospects.

Against this background, the African Development Bank asked Dr J.H.Frimpong-

Ansah, in the light of his interest in economic development and his experience as a central and commercial banker, to prepare a paper which would examine the role of domestic resource mobilization in Africa's economic recovery. This paper, together with the ensuing Discussion at the Abidjan Symposium, is reproduced in Part I of the present volume.

The Discussion at Abidjan was led by the Moderator of the Symposium, Dr Chu P.S.Okongwu, Federal Minister of Finance and Economic Development, Nigeria.

The main discussants were Professor Ali Ahmed Suliman, Dean, Faculty of Economic and Social Studies, University of Khartoum; Dr Denis Kessler, Director, Centre d'Étude et de Recherche, CEREPI, University of Paris; and Dr K.J. Moyana, Governor of the Reserve Bank, Zimbabwe. Invited contributions were also made by: Mr P. Derreumaux, Director-General, Bank of Africa, Mali; Mr Alain Lenoir, General Delegate for Africa, International Centre for Banking Training; Dr A.Mullei, Director-General, African Centre for Monetary Studies, Dakar, Senegal and Mr E.W. Zafu, General Manager, AFRICARE, Nigeria. From the ADB were Mr T. Gedamu, Vice-President, Central Operations; Mr G.R. Aithnard, Director and Mr S.S. Omari, Deputy Director of the Training Centre, and Professor O.Ojo, Principal Economist, Development Research and Policy Department.

The remainder of the present volume is divided into two further sections. Part II extends the scope of the previous section, with two chapters which aim to provide a theoretical and policy background for the case studies in Part III. The case studies in Part III cover aspects of domestic resource mobilization in eight African economies, Ethiopia, Kenya, Uganda, Malawi, Nigeria, Zimbabwe, Côte d'Ivoire and Cameroon. The case-study chapters are based on papers prepared for the Symposium on Domestic Resource Mobilization, sponsored by the Rockefeller Foundation, which was held subsequent to the Abidjan meeting, in Nairobi in August 1988. They provide an opportunity to review recent research into the issue of domestic resource mobilization in Africa and illustrate a variety of approaches to a subject of common interest. Most importantly, they provide the critical research foundation which the African voice in policy-making requires.

In his opening statement to the Abidjan Symposium, the Moderator focused on the economic decline in Africa and the need to reverse this fall in per capita income, to achieve recovery and to initiate sustainable growth. The magnitude of the task would be judged from the African Priority Programme of Action for Africa's Economic Recovery and Development 1986–1990. APPER requires financing to the tune of US$ 128 billion and two-thirds of this has to come from the African States themselves. This is a formidable task for domestic resource mobilization, requiring enormous concentration of efforts on ways and means of achieving increased domestic production, and the formation of relevant and effective policies. The Abidjan and Nairobi Symposia may have pointed the way forward. It is hoped that those who are closely involved in carrying out strategies of domestic resource mobilization will find the various contributions to this volume of value in the decision-making process.

J.H.Frimpong-Ansah
Executive Secretary,
African Capacity Building Foundation

Barbara Ingham
Director, Centre for Development Studies,
University of Salford

Abbreviations

AAF-SAP	African Alternative Framework – Structural Adjustment Programmes
ACEPOR	African Centre for Economic Policy Research
ADB	African Development Bank
AIH	Absolute Income Hypothesis
APPER	African Priority Programme for Economic Recovery
BCEAO	Banque Centrale des États de l'Afrique de l'Ouest
BCC	Bank of Credit and Commerce
BCCZ	Bank of Credit and Commerce Zimbabwe
BEAC	Banque des États de l'Afrique Centrale
BGF	Budget General de Fonctionnement
BIAO	Banque Internationale pour l'Afrique de l'Ouest
BIAOCI	Banque Internationale pour l'Afrique de l'Ouest (Côte d'Ivoire)
BIC	Benefice Industriel et Commercial
BICICI	Banque Internationale pour le Commerce et l'Industrie de Côte d'Ivoire
BNDA	Banque Nationale pour le Développement Agricole de Côte d'Ivoire
BNEC	Banque Nationale pour le Credit
BNP	Banque Nationale de Paris
BSIE	Budget Special d'Investissement et d'Equipement
BVA	Bourse des Valeurs d'Abidjan
CAA	Caisse Autonome d'Amortissement
CABS	Central African Building Society
CCI	Credit de Côte d'Ivoire
CCM	Cooperative de Credit Mutuel
CDB	Cameroon Development Bank
CDC	Cameroon Development Corporation
CFA	Communauté Financière Africaine
CNC	Comité National de Credit
CREP	Caisse Rurale d'Épargne et de Prets
CSSPA	Caisse de Stabilisation et de Soutien des Prix Agricoles
DEMATT	Development of Malawi Traders Trust
DFCR	Domestic Factor Cost Ratio
DMC	Direction de la Mutualité et de la Cooperation
ECA	Economic Commission for Africa
FAO	Food and Agriculture Organization
FF	French Franc
FINCOM	Finance Corporation of Malawi
FNI	Fonds National d'Investissement
FONADER	Fonds National pour le Développement Rural
FRR	Financial Rate of Return
FZ	Franc Zone

IBRD	International Bank for Reconstruction and Development
ITB	Institut Technique de Banque
IDA	International Development Assistance
IFC	International Finance Corporation
IMF	International Monetary Fund
Indebank	Industrial and Development Bank
Indefund	Industrial and Development Fund
K	Kwacha
LDC	Less-Developed Country
LFC	Leasing and Financing Company
N	Naira
NIC	National Investment Corporation
NTB	Non-Tariff Barrier
OAU	Organization for African Unity
OECD	Organization for Economic Cooperation and Development
PEL	Plan Épargne Logement
PMB	Produce Marketing Board
POSB	Post Office Savings Bank
RESGAP	Resource Gap
ROSCA	Rotating Savings and Credit Association
RSS	Rotatory Savings Societies
SAP	Structural Adjustment Programme
SCB	Société Camerounaise de Banque
SEDOM	Small Enterprise Development Organization of Malawi
SFTT	Share of Foreign Trade Tax
SGBCI	Société Generale de Banque en Côte d'Ivoire
SIB	Société Ivoirienne de Banque
SICN	Système Ivoirien de Compatabilité Nationale
SINT	Share of Income Tax
SME	Small and Medium-Sized Enterprises
SMPR	Société Mutuelle de Promotion Rurale
SNDP	Sixth National Development Plan
SONAFI	Société National de Financement
SSA	Sub-Saharan Africa
UCB	Uganda Commercial Bank
UDI	Unilateral Declaration of Independence
UMOA	Union Monetaire Ouest Africaine
UNCTAD	United Nations Conference on Trade and Development
UNICEF	United Nations Children's Fund
UNPAAERD	United Nations Programme of Action for African Economic Recovery and Development
USAID	United States Agency for International Development
Zimbank	Zimbabwe Banking Corporation

1 The Mobilization of Domestic Resources for Africa's Economic Recovery & Development

J. H. Frimpong-Ansah

Introduction: The Special Problems of the African Economy*

This chapter discusses domestic resource mobilization and its links to Africa's economic recovery and development. The chapter is presented in three sections. It first deals briefly with factors explaining the economic development, stagnation and decline in Africa in the post-independence period and discusses the basis for economic recovery, the reversal of past trends and the return to economic growth. The second section, which is the bulk of the chapter, analyses the resources needed to finance economic rehabilitation and the return to the growth path. The emphasis is on domestic resources and their mobilization. This section concentrates on three general characteristics of savings and their trends: the behaviour of the principal savings hypotheses, the principal determinants of savings, and the institutional performance in savings mobilization. The third section deals with the policy implications of the analyses for the African Development Bank and African policy-making generally.

Any attempt to provide a general description of the development problems of the African economy is subject to important constraints. First, there are significant differences in the levels of attained economic development. Some countries are still at the primary stages of development while others are at the threshold of export industrialization in light manufactured goods. Between the two extremes there is a wide spectrum of development. Secondly, there are significant differences in the facilities available for development. Natural resource endowment differs widely. There are also variations in climatic conditions that affect top-soils in the different countries, ranging from desert conditions to tropical rain forests. Thus for some countries adverse natural conditions have imposed severe constraints on attainable development.

Thirdly, African countries have opted for different macro-economic and management policies in the post-independence period that have shaped different paths of economic development. At the time of independence some countries decided in favour of a funda-mental alteration of macro-economic policies that implied trade and exchange restrictions, while others retained currency convertibility and relative free trade. Some opted for aggressive strategies of development that implied the utilization of larger domestic savings

---

*Presented at the 1988 Annual Symposium of the African Development Bank, Abidjan, Cote d'Ivoire, May 1988; and at the Nairobi Symposium on Domestic Resource Mobilization in Africa, August 1988.

and external borrowing for massive capital formation in social infrastructure and industrialization, while others pursued moderate and conservative investment policies focusing on agriculture. In some regions the old monetary unions survived decolonization and enabled greater restraints on fiscal expansion, while in other regions the common currency systems disintegrated, giving way to more expansionary fiscal and monetary policies.

Because differences in trends in economic indicators of domestic resource mobilization sometimes reflect these differing factors, generalizations are avoided except in those cases where common regional policies may be referred to, or where descriptions relate to a significant number of countries.

Some largely exogenous features are common to most African countries. First, Africa is the most balkanized continent in the world. It has a little in excess of 10 per cent of the world's population, but over 30 per cent of the world's countries. This handicap makes national self-reliance in economic development, in terms of modern manufacturing and markets, rather difficult for the majority of countries. Therefore, unless regional economic integration efforts are successful, African countries can have little choice but to pursue outward-looking trade policies in their quest for economic growth.

A second feature, a corollary to the first, is the well-known development problem associated with the effect of the international economy on developing countries generally and on African countries in particular. Since African independence in the early 1960s economic growth in the advanced countries has failed to reach its high post-war levels, thus reducing prospects for primary production, light and simple manufactured exports and, in more recent years, bilateral and multilateral resource flows and private sector financial flows together with their terms and conditions. Indeed, there is a growing fear that excessively outward policies pursued by individual nations, not buttressed by viable regional economic integration, could return African countries to a new and worse form of economic dependency and paternalistic colonialism under the advanced countries acting multilaterally and through their financial institutions.

Specifically, the evidence indicates that the real prices of primary commodities in which Africa has export dominance were at their lowest levels in real terms in the mid-1980s, the lowest since 1940, and that the cumulative losses from real price falls in that period amounted to US$13.5 billion (OAU–ECA, 1986). The evidence also shows that, notwithstanding the benefits of the Lomé Convention and the tariff reductions under the Tokyo Round, non-tariff barriers (NTBs) have generally been increased and most of the increases affect agricultural commodities of interest to African countries. Interest rate policies of the advanced countries have also thwarted the development efforts of both successful and struggling African countries. It has been estimated, for example, that Cote d'Ivoire's present debt burden is 16 per cent higher as a result of international interest rate increases, and Zambia's 11 per cent higher. UNICEF has estimated that there was a negative net real resource transfer to Africa in 1985 of US$ 5.4 billion compared to a positive US$ 8.6 billion in 1978 (UNICEF, 1987).

There are several lessons in economic development that must be learned from these experiences, but two are most important. The first is that greater efficiency in resource management should be given high priority if the negative effects of the above-mentioned handicaps are to be minimized. The second is that well-structured and managed sub-regional and regional economic cooperation at both operational and institutional levels will be beneficial to economic development in individual African countries. The success of the African Development Bank in promoting development in Africa is a useful example of institutionalized regional cooperation.

1. Economic Recovery and Development

A statement of the problem

In this section we analyse, in turn, the factors in economic stagnation and decline, and the factors in economic recovery. In discussing economic stagnation and decline the focus is on four issues: (1) those strategies that affected macro-economic management in the transitional phase to independence, (2) the strategies of industrialization, (3) the approaches to agriculture, particularly its modernization, and (4) the structural economic foundations as they relate to the pace of attempted modernization. When discussing economic recovery, two principal issues are focused upon: (1) the methods of reversing stagnation and decline, which include domestic factors such as economic and monetary stabilization, the rehabilitation of economic infrastructure, the rationalization of productive facilities, social and moral rejuvenation, and relations with the advanced countries, and (2) strategies to return Africa to the economic growth path. All these are major development issues, but here they are treated rather cursorily with the object of indicating the dimension of the problem that faces domestic resource mobilization.

Macro-economic policies in the transition to independence

It has been explained in the introduction that one cannot speak of a common set of African development policies. Where similarities exist within the variety of different patterns, these derive from similar economic history, common pre-independence trade and development policies, common problems of post-independence economic development, and the established economic relationships with some advanced countries dating from the pre-independence period.

Common features of economic history enable some rough classifications to be made of post-independence development policies in Africa. The most significant are the following. First, there were those countries that attempted a sharp break in the macro-economic policies and strategies of the colonial period. Colonial governments had been considered distant from the people and therefore had not undertaken any grassroots development. The need was also felt for aggressively self-reliant domestic development policies to reverse excessive reliance on the international economy. There had been a disproportionate emphasis on agriculture for raw materials; hence the need to shift the balance of investment in favour of local processing. The colonial governments had been rather passive in initiating development; hence there was the need for post-independence governments to be more involved in mobilizing economic and commercial activity for development. The long period of colonial poverty had not enabled the creation of indigenous capital and entrepreneurship for rapid modernization; hence the desirability of state initiative in industrial and business organization.

For the category of countries that decided on a sharp break in macro-economic policies, the development themes fashionable at the time encouraged massive capital formation and import substitution, and generally the formation of development ideologies and organizational structures that have not always proved to be viable. In many such instances, the structural importance of raising agricultural productivity as a condition for economic development *ab initio* (Lewis, 1944) had not been articulated and was either ignored or not understood in terms of viable methods. The empirical evidence indicates that the majority of countries opting for radical modernization at independence have not been as successful as their architects had hoped.

At the other extreme is the second category of countries that avoided a sharp break in macro-economic policies at independence. Some in this category retained the economic and monetary unions of the pre-independence period. Other countries maintained conservative economic policies, some as a result of moderate politics, others under financial constraint. In this category of countries, there is little evidence of fiscal excesses and where balance of payments problems have been encountered they have been largely the result of exogenous factors. This group of countries have not been able to escape from the temptation of import substitution modernization; the only difference is that greater reliance has been placed on direct investment from local and external sources and also that agricultural modernization has not been sacrificed.

Between these two extremes lie a variety of development beliefs. The fact, however, that in the past decade a very large majority of African countries has had to engage in drastic economic and monetary reforms, voluntarily or involunarily, does indicate that there are rather deep-seated problems of economic development that stubbornly resist present under-standing and remedies. Some authorities who have studied Africa in relation to the economies of the Pacific Basin admit that a general understanding of transition growth remains elusive but argue that economic history is an under-utilized tool for analysing contemporary development (Okhawa & Ranis, 1985). Economists now admit that development theories have concentrated on labour-surplus situations and that much work is needed to modify the general methodology, making it useful for the analysis of typologically different situations such as labour-deficit and small countries in Africa.

In the search for appropriate development methodology, one cannot fail to recognize the statement by Arthur Lewis that

> if the effort is not made [to save], either because the desire to economize does not exist or else custom or institutions discourage its expression, then economic growth will not occur (Lewis, 1955: 11)

Though Lewis was fascinated by the labour-surplus economies (Lewis, 1954) and made his best known contribution to development theory in that context, in so far as Africa is concerned, his greater contribution is to be found in his writings in the 1940s which have only now been resurrected (Frimpong-Ansah, 1987b; Ingham, 1987). In one of those early works Lewis states that 'in any programme of economic development, agriculture must come first' (Lewis, 1944). Lewis's focus was on agricultural productivity, modernization of methods of production and organization of agricultural management. His thesis then was that, in economic development *ab initio*, it was increasing agricultural productivity that could release labour and capital productively, generating the markets for the new industrial enterprises.

This prescription places the primary responsibility for development *ab initio* on the operational and institutional viability of savings generation from the agricultural sector, that sector being the only really established sector, however rudimentary, in the pre-industrial state. Taken together with the transition theory (Okhawa & Ranis, 1985) one can hypothesize that there are two stages of transition, each based on increasing productivity, and therefore increasing surpluses and savings, in the preceding sector. The first is from primary agricultural production for export, domestic food and industrial inputs to local manufacturing (without protectionism). The second is from viable manufacturing to export substitution (substituting exports of manufactured goods for agricultural raw materials). By our hypothesis, export-substitution is possible after efficient local manufacturing has provided the productivity, rising incomes and saving to support an export sector in the extremely competitive international markets. This, in turn, is possible only within the context of increasing agricultural productivity. Very few African countries have been able to attain successfully these development transitions but it is difficult to see how successful economic development from the pre-industrial state can follow a different path. The evidence indicates that productivity in all three principal economic sectors is either stagnant or declining in the majority of African countries (Table 1.1). In only four of seventeen countries studied has agricultural productivity been increasing and these also were the countries in which productivity in industry and services has been increasing. Under these conditions, the development transitions cannot be expected in the majority of African countries.

Table 1.1   Average annual rates of growth of per-capita production at constant 1965 prices in 17 African countries 1965–85

	Agriculture	Industry	Services
Positive growth rates:			
More than 5%	–	2	1
2% to 5%	–	3	1
1% to 2%	1	–	1
0% to 1%	3	–	2
Total	4	5	5
Negative growth rates:			
–1% to 0%	4	1	1
–2% to -1%	2	1	1
–5% to -2%	5	7	7
Less than -5%	2	3	3
Total	13	12	12
Total countries	17	17	17

Source: World Development Report (1986)

From this perspective, domestic resource mobilization for Africa's economic recovery and development ought to be conceived in a dynamic sense: within each development phase and between phases, increased savings and productivity are mutually reinforcing. The questions that we should attempt to answer are the following:
1. What have been the trends in domestic savings in recent years? The answer to this question will help us to relate trends in resource mobilization to those in economic growth and to determine the levels of potential that may exist.
2. What are the principal domestic policies and other factors that have affected these trends? The results of this analysis will help us to identify the areas where future policy thrust should concentrate.
3. What is the scope for increasing domestic savings for economic recovery and development? Under this question, the main limitations on financial mobilization are discussed with a view to their improvement and the identification of alternative methods.
4. Finally, questions are raised on the policy implications of these analyses for development banks in Africa and for the African Development Bank.

2. Recent Characteristics in Savings Mobilization

Trends in savings behaviour

The dynamic relationship between domestic savings and productivity is explained by the fact that it is the surplus incomes derived from increased productivity that, under normal conditions, would yield the savings for further investment in production. The higher the rate of increase in productivity, therefore, the greater should be the expectation of more productive investment. The evidence in Table 1.2 shows that between 1965 and 1984, in the sample of 19 low- and middle-income African countries, the number of countries with low savings rates has increased while the number of countries with high savings rates has declined. Table.1.5 also indicates that in that period the average rate of growth in both low- and middle-income countries has correspondingly declined with a clear shift towards lower growth rates.

Table 1.2   Distribution of savings as percentage of GNP in 19 low and middle-income African countries, 1965–84

Savings Rate	Number of Countries		
	1965–72	1973–78	1978–84
Less than 5%	1 (5.2%)	1 (5.3%)	5 (26.3%)
6% – 10%	5 (26.3%)	5 (26.3%)	3 (15.8%)
11% – 15%	5 (26.3%)	2 (10.5%)	5 (26.3%)
16% – 20%	4 (21.1%)	6 (31.6%)	3 (15.8%)
Above 20%	4 (21.1%)	5 (26.3%)	3 (15.8%)
Total	19 (100.0%)	19 (100.0%)	19(100.0%)

Source: World Development Report (1986)

The available detailed comparative analyses of savings patterns in Africa (Umo, 1981; Frimpong-Ansah, 1987a) confirm this general observation of domestic savings deterioration in Africa. There are three aspects of these studies that are relevant to our enquiry. First, both researchers have found that though savings rates have been declining in the post-independence period, the marginal propensity to save, the primary indication of savings behaviour, has remained positive for the majority of countries (Table 1.3). This means that in Africa, as in most parts of the world, people and institutions will save more as their incomes increase, and demonstrates that policies directed towards increasing profitability and incomes in the productive sectors have the best chance of increasing savings and productive investment. Secondly, the studies show that savings capability has changed significantly, in the latter half of the post-independence period. The tendency for generalized dissaving in the immediate post-independence period has eased noticeably. This is largely the result of the reduced rate of capital formation using domestic real financial resources, as such resources dried up. Of the 27 countries that have been studied, in only eight is there still the tendency towards dissaving.

Table 1.3   Some savings characteristics in African countries, 1971–85

		Number of countries	
Marginal propensity to save:	Positive	21	(78%)
	Negative	6	(22%)
	Total	27	(100%)
Potential to save:	Increasing	4	(20%)
	Stagnant	5	(25%)
	Declining	11	(55%)
	Total	20	(100%)

Source: ADB Records, Abidjan

Table 1.4   The changing savings potential in a sample of African countries, 1960–74, 1971–85 (comparisons of income elasticities of savings)

Country	1960–74		1971–85		Change
Algeria	1.04	(Stagnant)	1.28	(Increasing)	+23.1%
Cameroon	1.36	(Increasing)	1.28	(Increasing)	−5.9%
Cote d'Ivoire	1.03	(Stagnant)	0.86	(Declining)	−16.5%
Kenya	1.46	(Increasing)	1.01	(Stagnant)	−30.8%
Libya	2.08	(Increasing)	0.89	(Declining)	−57.2%
Morocco	3.35	(Increasing)	0.80	(Declining)	−76.1%
Nigeria	2.24	(Increasing)	0.90	(Declining)	−59.8%
Tunisia	1.89	(Increasing)	1.01	(Stagnant)	−46.6%

Sources: Umo (1981), Frimpong-Ansah (1987a)

Table 1.5   Distribution of growth rates in 19 low and 10 middle-income African countries, 1965–84

Growth rates	Low-income countries		Middle-income countries	
	1965–72	1973–84	1965–72	1973–84
1	2	3	4	5
Less than 1%	2	4	–	3
1%-3%	4	5	2	2
3%-5%	8	7	2	3
5%-7%	4	3	2	1
Above 7%	1	–	4	1
	19	19	10	10

Source: World Bank World Development Report, 1986

The third observation, and perhaps the most crucial for determining the limitation on resource mobilization for economic recovery and development, is that the potential to save has declined significantly in the majority of African countries in the period since the early 1970s. The analysis for the period before 1972 shows that there was potential to save (Umo, 1981). On the other hand, in the more recent study covering the period 1971 to 1985, the conclusion is that in the majority of African countries, the marginal propensity to save has been well below the average propensity to save, indicating that the propensity to save earlier observed by Umo has withered since the early 1970s (Frimpong-Ansah, 1987a). In the 20 countries surveyed, the potential to save has been stagnant in five cases and has declined in 11 cases; thus in 80 per cent of the sample the trend has been unfavourable (Table 1.3).

This analysis points to certain conclusions, and to certain questions that must be answered if the present declining savings-production trend is to be reversed. One explanation for the failure of saving to grow in the early post-independence phase when capital formation increased is the failure of most African economies to respond productively and adequately to development spending. The answer is to be found partly in the unavoidable concentration of development spending in social infrastructure such as health and education which do not yield goods in the immediate term. The answer is also to be found partly in the lack of adequate organization of the productive facilities to enable them to respond fully to the stimulus provided by either policy changes or financial injection. These problems suggest that there is a limitation on the pace at which development can occur from the pre-industrial state and also that a limitation may exist on the ability of public policy and public resources to effect the initial transition. These are questions which research in development economics has yet to address adequately. For example, is there a limit on the reliance which can be placed on financial resources as a means of promoting development in Africa and, consequently, is there a limit on the use of taxation to finance development?

The next major conclusion to be drawn from the analysis of the trends in savings behaviour is that it is unrealistic to expect a dramatic change in the present conditions of declining potential in the majority of African countries. What must come first is the discovery of methods to halt the stagnation and decline in production. Here the tasks to be accorded priority are the identification, in the respective economies, of those sectors and enterprises that have the capability to contribute most to production and to savings, and the public policies that would stimulate them towards optimum productivity.

The third significant conclusion is that for several years to come, and given the prolonged economic stagnation and decline in the majority of African countries, the processes of economic recovery and development will continue to depend on external financial and technical resources. Here special care is needed to distinguish between external resources that facilitate production and savings and those that discourage them. In the initial period of economic recovery, external resources are needed to stabilize exchange rates and to implement viable fiscal and monetary regimes. In the period of restructuring, long-term concessional resources are needed to rehabilitate productive facilities and economic infrastructure. Then, in support of these programmes, short-term commercial bank resources are needed to re-establish domestic and international credibility in the flow of essential trade. Domestic resource mobilization should therefore be conceived at two levels: the mobilization of domestically generated foreign exchange to supplement external resources, and the mobilization of domestic currency savings as the counterpart to external resources in the process of economic recovery and development.

The final conclusion from our analysis is that, for a discussion on the mobilization of domestic resources to be useful, it must focus on the identification and analysis of the principal determinants of resource mobilization and the state of the institutional mechanisms for mobilization. A discussion along these lines helps to specify those areas of public policy that require to be emphasized.

Determinants of Savings

Most research on this subject relating to Africa has concentrated on the conventional determinants of savings, such as international trade, external capital inflow, interest rates, taxation, price levels, demography and the effect of the international economy. This chapter not only adopts a similar approach, taking into account the results of recent research, but also draws attention to two determinants particularly relevant to the African condition and both occurring in the process of modernization, namely, changing domestic economic conditions and urban–rural population shifts.

Recent research has shown that the range of determinants that are significant to savings in Africa is rather limited. Exports and taxation have been shown to be the most significant. Total export values have been shown to correlate positively with savings but exports in Africa are still dominated by primary production in the agricultural and mineral sectors and the markets for these products are rather sensitive to the conditions in the international economy. The fact that exports overshadow all other determinants of savings therefore imposes a major limitation on savings mobilization in Africa. It manifests both the adverse effects of the lack of diversification in the sources of savings and the excessive influence of the exogenous trends in the international economy on the savings and investment patterns in Africa. It is thus logical to strive for diversification (Lagos Plan of Action), but because of the failure of development to make a viable transition from primary exports in most African countries, the primary export sector will continue to exert a major influence on incomes and savings and will therefore have to be kept at the centre of public policy in any programmes of savings mobilization for economic recovery and development.

The effect of *taxation* in Africa has been shown to be mixed in recent studies on the subject. In a study conducted at the ADB into the effect of taxation in 12 countries, it was found that in five countries taxation had no effect on savings; in four others the effect was negatively significant; in the remaining three the effect was positively significant (ADB, 1987). There is also considerable disagreement in the economic literature on the value of taxation to domestic resource mobilization. Some who support the idea of state intervention in the savings process through taxation argue, in the Keynesian fashion, that the state should act counter-cyclically to maintain long-term equilibrium in the flow of financial resources. Others who support taxation argue that until the formal savings habit has evolved fully, governments should use taxation and other involuntary techniques to mobilize financial resources for development. Some who oppose the idea of taxation for savings mobilization have questioned the ability and the means of governments to influence fundamentally a major economic variable such as savings and have argued that increases in public sector savings will ultimately result in decreases in private sector savings and consequently in productive investment. Others have argued that as governments cannot resist the socio-political pressures to spend, the marginal propensity of governments to spend will remain high and disqualify them as agents for savings mobilization.

The empirical studies that have been undertaken on African countries (Bhatia, 1967; Umo, 1981; Frimpong-Ansah, 1987a) have come up with three general results: (1) that only in a minority of countries in Africa have increases in public sector savings resulted in increases in total domestic savings, but that, notwithstanding this fact, public sector mobilization is next in importance only to exports; (2) that taxation has tended to reduce household consumption and in that sense increase public sector mobilization. Nonetheless, public sector saving has failed to increase and is in fact, in most cases, in an inverse ratio with mobilization; (3) that the larger transfers of financial savings to governments have been achieved at the expense of the few vital productive sectors of the African economy, some of which have declined seriously as a consequence. The African experience would therefore generally support the school of thought that argues against the use of taxation for savings mobilization.

Table 1.6   Marginal tax rates in 13 African countries, 1971–84 ratios

Country	Taxes on incomes	Taxes on consumption	Taxes on international trade
1	2	3	4
Cameroon	.15	.05	.13
Egypt	.07	.08	.15
Ethiopia	.05	.05	.32
Ghana	.01	.02	.21
Kenya	.06	.15	.13
Malawi	.07	.11	.13
Morocco	.04	.14	.13
Mauritius	.01	.06	.17
Senegal	.04	.07	.09
Sudan	.01	.04	.33
Tanzania	.05	.11	.10
Zaire	.06	.08	.16
Zambia	.03	.16	.04

Source: Frimpong-Ansah (1987a)

Ironically, taxation could be one of the easier ways of domestic resource mobilization in Africa. In Table 1.6. the marginal tax rates in a sample of 13 African countries show that the area where taxes are centred is international trade. Taxes on consumption and on incomes are low compared to other regions of the world. The higher taxation on international trade has historical origins in the colonial period; this is the area in which the collection of taxes is easiest to organize. Taxation on incomes is the lowest, reflecting the difficulties of assessment and of collection in the largely non-commercialized and non-monetized African economy. Taxes on consumption, reflecting excises and retail sales taxes, are not as developed as in other areas of the world.

Table 1.7   Tax base elasticities in 13 African countries, 1972–84

Country	Taxes on incomes	Taxes on consumption	Taxes on international trade
1	2	3	4
Cameroon	2.09	1.04	.83
Egypt	1.59	1.07	.68
Ethiopia	1.67	1.34	1.47
Ghana	.76	.76	1.06
Kenya	1.02	1.33	1.50
Malawi	1.20	1.49	1.93
Morocco	1.04	1.13	1.27
Mauritius	.28	.97	1.45
Senegal	1.04	1.18	.79
Sudan	.78	.72	1.21
Tanzania	1.07	1.21	1.14
Zaire	1.03	1.15	.99
Zambia	.38	.99	1.25

Source: Frimpong-Ansah (1987a)

To assess the potential for additional taxation we should consult Table 1.7 which provides analytical results for the same sample of 13 countries. The high elasticities (greater than unity) indicate, for the large majority of countries in the sample, that the potential for higher taxation may exist in all three categories of taxes. In the case of taxes on incomes and on consumption only the same four countries exhibit negative potential. In the case of international trade taxes, four other countries have low to negative potential. The conclusion that may be drawn from these analyses is that public policy must find a method of employing publicly mobilized saving for more productive use.

Interest rates have been examined rather more exhaustively than any other determinant for their effect on savings, largely because the interest rate is a price and one would expect the holding of money to be related to its price. However, the results of these examinations are the least convincing. Some results have been mixed (Umo, 1981); some have found only a weak relationship; and others, comparing both nominal and real interest rates with savings, have found a negative relationship in the majority of countries (ADB, 1987).

A number of explanations have been suggested of which the principal one is the imperfect nature of the capital markets in Africa. Another important idea is that the exclusion of informal interest rates leads to imperfect specification of the interest rate variable. It has also been suggested that in most low-income societies it is consumption that is the residual rather than savings because most people save for specific long-term objectives and are therefore less concerned with interest rates except in situations of high inflation.

Some of these arguments have been used extensively in Africa in the past, in situations where it had been thought that market-related interest rates would tend to fuel inflation. But as attitudes change with the introduction of monetary stabilization measures, some new arguments have emerged as to why interest rates must be given an important role in monetary policy generally, and in domestic resource mobilization particularly:

1. If a major drive for savings in Africa is to make sense, then there must be an appropriate reward for both savers and for those institutions which will bear the cost of mobilization;
2. Because of their disuse in policy formulation for several years, it is reasonable to argue that interest rates have lost their significance as an economic price and that therefore the interest rate instrument can be tested scientifically for its efficiency after it has been raised to its market level for a long enough period. In some countries where the interest rate has been high in recent years, most borrowers and savers have already become sensitive to marginal changes in its value.

Studies on *inflation* and savings in Africa have often produced unexpected results. It is reasonable to expect money savings to fall with inflation as people shift their resources into real assets to escape the loss of money value. In Africa, the results of the most recent cross-country study (ADB/ECA, 1987) have shown that savings have increased with inflation. Several explanations have been offered for this peculiar behavioural characteristic. Inflation in Africa is usually associated with economic restrictions and hence an expansion of informal market activities. In those circumstances people tend to hold on to more financial assets for transaction purposes and also for personal security and tax reasons. The phenomenon is also explained by the lack of alternative forms of holding increasing nominal financial assets: the property market is yet to develop.

As a corollary to these observations, one should expect reductions in both public sector and private sector real savings in a period of economic and monetary stabilization aimed at bringing an inflationary situation under control, while savings should respond more favourably to stable price trends, but unfortunately the latter condition has not been experienced in Africa to any degree that would make an empirical analysis meaningful.

The core argument in support of *external capital inflow*, which nevertheless had escaped rigorous testing until the mid 1960s, was that domestic saving would be maintained at its maximum capacity and therefore external capital would fill an essential gap and become a catalyst for economic growth. The recent literature has reviewed this assumption and has shown that under certain conditions external capital has induced less rigorous fiscal policies, reduced public sector savings and often altered the structure of production to the detriment of indigenous initiatives, production and savings. All these would tend to disturb the proper balance of economic growth.

The most recent study on this subject tested the relationship between domestic savings and external capital inflow in 12 African countries for the period between 1963 and 1984 (Frimpong-Ansah, 1987a). For five countries the results showed that there was no significant relationship. In three, external capital positively influenced domestic savings. In the remaining four the relationship was negative. These results are, of course, subject to the accuracy of the sample and the econometric specification, but the fact that in only 25 per cent of the sample was there a clear positive influence denotes that foreign capital inflow should be treated with considerable care. Further analysis resulted in the conclusion that foreign capital inflow becomes more supportive of domestic savings (1) if less restricted in its use and more competitive with indigenous capital; (2) if the economic conditions in the host country are more stable; and (3) if capital inflows are targeted specifically towards the repair of identified productive facilities, especially in periods of economic restructuring and rehabilitation. These are conditions which make external capital compatible with Africa's efforts at economic recovery at the present time.

Now we can return to those determinants that are of particular interest to Africa, namely changes in economic conditions and changes in the structure of populations as related to urbanization. Recent analysis has shown that changes in *economic conditions* can change significantly the relative weights of the factors that influence domestic savings. In Côte d'Ivoire the economic instability caused by the fall in the prices of primary exports since 1976 fundamentally altered the relative importance of the key variables and rendered the well-developed export sector an unstable factor in savings. For Nigeria a trend line to fit the whole period 1963–84 had less significance than those for the shorter periods before and after 1973, when the first oil price increase occurred. In Ethiopia a similar experience occurred after 1974 with the export sector and incomes losing importance to foreign capital inflows. For all three countries the long-term trends overlapping periods of major economic change produced a far less useful guide to the interpretation of the factors in savings than shorter-term analyses that distinguished between the periods. Thus, whether changes in macro-economic policies are induced endogenously or exogenously, they all have considerable influence on savings behaviour. This also indicates that stable long-term policies enable better identification and consolidation of those factors that most favourably affect savings.

It is not difficult to conceptualize the many ways in which stable economic and monetary conditions can assist the accumulation of savings.

1. Economic growth, development transitions and the consequent increases in incomes, are more orderly, even and better assured; accordingly, so are increases in savings, as has been illustrated by our analysis of savings behaviour in Africa.
2. There is greater monetary stability and hence greater exchange rate stability and currency convertibility. This significantly reduces speculative currency hoardings overseas, otherwise a great drain on national development.
3. Prices, as well as interest rates, move closer to their relative margins of advantage and enable financial intermediation in savings mobilization to be more cost-effective.
4. Economic stability also provides an atmosphere of political and social stability in which individuals and enterprises retain maximum confidence in their country and are more willing to develop their individual and corporate wealth to the benefit of their country.

Changes in the structure of populations and *shifts in population between rural and urban areas* exert some influence on the accumulation of domestic savings. In the post-independence period in Africa there have been rapid changes in these demographic factors due to accelerated modernization. A considerable amount of research has been done in other parts of the world, but very little in Africa, on the effect of these rapid changes on savings. The areas in which such work may concentrate include the links between the size of households and savings; the effects of youth employment and the extended working life of African populations; the effects of urbanization against the background of rural versus urban labour productivity; and the effects of the declining welfare of rural populations on savings.

As the larger percentage of savings in Africa continues to be generated from the rural sectors, studies that reflect the relative levels and patterns of consumption and savings in the respective sectors will remain important indicators of optimum targets for development policy. At the moment, accurate ratios for the movement and utilization of savings between the rural and urban sectors are hard to come by.

From the above analysis a number of *conclusions* can be drawn as to the key factors in the mobilization of savings in Africa. Only one positive determinant of savings can be identified – exports. Taxation is generally significant but negative. The effects of the remaining factors are, on a continent-wide basis, negligible. But exports, in their present form, are rather too susceptible to exogenous international conditions, and cannot be reliable until well diversified. Economic advancement to the stage of manufactured export substitution must be made before some measure of stability can be expected. This is a major dilemma for which immediate solutions are not easily available.

The greater chance for savings mobilization lies with the conversion of the negative significance of taxation to a positive one, and the implications are to be found in the following questions that are addressed in the concluding section:

1. In the effort to increase expenditures on social and economic infrastructure, governments have had to rely on the taxation of the agricultural sectors where the bulk of incomes are generated. This strategy seemed logical, but what are the appropriate tax strategies that can best preserve the agricultural foundations of the African economy and yet ensure optimum mobilization of national savings for modernization and industrialization?

2. Most governments have indirectly attempted to increase public savings through the ownership of commercial enterprises. In what ways do the experiences in these efforts help to enlarge total domestic savings?

3. An examination of the tax base of most countries reveals that there has been a major shift from external trade to domestic transactions. This is largely due to import compression as exports collapsed and informal parallel markets and consumption expenditures grew. The question that faces policy-makers is how tax policies can be improved to cope with increasing ratios of domestic private consumption?

4. Lastly, if taxation should be made a positive tool for savings mobilization, how can government consumption propensities be curbed?

On external capital inflow, the empirical evidence has pointed largely to negative or negligible benefits. Yet it has been shown that there are situations, especially during periods of economic recovery, when external capital inflows have become an important necessity. What are the ways in which external capital can be turned into a positive influence on domestic saving under conditions other than economic restructuring? Are there types of external capital inflow that are more beneficial to savings and development than others? Are there conditions that must be preferred and others that must be avoided? These and similar questions pertaining to the other determinants are the subject of the third section of this chapter. But before coming to that section it would be useful to discuss the role that financial intermediation can play in mobilization.

Financial intermediation for resource mobilization

Africa, like other regions of the world, has over the years evolved several of the traditional forms of financial intermediation. In earlier days postal savings banks were the most prominent. In more recent times it is commercial banks that have demonstrated a better ability to grow. Other important formal institutions include insurance companies and stock exchanges. In the less formal sectors the most common forms of financial intermediation are savings societies and clubs of various descriptions that have become very widespread in all African countries.

Whether or not the formal financial institutions are able to perform an optimum role in savings mobilization can be assessed in a number of ways. A study of the ratio of the deposits they collect to money supply helps to determine how deep or shallow are their operations; the ratio of deposits to the Gross Domestic Product (GDP) helps to determine the stage of development of financial institutions; estimates of real money stock illustrate the real lending capacity of banks; the ratio of their financial assets to the GDP helps to assess the real capacity of the financial sector to grow; the index of institutional density measures the intermediary role of financial institutions; the levels of real interest rates measure the optimality of the role of financial institutions; and the elasticity of demand for money with respect to the rate of inflation assists us to determine whether the financial system is buoyant or repressed. It is useful to know that all these indicators have been measured for various African countries in recent years and the literature has recently been surveyed (Frimpong-Ansah, 1987c). Here we need only list the results.

The studies on the depth of the operations of formal financial institutions have shown that in the majority of countries there is an unmistakable shallowness and that formal financial institutions in Africa are in a rather rudimentary stage of development compared with their counterparts in other parts of the world. Studies on the capability of the formal financial sector to grow have also yielded rather negative results. The formal financial sectors of the African economy have not been able to keep pace with even the slow growth of their economies. In several cases where economies have stagnated or declined, the formal financial sectors have declined even more rapidly. The results of these two major indicators show that the formal financial sectors as at present structured have a rather limited influence on the growth of the African economy. The studies on the intermediary capacity of formal financial institutions have shown rather low densities in all the African countries that have been assessed. The studies have revealed, in particular, problems of commercial viability, financial integrity and resource distribution, and have indicated that formal institutions are unable to penetrate the countryside at a pace faster than the rate of commercialization of the non-urban sectors of the African economy. Likewise, sub-optimal conditions have been much in evidence in most African countries. These are illustrated by the predominance of negative real interest rates for protracted periods. Thus the cost and revenue structures of most formal financial institutions have not been viable for optimal levels of operation or for the mobilization of deposits at maximum levels. Further evidence of financial repression has been assessed from the tendency of informal markets to expand under inflationary conditions and of formal capital markets to contract correspondingly, and from the reluctance of banks to accept deposits during periods of high inflation.

This analysis paints a rather grim picture for formal financial intermediation in Africa, and therefore questions should be raised as to why these conditions prevail and how they can be overcome. Why have commercial banks failed to make the desired impact on resource mobilization? Why have postal savings banks remained backward? Why have building societies failed to take root in African society? Why have the attempts to develop stock exchanges in Africa been largely unsuccessful? What have been the factors inhibiting the integration of savings societies and clubs into the formal financial system? These are large issues that require extensive study and discussion. The discussion that follows merely provides the framework for such detailed work. Commercial banks cannot claim that they are not attractive to depositors. Recent surveys place them highest in the preferred list (for example, Chipeta *et al*., 1986). All large organizations save with them. Though most small savers are not able to borrow from them they nevertheless prefer them for security of deposit, ease of withdrawal and their relative nearness to their places of business. Notwithstanding these attractions, commercial bank intermediation in financial resource mobilization is constrained by several factors.

1. Commercial banks, as at present structured, are urban commercial institutions and relate only marginally to the bulk of small households and their businesses that dominate the African economy. Where they have voluntarily or otherwise branched into non-urban areas, they are merely smaller versions of city banks and are culturally out of tune with local conditions and customs. This characteristic of banks derives from the history of their introduction to Africa in pursuit of international trade.
2. Where urban banks have seriously attempted to penetrate the non-urban market their operation has been skewed, tending to divert rural resources to the more commercialized but less productive urban areas.

3. State banking initiatives, and state direction to take banking to the bulk of the population, has not succeeded because the basic traditions and methods have not changed. Rather, in many cases, considerable losses were incurred, and many such banks are now retreating into larger urban and multinational operations.

The links that the postal savings banks have with postal systems have been beneficial in providing security and nearness to the population. That association has not facilitated the modernization that is needed, however. There are financial and accounting rigidities that make them uncompetitive against commercial banks. They also lack lending facilities. Most studies have estimated that less than 20 per cent of small savers and small businesses deal with the postal savings banks, but it is reckoned that the postal banks, if they could be modernized, could become a major vehicle for savings mobilization.

Building societies should be attractive because of the combination they offer of easy withdrawals, security and home loans. Building societies have been stunted, however, by the underdeveloped nature of the housing market in Africa. There, buildings do not change hands as fast as in other regions of the world; savings mobilization through the instrument of building societies should not be expected to grow significantly in the immediate future.

The principal reason why savings clubs and societies have remained in their relatively underdeveloped state is that, in Africa, it often takes some courage for public policy to recognize and modernize indigenous institutions. Borrowed traditions have somehow convinced most professional bankers to regard saving clubs and societies as primitive. There are very few exceptions: in Zimbabwe, for example, the state-promoted Savings Development Movement has, since 1983, brought together over 5000 savings clubs and centralized their needs for agricultural supplies and marketing. This effort has linked savings with production and dynamically expanded both. In other African countries, however, the results of fieldwork indicate that the saving clubs and societies have resented state intervention when it undermines confidentiality and raises problems of arbitrary taxation.

Like commercial banks, stock exchanges are urban-oriented institutions for capital mobilization. The objectives of stock exchanges in Africa, as in other regions, are to diversify financial instruments and thereby to facilitate changes in the pattern of savings; to provide more opportunities for productive investment for a wider range of savers; to provide greater marketability and turnover in the instruments of savings; and to attract non-indigenous savers into domestic productive investments. To achieve these results a number of pre-conditions are needed:

1. Successful local companies must be willing to be quoted on the markets and to accept a wide range of indigenous investors. Most successful companies have not shown this enthusiasm.
2. There should be a high degree of speculative turnover in shares and a high stock to bonds ratio. The reverse has been the case in Africa. The bond market has been much larger, has absorbed most of the resources, has given to the stock exchanges the undesirable character of a market dominated by long-term instruments, and created risk aversion in the markets with the incorrect perception that share prices must maintain their prices as bonds.
3. There must exist a well-functioning secondary market to support issues by guaranteeing minimum purchases. The attempts that have been made in this direction (in Côte d'Ivoire and Nigeria, for example) have failed to create enough technical sophistication by institutional investors prepared to intervene to support new issues or to moderate fluctuations in share prices. These experiences show that even in their urban environment the few stock exchanges that have been created have a long way to go before they can make a significant impact on savings mobilization.

From the evidence that is available, it is in the field of insurance that the greatest potential may exist for savings mobilization in both urban and rural areas. The potential lies in the rapid development of actuarial knowledge of African life that has reduced past inhibitions, in increasing literacy, in the greater intensity of energy use (and increased fire risk) linked with modern technology, and in better marketing among indigenous populations. Of significance, too, has been the continuing role of social security contributions.

The generally underdeveloped state of financial intermediation in resource mobilization raises important policy issues. If formal financial institutions, as at present structured, are better suited for urban operations, should they be encouraged to confine their role to that economic sector so that public policy can concentrate greater attention on finding alternative methods of financial intermediation in the non-urban areas? If the answer is yes, then what kind of financial institutions should be promoted in the non-urban areas, and in what ways can the expertise and resources of existing institutions be made more supportive of such efforts? Are there any instructive experiences to draw on, in Africa or in other parts of the world? If the answer is no, then in what ways can financial institutions, particularly commercial banking, be restructured – or new appropriate mechanisms created – to mobilize resources successfully in non-urban areas?

3. Policy Implications

In the previous two sections some conclusions were reached on the basis of our analyses, and a number of questions and issues were raised. In this concluding section, ideas on the policy implications which flow from responses to these questions and issues are invited rather than offered. This approach is intended to facilitate a fruitful exchange of ideas.

Economic development from the pre-industrial state

Two principal conclusions have been reached in this chapter on the problems of economic development from the pre-industrial state. First, that there is a process of transition from primary agriculture through import substitution to export substitution, and that the maintenance of increasing productivity in all the phases is essential for economic growth. Second, that most African countries appear to have been unable to maintain agricultural productivity during the transition from the first phase and therefore the transition to the high development phases has been difficult. The implications for saving mobilization as it relates to economic development are (1) that in the conditions of low and stagnant productivity in the primary sectors of most African economies, the optimum mobilization of financial resources has not been possible; and (2) that a lopsided approach to mobilization is implied by the greater concentration of effort on the less successful urban industrial sectors. This has diminished the productive capacity of the primary sectors even further.

If we accept that failure to grow at the desired pace, and in some cases stagnation and decline, are due principally to the impact of wider economic distortion on the primary agricultural sectors, then the problem of resource mobilization revolves around methods of mobilizing the allocation of resources so that the engine of development can be ignited where it would most easily respond. The area of discussion is, therefore, whether or not it is viable to restructure development strategies by focusing principally on the agricultural sector and shifting resources to that sector. Some would argue against such a strategy, given the social and political conditions that exist. Perhaps a more acceptable approach is to mobilize and redistribute resources in a manner that does not discriminate between agriculture and industrialization but seeks to facilitate and rationalize the existing agricultural and industrial investments to bring both to their highest possible productivity. Though this school of thought would favour a curtailment of the present trend of resource drain from the rural sectors, it would not support transfers of resources to the agricultural sectors in excess of those enabled through normal monetary adjustments, such as high producer prices resulting from appropriate exchange rate devaluations.

The policy implication for domestic resource mobilization which requires to be discussed is whether or not to accept current mainstream thinking that financial resources should be mobilized from surplus sectors to deficit sectors, the underlying assumption being that the demand for financial resources would ultimately determine the more productive use of such resources. There is a major difficulty with this line of reasoning: generally a surplus sector would indicate a sector that has attained high productivity and a deficit sector one which is rising on the productive ladder through increasing efficiency. It is under this condition that productivity is maximized and debts are repayable. In most of Africa the sectors that yield surpluses are by no means optimum producers, nor are the deficit sectors in a state of rising productivity. There is, rather, a lack of opportunities to employ resources in the rural areas and a corresponding surfeit of opportunities to dissipate resources in the urban areas. Thus the evidence exists that large amounts of urban bank lendings are non-performing.

There is, on the other hand, the more radical school which insists that rationalization of the non-agricultural sectors ultimately is impossible without major repairs to the agricultural sector. Those who hold this view advocate a planned shift of larger financial resources to agriculture to rebuild higher levels of productivity, at the expense of other sectors. This argument follows the principle of transition development and insists that larger resources should go to develop sectors that have demonstrated the potential for higher productivity. The implication for resource mobilization is that the formalization of resource mobilization should, as much as possible, take place within the so-called informal sectors and not outside them. In other words, there should be policies that aim at larger generation of incomes in the primary sectors than at present, that retain larger amounts there than at present, and that seek to commercialize those sectors at a faster pace that has hitherto been achieved.

The choice between the two approaches would, of course, differ in the different countries and would be determined by the state of decay of the primary agricultural sectors, the degree of success that has been achieved in the processes of transition through the development phases, and the social and political conditions that prevail.

Trends and strategies in resource mobilization

In our analyses of trends in resource mobilization a number of conclusions were reached, on the basis of which certain policy implications may be advanced.

Firstly, in Africa as in other regions of the world, people and their institutions will increase their rate of saving as their incomes increase. Studies indicate that declining saving is the result of declining per-capita real income rather than a disinclination to save. Therefore if economies were to return to increasing prosperity, the negative trend in the propensity to save would be reversed. What is, therefore, important in savings mobilization is not only the superficial public encouragement to save more, but public policies that would stabilize economies, increase productivity and enlarge per-capita real incomes.

Secondly, in discussing the principal factors that affect the levels of savings, it was observed that only two had any real significance, namely exports and taxation. Of the two, only the export factor has a positive influence. Taxation effects were mixed but largely negative. The impact of all other determinants was negligible or negative. This included interest rates and external capital inflows. There are important implications from these findings that public policy should address. First, the dilemma of primary export sensitivity argues a strong case for diversification and for secondary processing. There exist, however, tariff and non-tariff barriers against such products, particularly in non-EC advanced country markets. Thus if some successes are to be expected, African countries should be prepared to participate more actively in the current phase of trade negotiations. At the production level, greater efficiency is necessary to become competitive in international markets. Furthermore, public policy must recognize that until appropriate diversification, secondary processing and export substitution have been achieved, Africa's development will have to depend significantly on her disadvantaged primary export industry.

The second set of policy implications concerns the other important determinants of resource mobilization, namely, taxation, interest rates and external capital. Theories of taxation distinguish between different objectives. One objective is to levy taxes to the level where the real GDP is maximized, given the current structure of production. At this level of taxation the state involves itself only in basic services such as law and order, defence, administration, and the maintenance of basic infrastructure that facilitate production at a level higher than would have been possible without such centralized services. A second objective of taxation is more dynamic. The economic case for taxation beyond the optimalization of production in any given static situation, is that the process shifts the production curve to a higher level through the utilization of such savings for more efficient production, and thereby promotes economic growth. The economic viability of taxation, at both levels, is a function of the efficiency with which government revenues from taxation are administered. Some governments are convinced that taxation for development purposes cannot be efficient and minimize this form of mobilization. They allow the private sector to take most of the development initiatives. Others take a different view and tend to emphasize state initiatives. Whichever approach is adopted, taxation can become a positive determinant of savings mobilization only if such taxation does not damage production incentives, and if the revenues that accrue to governments are used solely to facilitate further production by those sectors of the economy best able to provide it.

It has been argued in this chapter that interest rates should be fixed at levels high enough to provide ample reward for both financial intermediaries and savers. For the interest rate determinant to become a positive factor in resource mobilization, present policies in most African countries to raise interest rates to their market levels should be maintained for extended periods. The ability of governments to sustain market-related interest rates for long periods will depend upon the success of current monetary stabilization policies. These, in turn, depend upon the rate at which the productive facilities in African countries respond to the current stablization and restructuring programmes. Hence it is the viability of the total package of economic measures that is of greater relevance in policy formulation concerning interest rates.

The negative and insignificant relationship between external capital inflow and domestic savings in the majority of African countries has been explained in this chapter in a number of ways. Principally, external capital will be supportive of domestic savings if the latter are mobilized at the optimum so that the former becomes a catalyst. Policies to make external capital become a positive contributor to domestic savings are therefore all those that have been discussed in the above paragraphs. However, it has been shown in the chapter that in the current period of economic stabilization and rehabilitation in most countries, when infrastructure and productive facilities are not able to operate at full capacity, maximum productivity, and therefore maximum domestic savings, will not be possible without considerable external capital inflows specifically aimed at economic rehabilitation. Public policy in support of a positive link between external capital and domestic resource mobilization is therefore to be seen in two principal ways: firstly, in the identification of economic sectors that would be most responsive to rehabilitation; and, secondly, in the restructuring of institutions that handle the use of external resources so that such resources could be most efficiently employed.

Financial intermediation

Some relevant policy questions on financial intermediation have been posed in this chapter. On the question of whether, given their inflexible structures, their underdeveloped nature, and the generally depressed and fragmented state of the financial sectors of the African economy, the present formal financial institutions can be depended upon to undertake the wider role of financial intermediation for savings mobilization, the evidence does not indicate an affirmative answer. A logical approach, it would seem, is to allow and encourage the present financial institutions to continue with whatever efforts they can make, but for public policy to consider seriously other approaches that are better suited culturally to the African environment. In coping with fragmentation, a possible approach is to consider institutions particularly suited to the disadvantaged sectors. In other parts of the world, for example in the Far East, the Philippines and India, small-scale independent rural banks have been relied upon extensively to overcome fragmention. In some countries in Africa – in Ghana, for example – that approach has indicated some promise of success.

In dealing with the existing forms of commercial banking, consideration may be given to the promotion of regional and provincial or district banks as a way of decentralizing decision-making and providing greater cultural identification. In some very large countries in Africa (Nigeria, for example) this process has already begun and some benefit may be gained from studying their experience. Another possible focus for public policy is the modernization of the postal savings system, giving due consideration to some degree of autonomy.

The modernization of savings clubs and associations appears to be a priority. Here the desired goal should be official recognition and facilities for their organization, such as registration and integration into the consultation and decision-making processes. The experience in Zimbabwe demonstrates well the potential role of savings clubs and societies.

On the specific role of development banks in domestic resource mobilization, the question is whether development banks can promote savings by mobilizing some of the 'excess' liquidity in the African economy for productive investment. The economist's view of excess liquidity is that it is inflationary and therefore injurious to the processes of development. There is, however, another approach that has been successful in some African countries which may be worth mentioning. In these countries (Ghana and Tanzania are examples) a part of central bank profits, which would otherwise accrue to the Treasury, is earmarked for development banks for their productive investments in agriculture and industry. In some cases the central bank or the government assists in the mobilization of the external resource counterpart of such investments.

Finally, the subject of domestic resource mobilization is very crucial to economic development, but remains largely unresearched. It is an area in which African institutions with responsibility for development should assist with their own inhouse facilities and with financial support for researchers in their respective countries.

References

ADB/ECA (1987). *Economic Report on Africa, 1987,* Abidjan & Addis Ababa, March.
ADB (1987). *Domestic Resource Mobilization in Africa,* Abidjan, January.
Bhatia, R. J. (1967). *A Note on Consumption, Income and Taxes,* DM/67/70, IMF, Washington.
Chipetac. M.L.C. *et al,* Kaluma, Khonyongwa & Mkandawire (1986). *Financial Savings, Government Spending*

for Production Activities and Macro-Economic Adjustment in Malawi, IDRC Macro-Economic Workshop, Harare, November.

Frimpong-Ansah, J.H., (1987a). *Domestic Resource Mobilization in Africa – Consultant's File, ADB,* Abidjan, January.

Frimpong-Ansah, J.H., (1987b). 'Professor Sir W. Arthur Lewis – a patriarch of development economics', *Salford University Discussion Papers in Economics, 87–8.*

Frimpong-Ansah, J.H. (1987c) 'Some problems of managing and financing of economic development in Africa; an overview', ADB/ACMs Symposium, Kinshasa, November 1987, *Salford University Discussion Papers in Economics,88-3.*

Ingham, B. M. (1987). 'Shaping opinion on development policy in Africa: the Lewis and Seers and Ross reports of the 1950s', *Manchester Papers on Development,* November.

Lewis, W. A.(1944). *Machinery for Economic Planning in the Colonies,* Public Records Office, London.

Lewis, W. A.(1954). *Economic Development with Unlimited Supplies of Labour,* Manchester School of Economic and Social Studies, May.

Lewis, W. A. (1955). *The Theory of Economic Growth,* Allen & Unwin.

Nokgues, Olechowski & Winters (1986). 'The extent of non-tariff barriers to industrial countries' imports', *World Bank Economic Review,* Vol. 1, Washington DC.

OAU/ECA (1986). Africa's Submission to the UN Special Session on the Critical Economic Situation in Africa, 27–31 May 1986, 13th Special Session, Agenda Item 6.

Okhawa K. & Ranis G. (eds) (1985). *Japan and the Developing Countries,* Yale.

Umo, J. U. (1981). 'Empirical tests of some savings hypotheses for African countries', *Financial Journal,* Vol. 2, ACHS, Dakar.

UNICEF (1987). *The State of the World's Children,* Oxford.

World Bank, World Development Reports, Oxford University Press, Oxford and New York. Annually.

Discussion[1]

The Main Discussants

Professor Suliman[2] thought that the paper had dealt well with the question of savings and the resultant role of financial institutions. His prime concern was consequently with the economic environment and changing development strategies. These initially were embodied in development or investment plans financed largely from abroad, although domestic counterpart funds also played a part. Less is heard of planning now. It has to be juxtaposed with the present situation in the African economies, which are plagued by external debt, growing financial deficits (and so dissaving) and a discouraging environment. The current preoccupation is with stabilization programmes to reduce inflation, unemployment and overvalued currencies. Given this, it was natural to question the scope for enhanced savings.

Echoing J. H. Frimpong-Ansah, Professor Suliman doubted that the African countries could fund the US$82 billion required by APPER in the remaining years of the programme period. He also noted that external contributions were running below target. Among intractable African problems were drought, desertification, locusts and political difficulties. Thus, although APPER was important, a longer time-scale was required. In the long term, domestic resource mobilization was important and called for innovative approaches. Policy reform was also needed, as was research.

In this regard, Professor Suliman felt that economic theory had yet to establish a convincing relationship between savings and interest. It could be that the postulated link had not been tested sufficiently in developing countries, so that this was a specific area that required more research.

Professor Suliman cautioned against reading too much into the effect of aggregate taxation on savings. For policy formulation he thought it more useful to disaggregate – to distinguish, for example, direct from indirect taxation – and to examine the relationship between particular taxes and savings. This approach could throw light on which tax rates to increase. Here, however, one had to be aware of the incentive effect of tax changes. This could be different for consumers and producers respectively. For this reason, how the government saves is an important question. It was unrealistic to classify the development budget as savings and the current budget as consumption. Private savings through taxation were not in many cases employed in productive activities. Budgets were financed by borrowing or deficit financing.

The Khartoum Declaration, Professor Suliman noted, asks governments to protect the socially vulnerable groups – the poor, street boys and certain women, for example – in the adjustment process. This was a call for human resource development and so brought the argument back to the need for more research into resource mobilization.

Dr Denis Kessler[3] saw domestic resource mobilization as a foremost objective of economic policy. It should be pursued by all economic agents – administrations, public and private enterprises, households and financial institutions. Among its virtues is the fact that its intensified pursuit could lead to the progressive end of recession; and that it is a more durable and self-sustaining strategy than long-term dependence on foreign capital. The developed countries also had to renew their efforts to accumulate. Indeed an important part of the world crisis could be explained by the spectacular slow-down in capital accumulation in the industrial economies. The disequilibrium between needs and capacity in world finance had contributed to the rise in real interest rates.

If wide and ready agreement can be had on the importance of mobilizing domestic resources, it is more difficult to secure accord on how this can best be done. In this regard

Dr Kessler identified three aspects of the question that seemed to him particularly important, and consideration of which he thought filled out J. H. Frimpong-Ansah's paper. These were: the development of a genuine accumulation culture; the establishment of an economic environment favourable to savings; and improvement in the working of the financial system.

The accumulation culture

Since savings, and hence investment, arbitrate between generations, if the rate of accumulation is to increase it is necessary that those who control the economy systematically favour tomorrow against today. Here, economists should recognize, cultural factors can be as important as the economic. Differences in the savings rate across countries cannot be fully explained by variations in income per head, the inflation rate and the level of exports. Religious, sociological, psychological and political factors are often what provide understanding. In this regard it is possible to cite fear of the future, political uncertainty, moral disapproval of riches, and weaknesses in financial institutions.

Accumulation is, therefore, in part a cultural phenomenon. The culture is, however, not fixed: it can be transformed. This has been seen in South East Asia. It is therefore important to put in place and to follow a genuine national savings policy aimed at convincing and encouraging as many people as possible to save and invest in the country in which they live. Accumulation must not be limited to a small fraction of the population or of the enterprises. The habit has to be widely disseminated.

The question for research is how to mobilize the largest total of savings. The required saving can take many forms: a field newly brought into cultivation, a house built by self-labour, and businesses and factories expanded by internal accumulation.

Favourable economic environment

Many believe that potential savings in Africa are large and insufficiently exploited. This potential should be quantified, albeit crudely; once it is clear that it exists, every effort should be made to realize it. Here, however, there are no general panaceas, and account has to be taken of variations across countries. In this regard, the important thing is less the volume of resources and more the uses to which these are put.

This proposition could be illustrated with reference to foreign capital, public revenue and exports. Foreign capital can either encourage or discourage domestic savings depending on how it is used. Revenues raised through taxation can also, if properly used, lift savings. They can equally, however, translate simply into an increase in public consumption. Exports – like capital flows and taxation – represent economic transfers in space as well as in time. These flows together with inflation and the interest rate, give rise to transfers from one economic agent to another – from a rural to an urban household, from a lender to a borrower, from a private to a public enterprise, and from a national to an international location. To know whether such transfers are desirable it is necessary always to ask whether accumulation would be greater before or after the transfer.

Financial intermediation

It is through the financial system that an optimal structure of savings, which is as important as its level, can be obtained. This system mediates between those who have funds and those who can show a need for them. J. H. Frimpong-Ansah had shown that the traditional financial institutions were not making adequate contribution to the collection of savings.

This relative inefficiency is in part due to how these institutions are run. It is also, however, to be explained by the character of financial regulation and the economic environment in which the institutions have evolved. Attention should be paid, therefore, to management, regulation and the environment.

Dr Kessler concluded by identifying a few areas for action, with the emphasis on the development of innovative financial markets: the use of simple institutions in the rural areas, for example; the encouragement of savings, and a better choice of investment, by allowing the rate of interest to reflect market forces; the stimulation of the financial institutions to develop a range of financial services, including consultancy and advice; redoubled effort in the rural areas; simplification of procedures and decentralization of decision-taking; and the enlargement of the insurance sector.

Dr K. J. Moyana[4] saw in J. H. Frimpong-Ansah's paper the implication that the best that Africa could expect from external aid flows, debt relief, foreign investment and export earnings was a maintenance of the existing unsatisfactory economic situation. As in *Alice in Wonderland*, Africa had to run to stay in the same place; it would be necessary to run even faster to get anywhere. Dr Moyana identified two preconditions for successful domestic saving: financial stability, to guarantee rising production, risk-taking and the ploughing back of surpluses; and a price system that fully reflects input costs and basic resource scarcities, whether the price in question is that of a commodity, an interest or an exchange rate.

The mobilization of savings required a proper set of financial institutions to take deposits and lend money, for short and longer periods, for directly productive activity, for domestic and foreign trade, for housing mortgages, for the purchase of capital goods and for the overnight placement of funds. It was necessary to mobilize resources in a way that provided a natural channel for their quick and easy application in production.

Dr Moyana said that it was unclear whether the way forward lay in financial engineering. He made a number of practical suggestions that would raise savings and engage productive forces not only in the traditional formal sectors but also in the currently popular rural and non-formal sectors.

Savings clubs and credit unions

These enable peasants to mobilize and pool their resources to better their lot. In Zimbabwe, with the active encouragement of government, such institutions employ a treasurer who places funds with the conventional institutions, especially the commercial banks. The funds have financed the purchase of fertilizers and other inputs, the construction of grain stores, and the purchase and hire of delivery trucks.

Central bank financing of development banks

Too much should not be made of this. It could, however, be acceptable to use Central Bank profits to finance the operations of development banks in the rural areas and in support of the informal sector – provided this accords with national policy.

Increasing the monetization of the economy

This could come from the Central Bank requiring the existing commercial banks to extend their services in the rural areas. This could be helped by government paying teachers and other employees through salary accounts at the rural branches of the commercial banks. The marketing board could pay farmers in similar fashion. These measures would guarantee a certain deposit in the commercial branches. And this, together with deposits in the rural branches of postal savings banks, would generate finance for individual farmers, entrepreneurs and local authorities engaged in productive activities.

Insurance companies could be encouraged to underwrite more policies in the rural areas. This is important since it could provide the collateral security that many would-be borrowers in the rural areas now lack.

The extension of rural banking through an increase in the number and range of services provided by the postal banks, and the creation of rural banks, is expensive and requires intensive deployment of otherwise scarce banking skills. More useful, probably, is the setting up of mobile units and the lowering by the Central Bank of the minimum deposit and withdrawal requirements. Moreover, the Central Bank and the commercial banks can introduce a 'credit guarantee scheme', in which the risk of lending to a scheme is underwritten by the Bank. This has been very successful in Zimbabwe.

Encouragement of venture capital and equity

Governments and the Central Bank could set up venture capital companies to encourage new projects and help expand existing enterprises. Such companies would be formed as joint ventures with domestic financial institutions and external organizations such as the IFC. Governments could encourage savings in equity firms by regularly selling on the market its own shareholding in firms.

Dr Moyana warned against the danger of being over-zealous in deprecating the existing financial institutions. Much had been invested in these and it would seem rational to reform and re-orient them rather than abandon them in favour of new formulae. Innovation with continuity was what was called for.

Interventions by Invited Speakers

Mr Alain Lenoir[5] discerned three important links: between savings and trust; savings and income; and savings and collection structures. The first ranged from how customers were handled to the stability of the national currency. The second was the classical relationship that suggested in the developed countries that it was the middle income groups that did much of the saving. Of interest, here, however, were immigrant Malian workers in France who regularly saved more than half of their salaries. In Mali itself the BIAO had seen high savings by rural workers. As for the third link, the structures in Africa were cumbersome. Adaptation (to local conditions), accessibility and flexibility were essential.

In the view of Dr Mullei[6], the mobilization of savings was a challenge to governments and financial institutions. Governments should be concerned with the appropriateness of the economic environment. They had a range of policy options and could consider the role of the private sector and the balance between market and other forces in resource allocations.

It was important to distinguish between the mobilization of saving and the mobilization of resources. It was time that banks and other institutions developed sophisticated financial services. These could include underwriting business, negotiable securities and promissory notes, bills of exchange, discounting and merchant banking, futures markets, consortia to finance inter-regional trade, commercial bank lending linked to harvest timing in the rural areas, and the provision by rural banks of advisory as well as lending services.

It was doubtful, according to Mr Zafu[7], whether African countries could meet their contribution to the UNPAAERD. Nor did the developed countries look like producing their share. Moverover, East-West detente could open up new markets for the West and so provide competition for funds that could have come to Africa. This placed increased emphasis on African resources. He noted that insurance had been identified as the area of the greatest potential for savings and he elaborated on this point.

At its present stage of evolution, the African insurance sector may be considered small. However, considering its relatively late introduction to the continent, at least in its present organized form, it has recorded phenomenal growth – 25-fold in as many years (1960 to 1985). Although it was not considered as its primary objective, its potential for mobilizing domestic resources for national economic development is in no danger of being over-emphasized. Indeed, today a significant portion of resources reported as mobilized by banks may be traced back to depositor insurance and reinsurance companies. The sector's income structure reflects weaknesses not unrelated to those of the region of which it is a part. Its premium mix contains relatively less of the high-savings ratio and longer duration life assurance funds and relatively more of the high-loss ratio and shorter duration motor insurance portfolios.

Partly because of its portfolio mix, partly because of limited reinsurance capacity, but most importantly because of poor reinsurance planning at all levels, lack of commitment by industry professionals and failures of appropriate government authorities to follow up the implementation and performance of the institutions they create and in which they would have invested valuable resources, the African insurance industry has become a perpetual net exporter of embarrassingly large capital in the form of reinsurance premiums.

Where insurance is not considered irrelevant, its services may be found to meet a variety of complex individual and collective needs:

• The protection of national assets including investments;
• The provision of security/guarantee to individual and collective ventures in commerce, industry, agriculture, etc.;
• The facilitation of the movement of goods and persons;
• The provision of benefits – social security, pensions, health, etc. – either in full or as supplements to those being offered by governments.

In the process, insurance could mobilize considerable domestic resources, and the direction and tempo of investment could be influenced by appropriate tax and reward incentives, including market-oriented interest rates.

The seemingly unhealthy premium structures of today could gradually change along with changes in the economic structures of the African countries. What may perhaps require immediate attention in this regard is the Life sub-sector which over the last 25 years has held a static 20 per cent share of the sector's income. As the sub-sector with the most promising prospects for domestic savings mobilization, appropriate policy measures by governments may facilitate fuller exploitation of its proven potential.

Following considerable research and policy measures recommended by UNCTAD and the pioneering efforts of the ADB, capital transfer from Africa by way of reinsurance had attracted the collective attention of African states, so much so that in 1976 they established an inter-governmental financial institution, the African Re-Insurance Corporation, to gradually reduce that outflow. Today's premium export is ten times greater than in the early 1970s, though empirical findings clearly show that it could be reduced significantly were these governments to implement their commitments of 1976 and their annual resolutions since. As has been the case in previous years, reinsurance premium export from Africa in 1988 will be no less than US$5 billion. During the same year the African Re-Insurance Corporation will be writing no more than US$35 million, of which about 60 per cent will come from mandatory cessions and the balance from additional shares obtained by intensive marketing efforts.

The African Re-Insurance Corporation's level of shareholders' funds as at 31 December 1987 would have allowed a premium turnover of between US$55 million and US$75 million. Instead of consolidating institutions already created and conclusively proved profit-able, African states have embarked on the proliferation of sub-regional reinsurance corpora-tions whose viability is at best uncertain. The resulting market fragmentation, dissipation of limited skill and capital are all factors which militate against the success of such new efforts.

Besides, the reinsurance premium retention objective for which, presumably, such new ventures are being created could be achieved by an African Reinsurance Exchange, the forerunner of which the African Re-Insurance Corporation had already launched in the form of the African Retro Programme, a mechanism by which several large insurance risks from the continent are being distributed among African companies in several member states. Strict scrutiny of the need for, and the commercial viability of, new ventures may save the continent from the burden of unprofitable parastals, of which it already has far too many.

Who is to say Africa is not borrowing – at a very high cost – part of the resources it once had and could have retained?

Africa's interaction with the international reinsurance market is bound to continue but the level of its dependence could be reduced significantly were African governments to require companies operating in their territories not to resort to extra-regional markets before adequately engaging Africa's existing national, sub-regional and regional reinsurance capacities. Here, one is not talking about ways of mobilizing more domestic savings. Rather, one is suggesting a way of retaining more of what we mobilize for domestic investments.

In conclusion, the long-run potential of the insurance sector is certainly there. For the present, however, there are problems. Life assurance in particular is poorly developed since the level of disposable income is low and because of religious and cultural inhibitions. The industry also suffers from a multiplicity of institutions in Africa. These should be consolidated and their dependence on the international reinsurance market reduced to a minimum.

Notwithstanding the limits that had been perceived on taxation as an instrument of saving, Mr Tamrat Bekele thought that it and other mandatory means would be used until individuals had cultivated the formal savings habit. The African tax system needed to be reviewed in order to increase proceeds and bring these into line with those in other parts of the world. The system of economic relations between countries should also be overhauled so that surplus and deficit countries could be brought together to harmonize the spending needs of surplus countries and the borrowing needs of poorer ones. In the meantime, African governments should match deficit financing with less consumption and channel funds to income-generating activities. Mr Bekele also noted that the attraction of financial assets depended on how financial instruments were fashioned to take account of the population's savings habits.

Mr P. Derreumaux[8] said that the Bank of Africa, Mali, was truly indigenous. It was a private, independent, absolutely African bank with well-distributed shares. There was mutal understanding between it and the people. Its successes notwithstanding, it had certain limitations. Because it was an urban bank it could not extend its services to the agricultural sector. Being privately owned, it was possibly over-cautious in its investment policy.

Other Contributions

A number of speakers expressed doubts about Africa's savings capacity in present circumstances. African socialism, which draws inspiration from Marxism, argues for an equitable distribution of wealth, but income had to be created before it could be distributed and consumption needs met before savings could take place. It was, however, suggested that the real constraint was not the lack of savings but weakness in the policies governing savings. These inhibited investment. The factors in question included insufficient national recognition of the importance of savings; inefficient mechanisms and institutions, which generated lack of confidence; lack of clarity about identified needs; and a lack of investment opportunites. Again, customers baulked at the discourtesy and poor performance of the banks. The agricultural marketing boards were inefficient and the restrictions on the private sector had harmed growth. The solutions were to be found in more liberal economies.

Colonization had, it was argued, balkanized Africa and created mostly small and poor countries that were incapable of generating enough resources even for their own consumption. A plausible solution could be a Marshall Plan for Africa. The mobilization of external resources was indispensable if African economic recovery was to proceed.

Another view was that progress – without adverse consequence for the physical and cultural environment – could come from the development of 'niche' industries. These would be based on Africa's unique natural resources; the pharmaceutical and perfume industries and crocodile farms were cited as examples.

A number of speakers were concerned with improvements in the mechanisms of saving and with the environment in which it was undertaken. In this regard, public and private savings were seen as complementary. It was suggested that more attention should be given to the composition of the budget than to whether it was in deficit. The success of efforts to save depended more on stability and security than on returns. Among the aims should be an appropriate price structure, improved stock markets and realistic exchange rates. One speaker wondered if a claim in J. H. Frimpong-Ansah's paper that African savings had grown with inflation had been well-founded. Another urged that it was most important to strike a fair balance between savings and government consumption requirements. Yet another contribution emphasized the importance of fiscal policy, and an increase in expertise in financing insurance and export credit was also mooted.

Echoes of earlier statements were heard in the contributions from the floor. Overvalued currencies and capital flight, it was repeated, were not good for savings. One question was: what short-term measures can be put in place to counter these disincentives? The Banque Populaire Rwandaise, it was noted, had been successful in its efforts to win customers in the rural areas. Stress was placed, however, on the importance of variations across countries and the consequent limitations on any general model. Caution was urged, particularly in the transfer of models – and practices – from developed countries.

Another echo was the repeated doubt about the possibility of mobilizing domestic resources in the short run. This made external resources helpful, but these were exorbitant in their cost and were urban-biased. So how can the perverse effects of structural adjustment loans be curbed? Two measures suggested were: the creation of rural savings schemes, taking heart from the experience of Rwanda; and the recognition of informal enterprises as effective means of internal resource mobilization. The author of these propositions disagreed with the claim that African socialism was at the root of Africa's economic problems. The World Bank had no interest in agriculture in the 1960s and was now trumpeting structural adjustment programmes. Each of these policies had been presented dogmatically – as sacrosanct and unquestionable. Dogmas were to be avoided as no policy is without fault.

The Moderator's Conclusions

Dr Okongwu[9] felt that the proceedings had demonstrated clearly the need for more research. It was necessary to have the basic facts. What was the quantum of savings? He posed this question since the symposium had been told that African savings both did and did not exist. What, moreover, were the economic and non-economic determinants of savings? What were the relationships between savings and inflation and between investment and growth? How much income could be generated in the African economies, and how much of that income is taxable? Other issues that should be considered included the fundamental question of how economies could be developed and an accumulation culture sustained, the inducement of an optimal work ethic and so maximum productivity, the renovation of the banking sector and its adaptation to savings needs, and the modernization of the informal sector.

It was the judgement of Dr Okongwu that more should be known of the relationship between mass saving and production. Taking stock of the world economy, what technological niches were likely to be found in Africa in the next 15 to 20 years? How could the benefit of these be captured? What tax regimes are optimal in the African economies? How do these decompose across economic agents and goods and services?

How can the public sector be made more efficient and its undue appetite for foreign capital curbed? How can dualism, comprising predatory urban and submissive rural economies, be mitigated, and the internal terms of trade made more favourable to the rural areas? And lastly, since economic stabilization and adjustment call for sacrifices, how can these be more evenly spread than at present?

Dr Okongwu expressed the hope that the banks, together with regional and international organizations, would finance research in these and related areas and that the proceedings of the symposium would shed much-needed light on a most important topic.

Notes

1. This report was drafted and edited by staff of the Training Centre, Central Projects Department and the Development Research and Policy Department of the African Development Bank. Every care has been taken to render accurate summaries of the discussion. The views and interpretations thus reflected, and the conclusions reported, are the responsibility of those who offered them and not of the Bank, nor of any person acting on its behalf.
2. Dean,Faculty of Economic and Social Studies, University of Khartoum.
3. Director, Centre d'Étude et de Recherche, CEREPI, University of Paris.
4. Governor of the Reserve Bank, Zimbabwe.
5. General Delegate for Africa, International Centre for Banking Training.
6. Director-General, African Centre for Monetary Studies, Dakar.
7. General Manager, African Re-Insurance Corporation.
8. Director General,Bank of Africa, Mali.
9. Federal Minister of Finance and Economic Development, Nigeria.

2 The Mobilization of Domestic Resources for Development: Some Current Theoretical Issues

Robert Simmons

Introduction

The economies of sub-Saharan Africa are characterized by openness, with dependence on imports for raw materials as well as for consumption and investment goods. Sources of foreign exchange for most of these economies are earnings from a narrow range of primary exports supplemented by foreign aid and, in a few cases, commercial lending. With terms of trade moving against primary producers in the 1980s, net external financial flows have fallen and foreign exchange has been insufficient to purchase essential imports required to sustain even modest economic growth. Resort to external borrowing has resulted in debt problems for several African economies with a heavy burden of debt service exacerbated by high world real interest rates (Lancaster & Williamson, 1986).

Faced with such a bleak international economic environment, it is not surprising that African policy-makers should perceive the increasing importance of domestic savings mobilization (FAO, 1986). Often a ratio of gross domestic saving to GDP of above 20 per cent is taken as a target. Policies designed to achieve this objective cover two related problem areas. Firstly, there is a perceived requirement to improve the flow of savings from the household sector towards productive investment and to loosen finance constraints on investment. Discussions on this problem revolve around the extension of banking services to rural areas, innovations in savings instruments and the respective roles of Rotating Savings and Credit Associations (ROSCAs) and informal money-lenders (FAO, 1986). Secondly, some commentators have called for deregulation of financial markets, in particular the removal of interest rate ceilings on deposits, so as to promote greater efficiency and intermediation in the financial sector.

This chapter examines the analytical basis for these policies and, in so doing, attempts to unravel the relationships between saving rates, credit constraints and economic growth in less-developed economies. The chapter is organized in five parts. In the first part, we show how official pronouncements in support of financial liberalization derive from the financial repression hypothesis of McKinnon (1973) and Shaw (1973). In the second part, we consider the structuralist/Keynesian models of Taylor (1983) and van Wijnbergen (1982) which offer a critique of the financial repression hypothesis. Both Taylor and van Wijnbergen highlight the role of the interest rate as a component of costs of working capital. An increase in time deposit interest rates raises the cost of working capital and may reduce growth of output, where bank loans and informal sector loans are substitutes.

If interest rates were deregulated there is still no guarantee that the state of credit rationing, identified by McKinnon as an outcome of statutory nominal interest rate ceilings, will be eliminated. In the third part of the chapter, we report the work of Stiglitz and Weiss (1981) who showed how credit rationing can emerge as an equilibrium outcome of adverse selection problems in bank lending. If the aggregate economy is credit rationed, a policy of varying the quantity of credit supplied by the central bank may be more effective in raising output than altering the price of credit.

Proposals for interest rate deregulation implicitly assume that total domestic saving will be responsive to interest rates, yet empirical evidence fails to provide conclusive support for this result. In the chapter's fourth part, we review the scanty evidence on the empirical relationship between interest rate and domestic saving in developing economies, with particular reference to work on African economies.

As mentioned above, attention devoted to domestic resource mobilization through increased domestic saving partly reflects reduced flows of foreign resources. This might tempt some to think that foreign aid and lending may actually harm the growth potential of African economies by acting as substitutes for domestic saving. In the fifth part of the chapter, we consider some recent evidence, specifically related to Africa, on the familiar issue of whether or not aid is complementary to domestic saving in promoting economic growth.

Our survey, which concentrates on the relevant analytical and empirical work on these problems published in the 1980s, concludes by summarizing the main themes and by suggesting areas for further research.

1. The Financial Repression Hypothesis and Proposals for the Reform of Financial Markets

It is often suggested that direct controls on nominal interest rates are operative in most African economies at below-equilibrium levels (World Bank, 1987).[1] Such controls stimulate investment demand, help finance government deficits, are a means of provision of low interest loans to state firms and facilitate monetary regulation whereby commercial banks may be required to place some assets as low-interest bearing reserves at the central bank.

The main objection to these controls is the distortion in the price of capital brought about by below-equilibrium real interest rates which do not reflect the opportunity cost of capital. This distortion spills over into inefficient investment allocation where investment is promoted in low-return projects and commercial banks lend to known borrowers who are typically large. Since the share of overheads to total lending costs is relatively high for small borrowers, and these are perceived as relatively risky, typically they are denied credit in favour of large borrowers when credit is rationed by quantity. Hence, funds for investment are not only inefficiently allocated but smaller borrowers are subject to discrimination. In contrast, the beneficiaries of institutional loans are effectively subsidized.

These points against nominal interest rate ceilings are raised in the 1987 World Development Report (World Bank, 1987) and in the FAO symposium (FAO, 1986). The latter approvingly cites Fry's studies of Asian economies in support of claims that increased real deposit interest rates can stimulate financial savings, improve financial intermediation and raise the efficiency of allocation of investment funds (Fry, 1988).

The phenomenon of real interest rates at below-equilibrium levels is termed *financial repression* and can be explained most simply using a loanable funds theory of interest rate determination.[2] In a simple, one-good economy, aggregate saving is positively related to the

Figure 2.1   The market for loanable funds

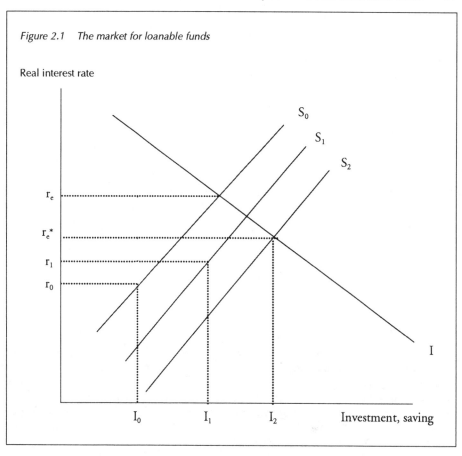

real interest rate, whereas aggregate investment demand is negatively related to this variable. In equilibrium, the supply of loanable funds (saving) equals demand for funds, at r_e in Figure 2.1 above.

If a nominal interest ceiling, together with an exogenous and constant inflation rate, results in a real interest rate below equilibrium at r_0, loanable funds are quantity-rationed and investment is constrained by supply of saving to I_0. This position is clearly inefficient. Suppose financial reform results in a higher real interest rate of r_1. Not only will the rationing of investment ease somewhat through a movement along the saving schedule, but the curve will shift to the right as high growth will occur due to low-yielding investment being removed from business plans. That is, the supply of saving responds positively to high growth promoted by a more efficient allocation of funds for investment. Complete deregulation of interest rates, again for constant exogenous inflation, results in an equilibrium real interest rate of r_e^* and both saving and investment are higher than their initial values where interest rate controls were imposed.

Current discussion of the financial repression hypothesis strongly emphasizes the existence of inefficiencies in the regulation of financial markets. The impetus for this analysis came from the important work of McKinnon (1973) and Shaw (1973). McKinnon defines financial repression as a state where 'bank credit remains a financial appendage of certain enclaves . . . even ordinary government deficits on current account frequently pre-empt the limited lending resources of the deposit banks. Financing of the rest of the economy must be met from the meagre resources of money-lenders, pawnbrokers and co-operatives' (1973: 68–9).[3] McKinnon saw a close connection between growth of the real stock of money and ratios of savings and investment to GDP. According to him, real money balances and physical capital should be regarded as complements in asset portfolios rather than substitutes, as is conventional. Less-developed economies are characterized by fragmented financial markets with reliance on self-finance for expansion of production. The absence of complete financial markets leaves money, broadly defined, as the only financial asset available to wealth-holders – in other words, McKinnon assumes cash balances are the only available financial instrument. Further assumptions are indivisibility of investment and absence of public investment.

McKinnon writes demand for real balances as positively related to (i) real income (Y); (ii) investment–GDP ratio (I/Y); and (iii) real deposit interest rate (r_D).

$$(M/P_D) = f(Y, I/Y, r_D)$$
$$+ \quad + \quad +$$

$$(1.1)$$

The investment–GDP ratio is taken to be positively related to the average return to capital, r_K. Therefore, (1.1) can be rewritten as:

$$(M/P_D) = g(Y, r_K, r_D)$$
$$+ \quad + \quad +$$

$$(1.2)$$

With money balances and physical capital as complements, an increase in average return to capital will raise the demand for both assets. Similarly, an increase in the real return on money (r_D) will raise self-financed investment and simultaneously provide an increased flow of savings since the opportunity cost of saving will have fallen. Hence, an increase in real return to money, which can be brought about either by an increase in nominal deposit interest rate or by reduction in the rate of expected inflation, will raise demand for real balances and provide greater intermediation together with higher average propensities to save and invest.

Beyond this simple logic, McKinnon proposed two further beneficial outcomes of financial liberalization: increased efficiency of investment and improved financial intermediation. The former point can be seen by reference to an extension of the simple loanable funds model by Galbis (1977). In this model there are two sectors with different technologies. The advanced sector, A, has a higher marginal product of capital than the backward sector, B. Investment in each sector depends on real return on own investment and real deposit rate with banks. Financial savings, equal to accumulated real balances and to real value of output not used in sector B, are available for sector A investment. However, a real return on deposits maintained below equilibrium by the authorities' interest rate ceiling will result in an excess demand for investible resources in sector A. With credit rationing, investors in sector A can neither finance their investment plans (since bank credit is limited) nor satisfy their complementary demand for financial assets. Potentially high-yielding investment in sector A is foregone while relatively low-yielding investment in sector B is carried out. The excess demand for investible resources in sector A at an interest rate of r* is depicted in Figure 2.2.

The flow of savings generated within sector A is S_A and as the real rate of interest rises from zero, these savings are supplemented by additional real balances accumulated from sector B. At some point G, real balances, by hypothesis, become inelastic with respect to the interest rate. At a real interest rate of r*, imposed by the authorities, the total volume of

Figure 2.2   Credit rationing in the advanced sector

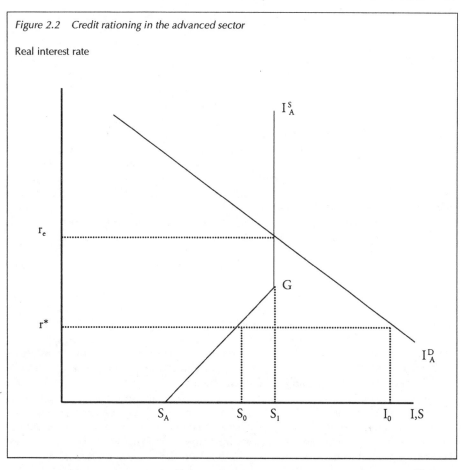

saving in sector A is S_0 but the total demand for investment is I_0 and this demand cannot be made effective. Equilibrium between planned saving and planned investment requires a a deregulated real interest rate of r_e. At this rate, a greater effective demand for investment in the advanced sector is permitted and, since this is more productive, the allocation of total investment is improved. Investors in sector B also gain from a higher real return r_e relative to r^*. The increased bank deposits gained in sector B permit a transfer of resources to sector A investment, promoting increased growth of capital and output.

Since bank deposits increase with removal of interest rate ceilings, improved financial intermediation should follow, according to McKinnon. The organized banking sector should respond to demands placed upon it by rural and small-scale urban borrowers who were hitherto compelled to use the informal sector, having been excluded from bank loans by lack of collateral and/or creditworthiness. Resort to informal money-lenders is itself seen as an endogenous response to interest rate ceilings and collateral requirements of the regulated formal financial sector.

The financial repression hypothesis relies on the presumption of a positive association between real deposit interest rate and aggregate saving. Elementary microeconomic theory teaches that there will be offsetting income and substitution effects following an increase in real interest rate; hence the net impact on saving must be ambiguous. As put by Dornbusch and Reynoso (1989), 'it is surprising to find so strong a belief in the ability of higher interest rates to mobilize saving'. A more sophisticated rationalization of an upward sloping aggregate saving schedule can be shown using a two-period life, overlapping generations model (Blanchard and Fischer, 1989: Ch. 3). Even though income and substitution effects are offsetting, if labour income is received throughout life then human wealth falls as the interest rate rises. Consumption also falls and the saving rate increases. The human wealth effect then provides the rationale for a positive interest elasticity of saving. Not surprisingly, considerable effort has been devoted towards empirical verification of this result and we shall consider some of this work in the fourth part of this chapter.

From a Keynesian standpoint, the variable which adjusts to ensure equilibrium between planned saving and planned investment is real income rather than interest rate. Moreover, the primacy of saving in the accumulation process is rejected in favour of a theory based on mutual interaction between investment and growth (the multiplier–accelerator model) with saving as a purely passive variable.

Financial constraints may still exist but these are examined by Keynesians in an entirely different manner to proponents of the financial repression hypothesis. Growth of capital markets and financial intermediaries in developing countries can aid the savings–investment-growth process but new markets in financial instruments also create opportunities for speculation and financial arbitrage. Ideally, functioning capital markets would enable the fundamental risks of firms to be taken by those least averse to risk while helping people shift time patterns of spending in accordance with their preferences. However, the volume of activity in markets for financial instruments may reflect short-term, inefficient speculative behaviour which dominates the role of economic fundamentals. This is, of course, the essence of Keynes' critique of the ineffective role of the British stock market in facilitating productive investment in the inter-war period (Keynes, 1936: Ch. 12). Amongst many others, Tobin (1984) has recently revived this critique. One particular consequence for developing countries is that real resources are absorbed in the process of financial intermediation, both private in the form of operational costs and public in the form of monitoring or regulation costs. Even where interest rate ceilings are abolished and direct intervention by governments is avoided, some supervisory role may need to be retained to avoid financial malpractices. This function also absorbs real resources.

It is standard World Bank–IMF practice to recommend to its lenders a policy of increased nominal interest rates towards market-clearing levels (Taylor, 1988). But, in the analysis of financial repression above, it is the real interest rate which is held to determine aggregate saving and investment. In so far as a positive real interest rate to reward savers is a desirable objective, this may be better achieved by reduction of inflation rates rather than raising nominal interest rates. Deregulation of interest rates may then be secondary to the primary objective of controlling inflation.[4]

McKinnon initially proposed complete, rather than partial, measures for financial liberalization together with the removal of tariffs and quotas. More recently, he and other advocates of financial reform have been more cautious. The 1987 World Development Report suggests that movement towards a more competitive financial sector is easier when inflation is low and the real exchange rate is stable. Hence, stabilization policies should be in place prior to financial reforms. This lesson appears to have been learnt from the unfortunate consequences of financial liberalization in South America, where increased financial inter-mediation did not occur and in some countries (Chile, for example) saving rates actually fell (Arrieta, 1988; Dornbusch and Reynoso, 1989) It is also recognized that it may be desirable to retain controls on international movements of capital until financial reforms are complete. Prior to interest rate deregulation, sudden removal of exchange controls would result in capital flight.[5]

A gradualist approach to financial reform would rely on discrete upward adjustments of interest rate ceilings to reduce the risk of company and bank insolvencies as balance sheets adjust. The policy package would be supported by supervision of the financial system to monitor the creditworthiness of business. In this gradualist programme, credibility requires that potential investors be assured that the policy is time-consistent and hence that the reforms will be implemented fully.

An advocate of financial liberalization could consider the above points as qualifications requiring refinement of McKinnon's original analysis rather than as damaging criticisms. In the next part of the chapter we explore the possibility that even gradual financial liberalization may have unintended, adverse consequences for capital accumulation and growth.

2. Structuralist Models of Goods and Credit Markets

McKinnon's discussion of financial repression is inherently classical in conception and is a long way from Keynes' General Theory where the paradox of thrift and the euthanasia of the rentier are ingredients (Keynes, 1936: Ch. 24). In this section, we address two questions. Firstly, can an increase in average propensity to save stimulate economic growth in a structuralist-Keynesian framework? Secondly, what are the potential adverse effects of increased nominal deposit interest ceilings on inflation and economic growth advanced by structuralist theorists? These questions will be addressed by examination of the models of Taylor (1983) and van Wijnbergen (1983).

Taylor's model, without a credit market, has prices of goods set by mark-up on unit costs where these include unit labour costs plus unit costs of intermediate imports. Output is determined by a fixed-proportions production function. The flow of saving available for investment is given by the familiar Keynesian equilibrium condition, where Z denotes imports and X denotes exports:

$$I = (Z - X) + S \quad (2.1)$$

It is convenient to assume that all saving is generated from producers' profits and that wage income is entirely consumed in the manner described by Kalecki (1971). Relaxing this to allow for saving propensity out of wage income less than propensity to save out of profits does not alter the essential model properties. Total saving is given by:

$$S = s_C r p K \quad (2.2)$$

where s_C is average propensity to save out of profits, r is average rate of profit, p is aggregate price level and K is capital stock. In equilibrium, the growth rate of output, g, equals growth rate of capital stock (I/K). From (2.1) the function relating growth of capital (and hence output) to supply of saving is:

$$g = F(r) \qquad dF/dr = s_C \quad (2.3)$$

Investment demand is positively related to both rate of profit and capacity utilization rate, expressed by output–capital ratio, v. But the latter is positively related to rate of profit via the mark-up parameter, k:

$$v = (1+k)r/k \quad (2.4)$$

Demand for investment then translates into a second expression relating growth rate of capital, and output, to rate of profit:

$$g = G(r) \quad (2.5)$$

For stability, the saving supply relation (2.3) must be steeper than the investment demand relation (2.5) – that is, $dF/dr > dG/dr > 0$.

Assuming less than full capacity utilization, an increase in saving propensity out of profits will tilt the saving supply schedule in Figure 2.3 anti-clockwise. The rate of profit and rate of growth will both be lower in the new equilibrium (point B). This provides a dynamic version of the Keynesian paradox of thrift.

At full capacity utilization, macro-economic adjustment is via forced saving. Consider a state of excess demand for goods with a capacity shortage or a foreign exchange constraint. Inflationary pressure, with nominal wage rates relatively sticky, will lead to a change in income distribution in favour of profits. Total saving will increase even though the propensity to save out of profits (s_c) is constant. This ensures balance between aggregate supply and aggregate demand.

Next, we extend the model to allow for bank loans taken by firms. These loans are used for working capital, which is required to pay the wage bill in advance of revenue. With a

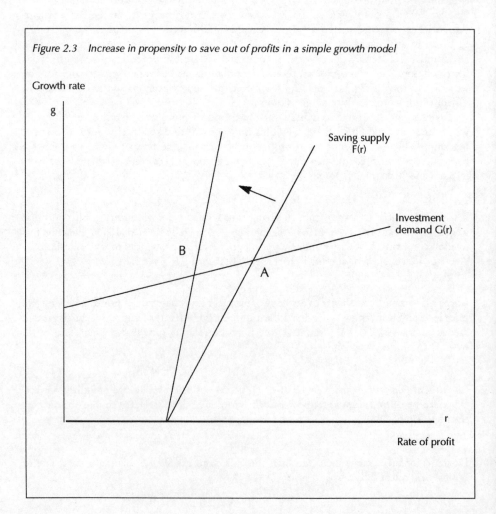

Figure 2.3   Increase in propensity to save out of profits in a simple growth model

fixed money wage, w, costs of working capital are iwL where, i, is nominal interest rate on bank loans and N is employment. (Taylor assumes that working-capital costs are measured by the nominal rather than the real interest rate).

In commercial banks' balance sheets, equality of assets and liabilities gives:

$$H + L_b = D_p + D_f \qquad (2.6)$$

H denotes bank reserves, L_b is firms' loans from banks, D_f is firms' deposits set equal to working capital and D_p is the public's deposits. Total wealth is the sum of bank reserves, H, which are determined by a statutory reserve requirement, $u(D_f + D_p)$, with $u < 1$ and nominal capital stock, pK. We ignore fixed assets such as land or gold. Capacity is fully utilized and the price level is variable. It is assumed that banks do not hold excess reserves.

Suppose an increase in general price level. Nominal wealth will be revalued. With absence of equity markets typical for African economies, the demand for loans must increase. However, the reserve requirement (with no excess reserves) means that bank lending is limited and lending to firms by the public must increase. This comes about through a reduction in bank deposits which, in turn, requires an increase in interest rate on loans. Therefore, the increase in price level must be associated with an increase in interest rate for loan market equilibrium.

The crucial mechanism in the loans market has offsetting impacts of price change on nominal wealth and interest rate change on the fraction of total wealth held by the public as deposits with banks. The public's desired deposits–wealth ratio is given by $z(i, i_d, \overset{\circ}{p})$ with its arguments as interest rate on loans, interest rate on deposits and inflation, respectively. The responsiveness of price to interest rate in loan market equilibrium is:

$$dp/di = -dz/di.w/zK \qquad (2.7)$$

Since $dz/di < 0$ it follows that $dp/di > 0$.

In the goods market, an increase in interest rate pushes up the price level by raising costs of working capital. However, it is also possible that investment demand may fall, causing a state of excess supply of goods and resulting in a price reduction. Following Taylor, we assume that the former effect outweighs the latter.

Taylor further assumes a strong impact of interest rates on the price level through working-capital costs but nevertheless that the loan market locus is steeper than the goods market locus, since the converse would imply instability in the neighbourhood of an equilibrium.[6] The formulation of growth rate is different to that of the simple model without loans; growth of capital, and hence output, depends positively on the excess of rate of profit over real interest rate. This follows Kahn (1959) who suggested that, in long-period equilibrium growth, the risk-free real interest rate should lie below the rate of profit to allow for the 'risks of enterprise'.

An expansionary monetary policy can occur through a reduction in reserve requirements (u). This will tilt the loans market locus anti-clockwise in Figure 2.4. At the new equilibrium B, both price level and nominal interest rate are lower. The latter creates conditions for higher growth since the profit rate differential over real interest rate has increased.

An increase in saving propensity out of profits will tilt the goods market locus clockwise. Again, price level and nominal interest rate are brought down, this time with a new equilibrium at C. It would appear that an increased saving propensity (out of profits) can indeed raise the growth rate of output in a structuralist-Keynesian framework and the paradox of thrift which arises in a simple one-good model is overturned.

However, Taylor's model is silent on the key issue of the role of financial structure in facilitating investment plans. Existence of only a narrow range of non-bank financial

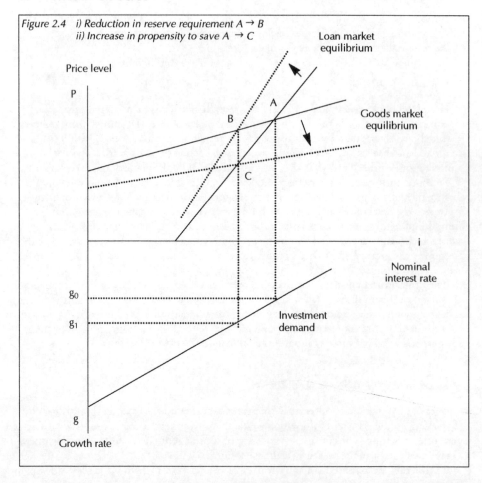

Figure 2.4   i) Reduction in reserve requirement A → B
             ii) Increase in propensity to save A → C

intermediaries may impose a constraint on firms' investment plans. Firms must be assured about the availability of long-term finance to match investment plans together with availability of short-term finance to provide working capital for current production. Even if current production and investment are financed completely out of retained profits, potential access to external finance is required should internal funds be run down. This suggests that an improved network of financial institutions can facilitate the savings–investment process by overcoming finance constraints. As Asimakopulos (1983) suggests, non-bank financial intermediaries can help provide investing firms with long-term finance before the full multiplier impacts of increased investment are completed. This can be done by purchase of long-term bonds with the proceeds of short-term bank loans. In addition, greater density of non-bank financial institutions helps reduce the spread between short-term and long-term interest rates and this also encourages investment.

Encouragement of growth of the financial sector, appropriately regulated, can overcome finance constraints for investment and growth, even in a Keynesian-structuralist framework. As Asimakopulos states, there are 'limits, related in some ways to the propensity to save, to the extent to which firms are in a position to increase their rate of investment even if short-term credit is available to finance such an increase' (1983: 232).

A well-established network of financial intermediaries can overcome finance constraints by screening borrowers to differentiate between levels of risk and by pooling and spreading risks (Tobin, 1984). The extension of financial intermediaries can improve the efficiency of allocation of funds to investment, hence raising output, even without an increase in average propensity to save (Stiglitz, 1988). If the saving rate does increase, this need not necessarily have adverse impacts on aggregate demand, provided that sufficient investment is forthcoming. This observation need not deny the fundamental role of investment in driving both growth and cyclical fluctuations in output in developing economies (Asimakopulos, 1983). There remains the critical question of exactly why financial markets are so thin in Africa; some clues are provided in the third part of this chapter.

Interest rate regulation in van Wijnbergen's structuralist model

We turn now to a full examination of the structuralist treatment of interest rate ceilings where cost of working capital effects co-exist with an informal sector as an outlet for lending to firms rationed in bank credit. Van Wijnbergen's 1983 model provides an effective critique of McKinnon's analysis, outlined in the first part of this chapter. In that presentation, an increase in nominal deposit interest rate attracts deposits, increases financial intermediation, facilitates greater saving and promotes growth of output. Financial intermediation is measured by the real size of the banking system.

Van Wijnbergen points out that an implicit assumption of McKinnon is that increased deposits represent a portfolio reallocation away from unproductive assets such as gold and money and commodity hoards. But, in McKinnon's own analysis, excess demand for institutionally rationed bank credit spills over into informal loans. Two important points follow from the integration of the informal sector into the economy's financial balance sheets. Firstly, the assets of the informal sector provide greater intermediation than the banking system since they are free from reserve requirements. Secondly, bank deposits may be closer substitutes to informal loans than to unproductive cash and gold hoards. This last point seems particularly relevant for credit-rationed developing economies where customers of the thriving informal sector may well include rejected applicants for bank loans.

The notation now has i as interest rate on informal sector loans, i_D as bank deposit (nominal) interest rate and $\mathbb{p}$ as inflation rate. Demand for currency, C^D, is given by:

$$C^D = f(\mathbb{p}, i, i_D, Y)W \qquad (2.8)$$

Demand for deposits is:

$$D = g(\mathbb{p}, i, i_D, Y)W \qquad (2.9)$$

Demand for informal loans is:

$$L^D = h(\mathbb{p}, i, i_D, Y)W \qquad (2.10)$$

Where W is real wealth and Y is real output.

With inflation held constant, demand for each asset depends positively on own return and negatively on alternative returns. This is Tobin's gross substitutability assumption which gives $df/di_D < 0$, $dg/di_D > 0$ and $dh/di_D < 0$. Total assets exhaust total wealth and the sum of partial derivatives in (2.8) to (2.10) with respect to any argument must be zero.

The supply of loans by banks, L^{SB}, is given by:

$$L^{SB} = b(\mathbb{p}, i_L)(1 - u)D \qquad (2.11)$$

where i_L is interest rate on bank loans and u is a reserve requirement with $0 < b < 1$ and $0 < u < 1$. As in Taylor's model, firms require credit to finance working capital and real demand for this, with w as the real product wage, is:

$$D_f = D_f(w, Y) \tag{2.12}$$

Asset equilibrium is characterized by three conditions. Firstly, the monetary base, MR, equals demand for currency:

$$MR = f(.) + uD + (1 - b(.))(1 - u)D \tag{2.13}$$

Secondly, deposits are demand-determined with banks off their supply schedules for notional deposits due to deposit rate ceilings:

$$g(.) < D^s \tag{2.14}$$

Thirdly, the total supply of loans, from both formal and informal sectors, must equal demand for working capital:

$$h(.)W + b(.)(1 - u)D = D_f \tag{2.15}$$

Substitution of (2.9) into (2.14) gives an LM curve:

$$h(.)W = D_f(.) - b(.)(1 - u)g(.)W \tag{2.16}$$

The impacts of an increase in deposit rate ceiling can be shown firstly for a static IS-LM model (Figure 2.5). Suppressing any cost of working capital effect on aggregate supply, we have an IS schedule with real output negatively related to interest rate on informal loans. An increase in deposit rate will leave the IS curve stationary. The LM curve will shift and its direction of movement can be identified for two distinct cases. Firstly, people shift mainly out of informal loans into bank deposits as the interest rate ceiling is raised. It will be true that:

$$\frac{dh/di_D}{df/di_D} > \frac{b(1 - u)}{1 - b(1 - u)} \tag{2.17}$$

with $df/di_D < 0$, $dh/di_D < 0$. The informal sector has zero reserve requirement and one-for-one intermediation. An increase in nominal deposit rate, with inflation exogenous, will draw funds away from this sector into banks where intermediation is partial ($u > 0$). Total supply of funds to firms will fall, the interest rate on informal loans rises and output falls.

In contrast to these results, if people shift mainly out of currency into bank deposits, the inequality in (2.17) is reversed and the LM curve shifts to the right. Informal lending rates fall and output increases as McKinnon's analysis predicts.

Increased interest rates on bank loans can raise the cost of credit for working capital and stimulate inflation (Figure 2.6). The IS and LM curves can be reconstructed to allow for endogenous inflation. If the supply-side impacts of tight credit conditions on output dominate their deflationary impacts on aggregate demand (as was assumed by Taylor) then the IS curve is downward-sloping in inflation–output space.

The LM curve is upward-sloping with inflation endogenous. Increased real output would raise both demand for loans and demand for money. The supply of informal loans is reduced, giving excess demand for credit. Informal sector interest rates are bid up and inflation must increase more than proportionately to maintain money market equilibrium (otherwise the real interest rate increases and output cannot be rising).

Following an increase in bank deposit rate, the LM curve shifts left when the portfolio reallocation is away from the informal sector.

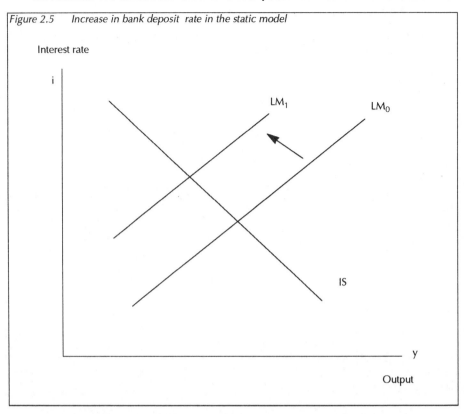

Figure 2.5   *Increase in bank deposit rate in the static model*

Informal lending rates and inflation will increase as funds are diverted to banks while output falls. These unpleasant stagflationary effects do not hold if the portfolio shift is mainly out of currency since in that case the LM curve shifts to the right.

In the long run, growth of output depends positively on the level of financial deepening given by ratio of monetary base to capital stock (mr), and negatively on a terms of trade index, q. An increase in q is brought about by an increase in inflation differential between domestic and world economies and this lowers competitiveness. With strong cost of working capital effects on inflation following an increase in bank deposit rate, van Wijnbergen shows that equilibrium competitiveness declines and also that the level of financial deepening will fall. The latter result comes about through higher real interest rates in the informal sector. Although an increased real interest rate will raise the rate of saving and increase the volume of financial assets, this will be more than offset by lower total savings as the growth rate of output declines. Overall, the level of financial deepening will decline in the case where portfolio reallocation is away from the informal sector. With fixed exchange rates and exogenous world inflation, lower competitiveness simply reflects greater inflation in the domestic economy relative to the rest of the world. Reduced competitiveness and reduced financial deepening combine to generate lower steady-state output growth.

It is possible that the increase in saving rate dominates the impact of lower growth of output on total saving. In this case, more favourable to McKinnon and relying on small impact of cost of working capital on inflation, financial deepening will increase. But growth of output will only increase if the deterioration in competitiveness (lower q) is not too large. If the favourable effect of improved financial deepening on growth dominates the adverse

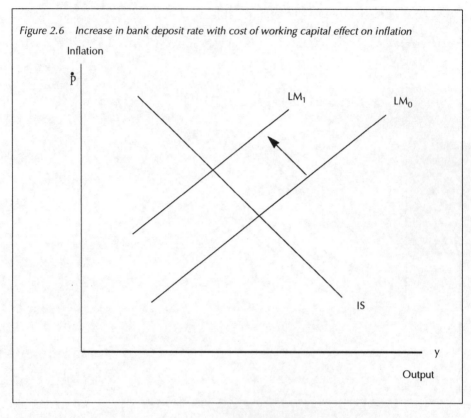

Figure 2.6   Increase in bank deposit rate with cost of working capital effect on inflation

impact of lower competitiveness then growth will increase, but there is no guarantee that this will occur, even in this specific version of the model favourable to McKinnon's case.

Practical relevance of the structuralist approach to financial markets

Some support for the structuralist themes outlined above comes from Wijnbergen's (1982) study of the South Korean economy following financial reforms in 1965 which led to increased interest rates on time deposits. Van Wijnbergen found that the huge increase in time deposits was caused by a switch from informal sector loans rather than increased savings diverted from currency and other hoards. Hence, time deposits were close substitutes to informal loans and this supports the case for the stagflationary effects of tight monetary policy outlined above.

In Egypt (Abdel-Khalek, 1987) it was found that the effective after-tax nominal interest rate on time deposits increased in the late 1970s following removal of a 40 per cent tax on interest income from deposits. The real return on deposits rose, becoming less negative, and loanable funds increased, but the banking system continued to be averse to illiquid lending. Loans to industry, which were more than 50 per cent of bank lending in 1979, fell to below 33 per cent in 1985 and it is not clear that rising real interest rates were associated with increased investment.

Taylor (1988) suggests that working capital effects on inflation are important for African economies. A 25 per cent bank credit–GDP ratio with 50 per cent of this going to working capital is not untypical. In high inflation economies, interest payments on working capital can form 10 to 20 per cent of GDP. Particular countries where restrictive monetary policy is contractionary and inflationary are Tanzania and Côte d'Ivoire.In these economies, there may be complementarity of public and private investment with 'crowding in'. Policies to control government spending should therefore be directed at consumables rather than public investment and with strong cost-push pressures from working capital effects, reducing interest rates may actually be a desirable policy. To avoid unduly large negative real interest rates it is desirable, however, to secure lower inflation rates with fiscal and monetary restraint and, possibly, the use of an incomes policy.

In the World Development Report of 1987, it was suggested that financial deregulation should be pursued after stabilization programmes had been enacted, since liberalization is likely to be more beneficial when inflation is low. However, even assuming that stabilization programmes can deliver lower inflation, the analysis of van Wijnbergen suggests that removal of interest rate ceilings may well rekindle inflation. Hence, even the more 'moderate' World Bank policy recommendations (favouring a gradualist approach to financial reform) may be questioned.

3. Credit Rationing as an Equilibrium Phenomenon

In McKinnon's analysis, credit rationing is the direct result of interest rate ceilings. In this section, we show how credit rationing can arise as a result of imperfect information in financial markets, as set out in Stiglitz (1985, 1987b) and established formally in Stiglitz and Weiss (1981). An excess demand for credit can occur, and persist, independently of any government intervention. Removal of an interest rate ceiling may not, therefore, eliminate credit rationing, contrary to current orthodoxy.

In making loans, banks are concerned about the interest rate payable and the riskiness of a loan, since borrowers may default. The interest rate charged and the riskiness of a pool of loans are related in two ways. Firstly, the interest rate may help sort potential borrowers. Different borrowers have different probabilities of repayment of a loan and the interest rate serves as a screening device here. Those willing to borrow at high interest rates are poor risks since their probability of repayment is low, and hence the expected return to the bank is low. This is an example of an *adverse selection* problem.

In addition, an increase in interest rate attracts borrowers with projects that have high payoffs if successful but low probability of success. The average riskiness of a loan will tend to increase as interest rate rises. Hence, there is an incentive problem facing banks. Clearly, banks will wish to design loan contracts so as to encourage borrowers to take actions in the banks' own interests. This will typically entail measures to attract low-risk borrowers with low probabilities of default on loans. Banks, of course, do use collateral requirements but these will typically be supplemented by the role of the interest rate itself in affecting the behaviour and distribution of borrowers.[7]

The hypothesized relationship between a bank's expected return per loan and the interest rate is shown in Figure 2.7. As the interest rate increases from zero, the expected return per loan rises less than proportionately since the probability of default rises. Beyond r^*, the expected return actually falls since relatively safe borrowers are less willing to borrow at higher interest rates. It is optimal for a bank to reject loan applications at interest rates above r^* since these are associated with higher probability of default compared to applications at r^* or below. The bank's expected return per loan is maximized at r^*. Above r^*, the adverse selection effect means that an increased interest rate is associated with a poorer mix of applicants. An optimum interest rate, r^*, may coexist with an excess demand for loans, or credit rationing. If so, raising the interest rate will not eliminate this excess demand since banks' expected return per unit of loan will fall. The reader should note that this argument does not imply that there will always be credit rationing in equilibrium but, rather, that if a credit-rationed regime exists (the supply of funds is insufficient to meet demand), the usual market response of increased interest rate on loans is ineffective in removing the excess demand.

In the first part of this chapter, we reported one standard objection to interest rate ceilings, namely that small borrowers are subject to discrimination when credit is rationed. Here, we point out that this is possible regardless of state intervention. In Figure 2.8, there

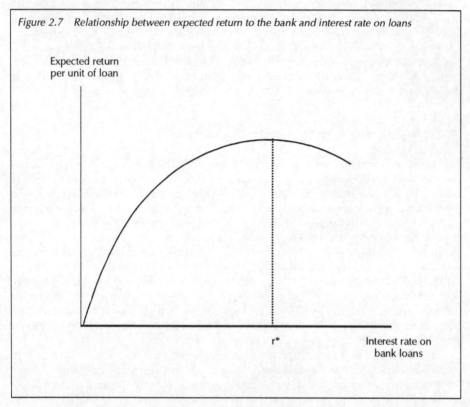

Figure 2.7   Relationship between expected return to the bank and interest rate on loans

Expected return
per unit of loan

r*

Interest rate on
bank loans

are groups of individuals who differ in observable characteristics. The functions relating expected return per unit of lending to the bank and interest rate charged will vary across social groups. Group B is excluded from the capital market since at no interest rate will the bank's return on lending equal equilibrium expected return rho*. These people, small rural borrowers perhaps, will be denied loans.

In contrast, Group A's maximum expected return just equals rho* and, here, some members receive loans while others are rejected.

We can use the imperfect information framework to consider possible approaches to policy towards the financial sector in less-developed economies. Our discussion will cover macro-economic policy, the role of government agencies in the financial sector and appropriate policy towards the informal sector, which has yet to be integrated into the above discussion..

Macro-economic policy under credit rationing

Blinder (1987) offers some useful observations on the role of monetary policy under credit rationing in a simple macro-economic model of a closed economy. Blinder follows Stiglitz and Weiss in considering banks as specialized institutions developed to make loans on the basis of information acquired on the risk of customer default. Loan contracts will make the future cost and availability of credit dependent on borrowers' previous performance. As in the Stiglitz and Weiss model, banks may find it unprofitable to raise lending rates to clear markets. Blinder's model is simplified by assuming no outlet for excess demand for credit – that is, no close substitute for bank loans in the form of informal sector loans. Denial of credit by a borrower's bank makes credit inaccessible.

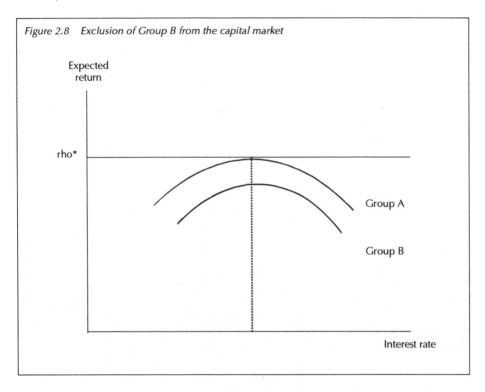

Figure 2.8   Exclusion of Group B from the capital market

Under credit rationing, Blinder finds that the effectiveness of monetary policy is enhanced compared to a Keynesian regime where the credit constraint is non-binding.[8] In contrast, the autonomous spending multiplier is reduced in the credit-rationed regime, although it is still positive. This is because increased autonomous spending will (partially) crowd-out private investment when credit is rationed, whereas 'crowding in' occurs in the Keynesian regime.

The notion that expansionary monetary policy can have strong impacts on the real sector where credit conditions are tight, but only weak effects where credit is plentiful, seems to be consistent with good economic intuition. Greenwald and Stiglitz (1987) follow this up, arguing that it is the availability of credit, and not the interest paid, which restricts investment or limits production in a credit-constrained economy (with curtailment of working capital). Restrictions on the supply of bank credit, brought about by higher reserve requirements or restrictions on the supply of high-powered money, will tend to lower investment and growth in a credit-rationed regime.

Tight monetary policies may raise uncertainty about the probability of default as bankruptcies begin to be anticipated. The effective cost of capital is equal to the cost of borrowing plus the cost associated with increased probability of bankruptcy arising from increased debt, and this variable increases when monetary conditions are tightened. There will be a tendency towards destruction of 'informational capital' as lenders face increased uncertainty about the prospects of their customers. Their rational response is to reduce their supply of credit, refusing to lend to some borrowers to whom they may previously have lent. Marginal borrowers are either unable to get funds or, more likely, are driven to the informal money-lenders who charge higher interest rates than the banks (see below). Either way, investment demand falls. Spill-over effects occur throughout the economy as inter-dependent suppliers are threatened by the increased prospect of bankruptcy in their chains of transactions. In this respect, the anticipation of bankruptcy may be more important than the event itself. Increased expectations of bankruptcy will be sufficient to induce producers to cut back their plans for output and investment.

It should be stressed that the effective (marginal) cost of borrowing can increase even if nominal interest rates are held constant. As the effective cost of borrowing rises, working capital is reduced and the real effects on the economy may be strong (Blinder, 1987). This is particularly the case in many less-developed economies where markets for financial assets are thin, and interest rate adjustment plays a minor role in establishing equilibrium between planned saving and planned investment.

Government intervention at the micro-level

In less-developed economies, firms are constrained in the forms in which they can raise capital as well as in the total volume they can obtain. The absence of equity and futures markets, including those for insurance, means that producers find it difficult to divest risks. With use of working capital prevalent, every production decision is inherently risky (Stiglitz, 1988).

The absence of sufficient well-functioning financial institutions to channel savings towards long-term finance to match investment plans suggests a role for government-established agencies, such as development banks, to fill gaps left by missing markets. This role is reinforced by the possibility of market failure of those institutions that do exist in credit markets. With pervasive imperfect information problems, Pareto-efficiency of financial markets is unlikely to be achieved and this rationalizes the existence of a set of welfare-improving taxes and subsidies (Stiglitz, 1988). Even if the absence of some risk markets may be optimal, due perhaps to high transaction costs of organizing such markets, the allocation of investible resources, given absent markets, may be Pareto-inefficient.

However, the existence of information problems and market failure do not necessarily validate government intervention. Government failure is a real possibility and, some would argue, an actual outcome in African economies (Frimpong-Ansah, 1988). The government may not be in a better position than the private sector to screen investment projects and control the actions of borrowers. In the allocation of funds, state bureaucrats may simply take opportunities to maximize their own utilities by providing subsidies at their discretion without reference to proper cost-benefit appraisal. Stiglitz provides an eloquent summary of the problems of government failure:

> The information problems, of selection, of incentives, of co-ordination and information exchange, are no different for the government than for the private sector, and indeed in some dimensions they may clearly be worse. One may argue that there are market forces which work to ensure that those who are entrusted to the management of capital and human resources are those who have a comparative advantage in doing so. There is no reason to believe that the electoral process (when it works) works to select public officials who have a comparative advantage in designing incentive structures which ensure that individuals work hard, and that their work is directed (to) the national interest (1988: 155).

Although a potential role exists for governments to improve the allocation of funds for investment, this does not mean that actual intervention measures will be successful. Indeed, it is quite possible that access to credit on political rather than economic considerations will occur and this will not improve resource allocation, leaving high default rates on loans and low efficiency of investment projects as unfortunate results of the state's intervention. This is certainly an area where further analytical and empirical research is needed to establish how, and to what extent, government failure impedes the promotion of investment in African economies.

Policy towards the informal sector

Excess demand for bank credit usually spills over into demand for informal sector loans as we saw in our examination of van Wijnbergen's model in the second part of this chapter. Unlike the formal sector, transactions and information costs are fairly low and trust and knowledge of customers by money-lenders will be important features. The informal sector, of course, is not subject to controls on lending and borrowing by the central bank. Compared with the formal sector, credit for consumption purchases is more important and credit for investment plans less important (Chandavarkar, 1986).

Interest rates charged in the informal sector are typically higher than those in the credit-rationed formal sector. Advocates of financial liberalization suggest that removal of interest rate ceilings will reduce this interest rate differential. However, this differential may be a non-competitive, equilibrium property, where adverse selection problems create credit rationing in the formal sector while the informal market clears.[9]

As Chandavarkar (1986) points out, the reason for the high interest rates charged in the informal sector can be divided into four main categories: *high risk of default*, including the possibility that the borrower may abscond with his loan; *willingness to pay*, reflecting the spill-over of demand from rejected applicants for bank loans; *high opportunity costs* of money-lenders; and a residual category reflecting *monopoly rents*, since the informal sector may be characterized by significant barriers to entry including local knowledge, inaccessibility of rural locations and lack of social acceptance of new money-lenders. Space does not permit a full analysis of these points here, but Bell (1988) provides a thorough review of two types of model. The first of these has a principal–agent relation where money-lenders have substantial knowledge of clients but still incur high costs of monitoring borrowers' actions and a risk of strategic default as the borrower may abscond with the loan. Lenders' expected return depends on the borrower's choice of project and this, in turn, is influenced by the terms of a credit contract. The possibility of strategic default affects the optimal interest rate–lending combination where money-lenders have monopoly power but not in the case of free entry.

In the second type of model, emphasis is placed on monopoly power as opposed to lender's risk. Lender's risk is actually assumed to be zero, since collateral may always be recoverable, subject to administration costs. As would be predicted in a monopoly model, the interest rate charged exceeds the marginal cost of borrowing and the monopolist money-lender earns pure profit (Figure 2.9). In addition, borrowers' collateral assets tend to be undervalued (Bardhan, 1988).

The very informality of money-lenders' operations means that interest rate ceilings tend to be ineffective in this sector. Extension of commercial banks' activities to the rural sector is often recommended (FAO, 1986) but the fact that such extension is not widespread may reflect high transactions and other costs of rural operations. Commercial banks might not be able to match the money-lenders' availability of inside information and the social ties which maintain their credit relations. As Bell (1988) suggests, using commercial banks to challenge the market power of the informal sector may be expensive and inefficient. A possible alternative is to use private lenders as agents for banks. Credit associations and

ROSCAs could also operate in this way, although barriers to entry arising from inside information may still generate inefficiency. Bell's conclusion here seems particularly relevant to African rural savings mobilization: 'the establishment of rural banks should be motivated by the desire to encourage thrift and mobilize rural savings rather than challenge traditional lenders directly at the outset' (1988: 791).

Since barriers to entry in informal credit markets include geographical inaccessibility of rural areas and poor communications, public investment in rural infrastructure might help encourage entry and this aspect of policy should not be overlooked. As Bell suggests, well-functioning rural credit markets may be the consequence rather than the cause of economic

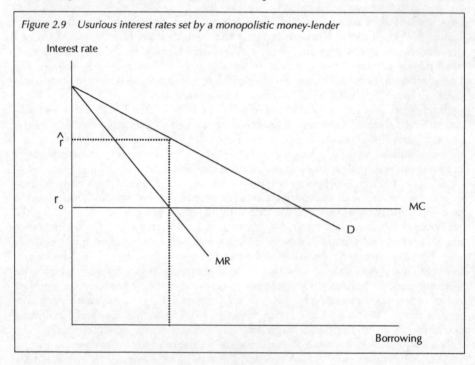

Figure 2.9   Usurious interest rates set by a monopolistic money-lender

development. Policy should be flexible, providing for a role for ROSCAs and other credit associations, rather than being over-reliant on the extension of commercial banks' (regulated) services.

4. The Interest Elasticity of Domestic Saving

If the McKinnon financial repression hypothesis is correct for developing economies, then typically an increase in real interest rate should raise the rate of domestic saving expressed as a proportion of GNP. It has been proposed (Fry, 1980) that an empirical finding of a statistically significant and positive interest elasticity of saving can be shown for some Asian economies, giving some support to the financial repression hypothesis.[10]

Fry's 1980 investigation employed a simultaneous equation model, recognizing the mutual dependence of domestic saving rate (S/Y) and growth rate on a set of exogenous variables. The domestic saving rate was held to be determined by growth of output, real deposit interest rate and the lagged dependent variable. The growth equation had saving rate, per capita real income level, ratio of foreign saving to GNP (considered as a substitute for domestic saving) and real interest rate on deposits as explanatory variables. Fry examined seven Asian economies, using pooled data over 10-year periods, on average, to give 70 observations and found that 'the cost of financial repression appears to be around half a percentage point in economic growth foregone for every one percentage point by which the real deposit rate of interest is set below its market equilibrium level' (1980: 324).

Giovannini (1983, 1985) tried to reproduce Fry's equations over a different sample period. In a simultaneous equation model, the domestic saving–GNP ratio was regressed against log of per capita income (1ny), $1/1ny^2$, $1/1ny^4$, the real interest rate, foreign saving–GNP ratio and the lagged dependent variable. Instrumental variable estimation was used. The coefficient of real interest rate was found to be 0.14 to 0.16 over Fry's country set and sample period. But Giovannini (1985) found there were two key observations from the years following the Korean financial reforms in 1965 which influenced Fry's results. With the same country set but a longer time horizon, giving a greater number of pooled observations, it was found that the coefficient of real interest rate became negative and insignificant. Hence, Fry's finding of a positive, significant real interest rate is vulnerable to changes in the sample period.[11] However, Fry (1988) reports results for an Asian 14-country sample for 1961–83 which suggest that a positive and significant real deposit rate coefficient remains when Korea is omitted. The value of this coefficient is about 0.1.

Fry attempted to extend his analysis of saving and financial repression to 61 economies for which saving, investment and growth data were available. African countries comprised over a third of this sample. Unfortunately, for most of these economies data on interest rates were unavailable. Fry did proceed to test saving and investment equations for this large pooled cross section-time series sample, without the interest rate as an explanatory variable. Again, instrumental variable estimation was used. In the equation for domestic saving rate (S/Y), the coefficients of growth rate, level of per capita real income, share of mining sector in GNP, purchasing power of exports and the lagged dependent variable were all significant and positive. The coefficients of foreign saving rate (Sf/Y) and anticipated inflation (estimated by a polynomial lag structure) were significant and negative. In the investment equation (for I/Y), growth rate, share of foreign exchange receipts in GNP, purchasing power of exports, ratio of actual and anticipated price and the lagged dependent variable all affected investment rates positively. In addition, two endogenous variables, the level and rate of change of domestic credit-GNP ratio, reflecting monetary policy, were found to be associated positively with investment share in GNP.

Fry's model structure is consistent with several possible explanations. His preferred interpretation follows Leff and Sato (1980) in suggesting an inherent tendency for developing economies, with interest rate ceilings, to have an excess demand for investment over *ex ante* total saving (domestic plus foreign). This gap, which cannot be ascertained simply by inspection of *ex post* saving and investment ratios, becomes wider under inflationary conditions since real deposit rates fall, the saving rate falls, the ratio of actual to expected price rises and investment increases, amplifying the initial disequilibrium. A further source of instability is the greater feedback effect of growth of output on investment rate compared to its impact on saving rate. Of course, Fry was unable to test impacts of government-imposed credit rationing on the growth process for his 61-country sample, since data for the real deposit effect were unavailable.

Fry's particular estimate of the cost of financial repression in Asian economies is not obtained from the full model reported above. In his 1980 paper, Fry uses two equations (for saving rate and growth rate) and one identity:

$$S/Y = a_0 + a_1g + a_2lnyn + a_3r + a_4Sf/Y + a_5S/Y(-1) \qquad (4.1)$$

$$I/Y = S/Y + Sf/Y \qquad\qquad (4.2)$$

$$g = b_1 I/Y + b_2 r \qquad\qquad (4.3)$$

Here, g is growth of real output; (4.1) is the basic saving equation estimated by both Fry and Giovannini. Since foreign saving is equal to the current account deficit by definition, (4.2) is an identity. In (4.3) b_1 is the incremental output–capital ratio for which Fry imposes plausible values ranging from 0.22 to 0.67 and b_2 is estimated from an OLS regression as 0.4. Fry then obtains his result that the short-run cost of financial repression is 0.48 to 0.66 percentage points in growth foregone for each 1 percentage point by which the real deposit rate is below equilibrium.

More recently, Fry (1988) has revised his earlier investment equation reported above, again for Asian economies:

$$I/Y = c_1 g + c_2 TG + c_3 TG(-1) + c_4 DCp/Y + c_5 r_w + c_6 I/Y(-1) \qquad (4.4)$$

Here, external impacts on the investment share are captured by change in the terms of trade (TG) and its lagged value. As before, credit conditions are included with the ratio of domestic credit to the private sector to GNP used as a proxy. Another new variable is r_w, the foreign (US) real interest rate included to show the cost of foreign borrowing. *A priori*, $c_1 > 0$, $c_4 > 0$ and $c_5 < 0$.

Fry does not revise his estimates of cost of financial repression in the light of this investment equation. Nor does he test a richer formulation of the growth equation (4.3) which, as it stands, is rather restrictive. Moreover, should the coefficients on real deposit rate, a_3 and b_2, both be not significantly different from zero then a Keynesian economist could readily accept this restricted version of the model. These points suggest the need for further progress towards better estimates of real interest rate coefficients in any measurement of financial repression in LDCs.

Unfortunately, as Giovannini is careful to point out, data inaccuracies tend to undermine any firm conclusions from aggregate econometric saving equations. Total domestic saving data are obtained from *ex post* equality of saving and investment, where foreign saving is deducted to obtain the domestic component. A further deduction of government surplus would reveal private saving as a residual. As Gersovitz (1988) observes, this computation of aggregate domestic saving is subject to several sources of measurement error. The allocation of goods to investment and consumption categories may be incorrect, particularly as investment may wrongly include inventories. Where investment data are used, the bulk of agricultural investment may be ignored. The use of official exchange rates which may be overvalued tends to understate the value of capital goods that are imported and this is reinforced by under-declaration of imports and smuggling. All this, together with problems of measurement of informal activities, means that investment and saving shares in GNP may well be understated in African economies.

The implicit aggregation of private and government saving in domestic saving data is forced upon researchers by the hazy nature of data on government budget deficits in African economies. But this aggregation is legitimate only if the Ricardian equivalence theorem holds and the conditions for this are quite strong in developed economies (Bernheim, 1987) and likely to be at least as strong in underdeveloped countries.

Lack of suitable data increases the probability of biased coefficients of explanatory variables due to the existence of omitted variables. This tends to be reflected in a high coefficient on the lagged domestic saving–GNP ratio which might well be due to serial correlation of the excluded variables.

Modern economic theory favours the inclusion of lifetime or permanent income as well as current income in econometric studies of consumption and saving functions. This is not compatible with the use of a simple, constant marginal propensity to save – adopted by Taylor (1983) in his structuralist models – although the use of a permanent income or life-cycle theory of consumption is not inconsistent with the van Wijnbergen (1983) model outlined in the second part of this chapter.[12]

Giovannini (1985) attempts to test a two-period optimization model of consumption behaviour. From the first-order conditions for inter-temporal maximization, the estimating equation is:

$$\ln(C_{t+1}/C_t) = k_0 + (1/d)\ln(1 + r_t) + e \qquad (4.5)$$

where r is real deposit interest rate and consumption, C, is expressed in per capita terms deflated by the consumer price index. The coefficient, $1/d$, is the marginal rate of intertemporal substitution with d as the elasticity of marginal utility. This equation is estimated separately for 18 countries with annual data, using both ordinary least squares and instrumental variable methods. Only 5 out of 18 countries have coefficients on the real interest rate term significantly different from zero. Values of the Durbin–Watson statistic are far removed from 2, indicating auto-correlated residuals and, hence, rejection of the rational expectations hypothesis. Of particular interest here, are the results for Kenya, the only African economy in the country set. The coefficient on the interest rate is positive but insignificant, the R^2 value is extremely low (0.09 to 0.13) and the Durbin–Watson statistic is 2.8 to 2.9, indicating negative first-order auto-correlation.

Generally, Giovannini's estimated equations based on the two-period consumption model show poor results. This may well be due to problems of measurement of consumption, inappropriateness of the deposit interest rate in economies where a substantial informal sector exists, and the possibility that many individuals in developing economies are liquidity-constrained, which is not allowed for in the derivation of equation (4.5). Since consumption by the very poor may actually be unrecorded in LDC data, it may be questioned whether construction of reduced form equations tightly derived from sophisticated rational expectations-based consumption theories is of great value. It may be noted that Giovannini's equation for Kenya has just 13 observations. Kidane's study of Ethiopia, in this volume, which uses a permanent income formulation of aggregate saving, also suffers from severe data limitations, as the author carefully points out.

In the absence of adequate data for African economies, pragmatic, parsimonious studies using simultaneous equation estimation techniques may be all that can be achieved. Use of cross section–time series pooled data can, of course, increase degrees of freedom provided one restricts use of dummies to intercepts and undertakes tests for homogeneity of the sample. Leite and Makonnen (1986) consider pooling of data for the BCEAO countries, Benin, Côte d'Ivoire, Niger, Senegal, Togo and Upper Volta (now called Burkina Faso), which represent a relatively homogeneous currency union, using the CFA franc as the common currency. The data covers the period 1967–80. Their fullest equation has real disposable income, change in real disposable income, real short-term interest rate and the lagged dependent variable as independent variables to explain total gross private saving. This is essentially a dynamic adjustment model and more restricted versions are tested without change in disposable income and with the additional deletion of the lagged dependent variable. All equations include the export–GDP ratio as an additional explanatory variable.

In their fullest specification, Leite and Makonnen allowed for different country intercepts and could not reject the homogeneity hypothesis. Under these circumstances, it is valid to pool the data to give a common saving function. They then used a correction for heteroskedasticity, using the standard error of each equation to normalize the observations for each country. In the full dynamic adjustment model, the real interest rate is not statistically significant although it has positive sign. In the restricted cases without change in disposable income, the real interest rate has a positive and significant coefficient. As the authors observe, this loss of explanatory power of the real interest rate may reflect a positive correlation between this variable and the growth rate, suggesting that simultaneous equation bias may be present.

A further source of bias in the Leite-Makonnen study lies in their method of calculation of the real interest rate. They simply use the nominal rate minus consumer price inflation and this defines the *ex post* real interest rate rather than the *ex ante* rate, which is the relevant variable. To calculate the *ex ante* rate, a process for determination of expected inflation is required, using adaptive or rational expectations methods as employed in the studies by Fry and Giovannini (see Gupta, 1984: Ch.4, for a discussion of the techniques involved in estimating expected inflation). As they stand, Leite and Makonnen's results are subject to bias as the actual (*ex post*) real interest rate is not necessarily a good proxy for the *ex ante* rate.

Empirical evidence on saving functions in African economies is extraordinarily thin and it is to be hoped that, as further data become available, more research, even on simple models, will be undertaken. Where possible, simultaneous equations techniques should be adopted, treating saving rates and growth rates as endogenous. However, choice of instruments is always hazardous, as there may be no particular case for a chosen instrument to be correlated with the independent variables yet uncorrelated both with the error terms themselves and the errors in measurement of the variables. It would be unwise to draw strong policy conclusions from the saving equations thus obtained.

5. Complementarity of Foreign Aid and Domestic Savings

In the FAO symposium (1986), considerable stress is placed on the need for African economies to generate increased domestic saving to help overcome increasingly tight foreign exchange constraints. This view can be rationalized using the standard textbook two-gap model (Williamson, 1983).

African economies import capital goods to support their capital accumulation. This reflects the comparative advantage of capital goods produced in developed economies using advanced technology and highly skilled labour and also the low level of demand for African capital goods relative to the minimum unit cost level of output, preventing realization of scale economies. The simplest two-gap model specifies an aggregate production function with fixed proportions of domestic and foreign capital.

Domestic saving is supplemented by foreign capital inflow and both are proportional to real income. The foreign capital–GNP ratio is given by an exogenous parameter, c. In Figure 2.10, this parameter appears on the horizontal axis and the growth rate is plotted on the vertical axis. With a fixed exchange rate, the savings constraint is shown by the line B_0B_0, the intercept of which increases with marginal propensity to save out of domestic income, s, and decreases with marginal propensity to import. The steeper line, A_0A_0, shows the foreign exchange constraint with the horizontal intercept determined negatively by exogenous export–GNP ratio and positively by marginal propensity to import.

If the domestic saving propensity increases, the saving constraint moves up to B_1B_1 and the maximum feasible rate of growth increases to g_1 from g_0. For the initial saving constraint, the higher growth rate, g_1, can also be obtained by an increase in aid–GNP ratio from c_0 to c_1, since this shifts the foreign exchange constraint from A_0A_0 to A_1A_1. Hence, either an increase in domestic saving rate or an increase in foreign aid can raise the feasible growth rate.

The two-gap model treats foreign capital inflow as exogenous and, as we shall see, this is questionable. Also, the model rules out import substitution strategies to reduce marginal propensity to import and alter the output–foreign capital ratio. The attractiveness of the model lies in its simplicity and good intuitive sense in that investment plans in many developing economies may well be frustrated by insufficient foreign exchange to purchase imports of capital goods. Taylor (1988) considers foreign exchange constraints to be tightly binding in the small, open economies of sub-Saharan Africa, referring to this problem as one of 'external strangulation'. Ghana is cited as a particularly strong case with an *ex post* investment–GNP ratio of only 8.5 per cent in the early 1980s.[13]

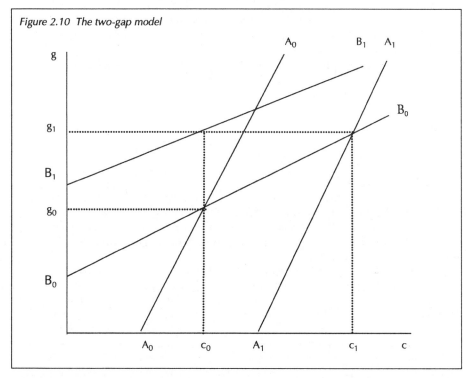

Figure 2.10 The two-gap model

It is an important feature of the two-gap model that foreign saving complements domestic saving. Levy (1988) examines some econometric relations between saving, aid, investment and growth in sub-Saharan Africa. His aid data refer to Official Development Assistance from 1968 to 1982 for 22 low-income and 6 middle-income sub-Saharan economies. The dividing line between middle and low per capita income was taken to be $600 at 1970 prices. The general pattern in the time series data was for growth of output to decline alongside the investment rate over the sample period. Aid flows typically increased as share of GDP while the domestic saving rate fell. For 22 low-income economies in a cross-section equation, based on data for the period 1968–82, Levy found a positive correlation between aid–GDP ratio and growth rates when per capita income was used as a control. The same positive association is found for change in growth and change in aid–GDP ratio. Hence, countries with above average foreign aid inflows had above average growth rates.

Again, across the 22 low-income economies, Levy regressed investment–GDP ratio against aid–GDP ratio and domestic saving–GDP ratio. Using pooled data, with 28 economies over 15 years giving 420 observations, and an error-component model, the coefficient of aid–GDP ratio in the investment rate equation was found to be 1.23. This appears to support the proposition that increased aid flow is correlated with an increase in investment–GDP ratio, once the effect of saving–GDP ratio is taken into account. Both independent variables have positive and significant coefficients.[14]

Next, Levy uses a growth accounting exercise to establish an equation for growth rate determined by investment–GDP ratio, annual growth of employment and annual growth of exports and changes in terms of trade. The latter is an optional independent variable. For estimation on a pooled cross section–time series data set, the coefficient of the investment–GDP ratio is found to be 0.13 for 1968–82 and 0.17 for 1974–82. The coefficient of growth of employment is positive and significant. Hence, countries with above-average investment rates and employment growth rates appear to have above-average growth of output.

In Levy's model, aid inflow, which is treated as exogenous, affects investment–GDP ratio which, in turn, affects growth rate. It remains to consider why growth rates were so poor in sub-Saharan African economies in the later years of the sample. One explanation, consistent with work reported in Taylor (1988), is that falling terms of trade contributed to slower output growth. Levy points out that in 1980–2, the prices of non-oil primary commodities fell by 27 per cent in current prices, giving a loss of income of 1.2 per cent of GDP across sub-Saharan Africa. In 1981 alone, the low-income countries in the sample faced a 9.9 per cent loss of terms of trade. In the growth equation, the change in terms of trade had a negative and significant coefficient when it was introduced.

Therefore, Levy concludes that aid is positively and significantly correlated with both investment–GDP ratio and growth rate and that investment contributes to growth in sub-Saharan Africa with evidence of a significant positive average rate of return. This positive impact of growth may have been outweighed in later years by deterioration of terms of trade.

The comments made in the fourth part of this chapter, on the importance of simultaneity in empirical investigations of the saving-investment-growth process, must be raised here. Levy's study, while extremely interesting, calls out for the use of simultaneous equation estimation techniques. Although Levy finds that the aid–GDP ratio has a coefficient insignificantly different from zero, when included as an independent variable alongside the rate of investment in his growth equation, simultaneous equation estimation of aid and growth equations using instrumental variables may still be appropriate. Extension of Levy's exercise in this way, using the most recently available data, would be a valuable research project.

Levy's evidence notwithstanding, there remains at least the suspicion that aid inflows are endogenous since donors may provide aid in response to adverse economic conditions, including low saving rates, in host countries (Gersovitz, 1988: 416–17). In addition, inflows of foreign aid, and foreign capital generally, may be diverted into government recurrent expenditure on consumables rather than towards public investment. These effects have been examined in work by Heller (1975) and Mosley *et al.* (1987).

In Heller's model, public officials maximize an objective function subject to a budget constraint. The choices are between various public expenditure categories: public investment for development, civil consumption (e.g., administration) and consumables associated with 'socio-economic' activities (e.g., hospitals). Heller estimated five equations for government revenue, the three expenditure categories just mentioned and government borrowing from domestic sources. Data were obtained for 11 African countries (Nigeria, Ghana, Zambia, Kenya, Uganda, Tanzania, Malawi, Ethiopia, Tunisia and Morocco) over

6 years. The data were pooled and estimation was by the two-stage least squares technique. Heller found that loans to the public sector were negatively correlated with government revenue while the coefficient on grants to the public sector was insignificant. In the investment equation, the grants term was significant while the loans term was insignificant on a two-tailed test at the 5 per cent level of significance. The coefficient on grants to the public sector was less than unity (0.7), suggesting that some aid inflows may have leaked into spending on consumables.

Heller's study cast doubt on the effectiveness of foreign aid in promoting investment and growth, contrary to the earlier claims of Papanek.Tentative evidence was found for the view that foreign aid might be shifted into consumables with an associated reluctance of governments in Africa to increase or collect taxes. This reluctance to exploit the full potential tax base in Africa, partly reflected in the narrowness of the tax base and the limited range of goods subject to indirect taxation (Frimpong-Ansah, 1988), may have forced governments to divert aid into the recurrent budget.

Heller's optimization framework was taken up and developed in a comprehensive study by Mosley *et al.* (1987). They estimate the following equation:

$$dY = a_0 + a_1A + a_2S + a_3I_f + a_4dX + a_5dL^* \qquad (5.1)$$

Percentage annual rate of growth of natural income is dY, A is aid inflow, S is domestic saving, I_f is foreign capital inflow, dX is percentage annual rate of growth of exports and dL^* is percentage annual rate of growth of literacy. This equation is estimated using ordinary least squares for the periods 1960–70, 1970–80 and 1980–3, with a sample of over 50 developing countries and various sub-samples including one specifically for Africa. Aid comprises gross aid inflows as measured by the Development Assistance Committee of OECD. This data does not coincide exactly with that of Levy, above, who uses the concept of Official Development Assistance which was introduced only in 1968.

In the aggregate sample for 1960–70, with a cross-section over period annual averages, the only variable significant in OLS estimate of (5.1) is growth rate of exports. For 1970–80, the only variables significant are export growth and saving ratio. In the equation for Africa, none of the variables are significant for 1960–70, while for 1970–80 only the growth of exports is significant.

Mosley *et al.* extend their single estimating equation into a three-equation model which captures the possible endogeneity of aid. In the first equation, the growth rate depends upon aid, other financial flows, saving rate, growth of literacy and growth of exports as in (5.1) above. In the second equation, aid depends upon per capita income at the beginning of the period, start of period mortality and growth rate. This equation is non-linear. Finally, change in mortality is taken to depend upon aid, per capita income at start of period and growth.

Using three-stage least squares to handle non-linearity of the aid equation, Mosley *et al.* find for their complete sample that aid flows are correlated with the level but not the growth of income. The coefficient on aid in the growth equation is insignificant and this appears to suggest lack of simultaneity between aid and growth. However, the mortality equation generates poor results and it is possible that change in mortality should be replaced by investment–GDP ratio as one of the endogenous variables in a three-equation system. This modification might then permit a further test of Levy's claim of direct causality from aid through to investment–GDP ratio and then to growth rate. It would also permit a synthesis of the modelling approaches of Levy and Mosley *et al.* Certainly, further work is needed before the hypothesis of simultaneity can be rejected.

In contrast to Levy's proposed interpretation that terms of trade movements have offset any beneficial impacts on investment and growth, Mosley *et al.* suggest that the lack of correlation between aid and growth reflects other offsetting impacts, with rates of return on both private and public investment falling as aid flows increased in the 1970s. The 1970s saw a multiplication of donor numbers and attempts to divert aid to projects in the rural and social sectors with lower rates of return. Against this, however, Mosley *et al.* argue that the crowding-out impact of aid on private sector investment actually fell in the 1970s, one factor being the lower probability of expropriation of private sector assets as the number of countries with nationalization measures without compensation fell in the 1970s, particularly in Africa.

In summary, whereas Levy emphasizes external terms of trade movements in the explanation of lower African growth rates in the 1970s, Mosley *et al.* are more concerned with factors determining the internal effectiveness of aid, along the lines of Heller (1975). Some synthesis between these approaches, together with further experimentation using systems techniques to test for simultaneity in the aid-growth relation, would appear to be in order. It would also be desirable to update the studies reviewed in this section to take account of observations since 1983. At present, though, the question of complementarity of aid and domestic saving remains unresolved.

6. Conclusions

We return to the dominant theme of the FAO symposium (1986), namely the mobilization of domestic saving for African development. There is a consensus that extension of financial institutions to improve the channels from household and company saving to fixed investment would be desirable. Disagreement remains over recommendations to remove interest rate ceilings on deposits and liberalize financial markets. Deregulation of interest rates to overcome financial repression may raise inflation, lower growth rates and actually reduce financial deepening, as we saw in our summary of van Wijnbergen's model. Those arguments, which apply both to 'sharp shock' and 'gradualist' approaches to deregulation of financial markets, seem to us to be strong but it remains necessary to obtain empirical support for van Wijnbergen's crucial assumption that time deposits and informal loans are indeed substitutes.

Bland recommendations to improve the provision of financial services to rural areas in Africa will achieve little unless the inability, or reluctance, of financial institutions to open branches in these areas are properly understood. Recent theories of credit rationing as an equilibrium phenomenon, drawing on imperfect information problems as outlined in the third part of this chapter, offer considerable insights; further work is needed to make these models operational in particular African credit markets.

The empirical sections of our survey have revealed a dearth of econometric evidence on key questions for macro-economic policy in Africa. Econometric studies of the saving-investment-growth process in African economies are urgently needed and even broad-brush, small macro-econometric models can yield some insights on policy questions. In the fifth part of the chapter, we saw that the relationship between aid and domestic saving is one area where some work has been undertaken of relevance to Africa and here there is a base for further work.

The twin problems of high (and still growing) levels of African debt and the application of stabilization policies, often connected with IMF conditionality, have attracted relatively greater attention elsewhere and have not been examined in our survey (see Clunies Ross, 1989, and Buiter, 1988, for overviews). Short-run stabilization programmes will have implications for long-term development strategy and it is important that these are better understood. In particular, domestic resource mobilization must be considered in relation to difficult trade-offs concerning, for example, the urgent need for public infrastructure in African economies against the requirement to set a path for growth of government spending consistent with single-digit, stable inflation.

The FAO symposium proposed an intensified drive to raise domestic saving as a response to foreign exchange constraints. But, in the two-gap model, and in structuralist models generally, even if measures to increase domestic saving are successful, the potential for higher growth rates must still be limited, precisely because of the foreign exchange constraint (UNCTAD, 1987). As Bardhan (1988) observes, small countries, including those in sub-Saharan Africa, may face foreign exchange constraints with export demand limited partly by insufficient growth of aggregate demand in developed nations and partly by unfavourable movements in terms of trade. Where capital movements take the form of interest-bearing foreign debt, credit rationing in world markets may sustain foreign exchange constraints for African economies. Not surprisingly, African economies are reluctant to open up capital markets for fear of capital flight. As Taylor and Arida suggest, 'instead of financial repression it is the financial openness of processes of interest rate determination which is the pressing problem for LDCs' (1988: 186).

If Taylor and Arida are correct, and further work is needed to substantiate their conclusion, then the prospects for domestic resource mobilization based on raising flows of domestic saving to stimulate growth will be modest. This claim is strongly argued in UNCTAD (1987). Nevertheless, it remains important for rational policy formation to extend analytical and empirical work on the economic mechanisms determining saving, availability of credit, investment and growth in African economies.

Notes

1. See Agu (1988) for a case-study of financial policy in Nigeria.
2. Our presentation follows Arrieta (1988).
3. Credit rationing is perhaps a more neutral term. The state described by McKinnon is one of excess demand for bank credit. It is also characterized by a low monetization rate measured by money/GDP ratio.
4. Abdel-Khalek (1987) makes this point in relation to IMF-recommended stabilization programmes in Egypt. McKinnon (1973: Ch.7), and IMF officials, recommend joint policies of financial reform and demand restraint to control inflation.
5. The experience of Chile and Argentina in 1980–2 is instructive here (Dornbusch, 1982). With open capital markets, and anticipation of substantial devaluation beyond specified magnitudes set by the authorities, real interest rates soared. Instability may well result when financial liberalization coincides with capital mobility and high inflation. This point is strongly emphasized in UNCTAD (1987).
6. An exact stability condition is for saving propensity out of profits to exceed responsiveness of growth of capital to rate of profit.
7. Beyond a certain point, increased collateral can actually reduce returns to the bank. This is because the average degree of risk aversion of borrowers will tend to fall and investors will be attracted who undertake riskier projects – as is the case for increased interest rates. It is not always profitable to raise collateral requirements when credit is rationed.
8. Expansionary monetary policy refers to increased bank reserves which raise the level of bank credit.
9. There is an analogy here with the result of equilibrium wage differentials between urban and rural sectors which are traced by Stiglitz to turnover costs in developing countries' labour markets (Stiglitz, 1987a).
10. See Gupta (1984) for a survey of empirical work on aggregate saving functions in the 1960s and 1970s and his own study, covering similar ground to Fry and finding only limited support for the financial repression hypothesis. More recent work is surveyed in Arrieta (1988) and Fry (1988).
11. This does not prevent some commentators (FAO, 1986; Frimpong-Ansah, 1988) from proposing interest rate reforms on the grounds that interest rates have not affected domestic saving rates in developing countries precisely because of the presence of interest rate ceilings. The impact of interest rates on saving can then only be ascertained once controls are lifted. This represents a fundamentally untestable assertion. Moreover, since interest rate ceilings are typically set in nominal terms, variations in inflation generate variations in real

deposit interest rates making possible econometric investigation of the real interest rate elasticity of domestic saving.

12.   Buffie (1984) criticizes Taylor's models for their lack of behavioural foundations, i.e., the lack of any derivation from individuals' maximization problems. This applies both to the aggregate saving function, which posits an exogenous saving propensity out of profits, and the investment function, where the average, rather than marginal, rate of profit is an explanatory variable. In contrast, van Wijnbergen leaves his aggregate demand specification open and the permanent income and life-cycle theories of consumption and saving are quite compatible with a standard IS schedule.

13.   Ghana's severe foreign exchange shortage is associated with, but not necessarily caused by, a negligible aid-GNP ratio over the period 1974–82. Ghana's problems may be due to a hugely overvalued exchange rate and the IMF did recommend a large-scale (maxi) devaluation in this case. Taylor (1988) deals with the problems of possible adverse effects of maxi-devaluations in Africa.

14.   The null hypothesis that all observations can be pooled without accounting for country and time random effects is rejected by F-tests.

References

Abdel-Khalek, G. (1987). 'Egypt', World Institute for Development Economic Research, Stabilization and Adjustment Policies and Programmes, Country Study No. 9, Helsinki.

Agu, C. (1988). 'Interest rate policy in Nigeria and attendant distortions', Savings and Development, 12.

Arrieta, G. G. (1988). 'Interest rates, savings and growth in LDCs: an assessment of recent empirical research', World Development, 16: 589–605.

Asimakopulos, A. (1983). 'Kalecki and Keynes on finance, investment and saving', Cambridge Journal of Economics, 7: 221–33.

Bardhan, P. (1988). 'Alternative approaches to development economics', in H. Chenery and T. Srinivasan (eds).

Bell, C. (1988). 'Credit markets and interlinked transactions', in H. Chenery and T. Srinivasan (eds).

Bernheim, B. D. (1987). 'Ricardian equivalence: an evaluation of theory and evidence' in S. Fischer (ed.) NBER Macroeconomics Annual 1987, MIT Press, Cambridge, Ma.

Blanchard, O. and Fischer, S. (1989). Lectures on Macroeconomics, MIT Press, Cambridge, Ma.

Blinder, A. (1987). 'Credit rationing and effective supply failures', Economic Journal, 97: 327–52.

Buffie, E. (1984). Book review of L. Taylor, Structuralist Macroeconomics, Journal of Development Economics, 16: 214–22.

Buiter, W. (1988). 'Some thoughts on the role of fiscal policy in stabilization and structural adjustment in developing countries', London School of Economics, Centre of Labour Economics Discussion Paper No. 321.

Chandavarkar, A. (1986). 'The non-institutional financial sector: macroeconomic implications for savings policies' in FAO (1986).

Chenery, H. and Srinivasan, T. (eds) (1988). Handbook of Development Economics, Vol. 1, North-Holland, Amsterdam.

Clunies Ross, A. (1989). 'Stabilization targets and instruments in developing countries', Journal of Economic Studies, 15, 2: 1–74.

Dornbusch, R. (1982). 'Stabilization policies in developing countries: what have we learned?', World Development, 10: 701–8.

Dornbusch, R. and Reynoso, A. (1989). 'Financial factors in economic development', American Economic Review Papers and Proceedings, 79: 204–9.

Food and Agriculture Organization of the United Nations (FAO) (1986). Third International Symposium on the Mobilization of Personal Savings in Developing Countries, held at Yaounde, Cameroon, 10–14 December 1984, United Nations.

Frimpong-Ansah, J. (1988). 'Some problems of managing and financing of economic development in Africa: an overview', Salford Papers in Economics, 88–3.

Fry, M. (1980). 'Saving, investment, growth and the cost of financial repression', World Development, 8: 317–27.

Fry, M. (1988). Money, Interest, and Banking in Economic Development, Johns Hopkins University Press, Baltimore.

Galbis, V. (1977). 'Financial intermediation and economic growth in developing countries: a theoretical approach', Journal of Development Studies, 13: 58–72.

Gersovitz, M. (1988). 'Saving and development' in H. Chenery and T. Srinivasan (eds).

Giovannini, A. (1983). 'The interest elasticity of savings in developing countries: the existing evidence', World Development, 11: 601–7.

Giovannini, A. (1985). 'Saving and the real interest rate in LDCs', Journal of Development Economics, 18: 197–217.

Greenwald, B. and Stiglitz, J. (1987). 'Money, imperfect information, and economic fluctuations', National Bureau of Economic Research Working Paper, February.

Gupta, K. (1984). *Finance and Economic Growth in Developing Countries,* Croom Helm, Beckenham.

Heller, P. (1975). 'A model of public fiscal behavior in developing countries: aid, investment and taxation', *American Economic Review,* 65: 368–79.

Kahn, R. (1959). 'Exercises in the analysis of growth', *Oxford Economic Papers,* 11: 143–56.

Kalecki, M. (1971). *Selected Essays on the Dynamics of the Capitalist Economy,* Cambridge University Press, Cambridge.

Keynes, J. M. (1936). *The General Theory of Employment, Interest and Money,* Macmillan, London.

Kidane, A. (1991). 'The determinants of saving in Ethiopia', this volume.

Lancaster, C. and Williamson, J. (eds) (1986). 'African debt and financing', Institute for International Economics, Special Report No. 5, Washington, DC.

Leff, N. and Sato, K. (1980). 'Macroeconomic adjustment in developing countries: instability, short-run growth and external dependency', *Review of Economics and Statistics,* 62: 170–9.

Leite, S. P. and Makonnen, D. (1986). 'Saving and interest rates in the BCEAO countries: an empirical analysis', *Savings and Development,* 10: 219–32.

Levy, V. (1988). 'Aid and growth in sub-Saharan Africa: the recent experience', *European Economic Review,* 32: 1777–95.

McKinnon, R. (1973). *Money and Capital in Economic Development,* Brookings Institute, Washington, DC.

Mosley, P., Hudson, J. and Horrell, S. (1987). 'Aid, the public sector and the market in less-developed countries', *Economic Journal,* 97: 616–41.

Shaw, E. (1973). *Financial Deepening in Economic Development,* Oxford University Press, Oxford.

Stiglitz, J. (1985). 'Information and economic analysis', *Economic Journal Conference Supplement,* 95: 21–42.

Stiglitz, J. (1987a). 'The wage-productivity hypothesis: its economic consequences and policy implications', in M. Boskin (ed.), *Modern Developments in Public Finance,* Blackwell, Oxford.

Stiglitz, J. (1987b). 'The causes and consequences of the dependence of quality on prices', *Journal of Economic Literature,* 25: 1–47.

Stiglitz, J. (1988). 'Economic organizations, information and development': in H. Chenery and T. Srinivasan (eds).

Stiglitz, J. and Weiss, A. (1981). 'Credit rationing in markets with imperfect information', *American Economic Review,* 71: 393–410.

Taylor, L. (1983). *Structuralist Macroeconomics,* Basic Books, New York.

Taylor, L. (1988). *Varieties of Stabilisation Experience,* Oxford University Press, Oxford.

Taylor, L. and Arida, P. (1988). 'Long-run income distribution and growth' in H. Chenery and T. Srinivasan (eds).

Tobin, J. (1984). 'On the efficiency of the financial system', *Lloyds Bank Review,* No. 153, July: 1–15.

United Nations Conference on Trade and Development (UNCTAD) (1987). *Trade and Development Report 1987,* United Nations.

van Wijnbergen, S. (1982). 'Stagflationary effects of monetary stabilization policies', *Journal of Development Economics,* 10: 133–69.

van Wijnbergen, S. (1983). 'Interest rate management in LDCs', *Journal of Monetary Economics,* 12: 433–52.

Williamson, J. (1983). *The Open Economy and the World Economy,* Basic Books, New York.

World Bank (1987). *World Development Report 1987,* Oxford University Press, Oxford.

3 Household Savings & Credit: A Long View of Policy*

Barbara Ingham

For the countries of sub-Saharan Africa, with relatively small corporate and public sectors, an active domestic savings policy necessarily entails strong commitment to the mobilization of personal and household savings. This is especially true of the savings of farming households. Numerous studies which have been made of savings in rural and urban areas have stressed the higher marginal propensity to save of rural, as compared with urban, families. The savings of farming households are critical in this respect, not forgetting the savings of many others who derive their livelihood from related occupations – fishing, hunting, forestry – or those who work as craftsmen and traders in rural areas.

It is a commonplace now in the literature, that despite widespread rural poverty in sub-Saharan Africa, there is a savings capacity which can be harnessed.[1] But to devise successful strategies for savings mobilization requires first and foremost a close study of the savings behaviour of the household. What does the evidence reveal? Most of the studies for sub-Saharan Africa support a positive relationship between household income and household savings. The influence of interest rates and price levels on savings is, however, somewhat indeterminate. Other influences on savings are undoubtedly important but are as yet imperfectly understood. These include such items as wealth, taxation, occupation and demographic factors.

A good understanding of the various influences on savings behaviour is a *sine qua non* of a successful savings mobilization strategy. In addition to the familiar influences of income, exchange rates, interest rates and agricultural prices, there are influences of an institutional kind. An example is the many 'informal' savings clubs, shaped to local conditions, which have long played an important role in savings mobilization and the provision of credit in sub-Saharan Africa.[2]

The present chapter sets debates on an appropriate policy framework for the mobilization of household savings in a long-run context. We begin by reviewing briefly early 'development policy' by reference to the attitudes to household saving displayed by colonial administrations in the last years of colonialism. Such policy as there was, does not appear to have been rooted in any systematic analyses of farmers' savings and investment behaviour. Rather, as a consequence of the inter-war depression, there was a preoccupation with rural indebtedness which tended to obscure the issue of rural savings and the potential

* Early drafts of this chapter were discussed in seminars at the University of London's School of Oriental and African Studies, and at the University of Bradford. I am grateful for comments received there from, among others, Chizuko Tominga, Gareth Austen, Ronald Toby and Colin Kirkpatrick.

therein. Farmers were assumed to be wholly reliant on outside sources, particularly on compulsory savings through producer cooperatives, to finance their investment expenditures.

Bringing the story up to date, in terms of national governments and influential policy-making bodies such as the World Bank and the United Nations, here too policy prescriptions may lack the detailed attention to farmers' motivations and responses, which a successful savings strategy would require. In this later case, however, the problem of rural indebtedness may be in danger of being forgotten altogether. Too often, for instance, bodies such as the IMF and World Bank, in advocating interest rate adjustments to facilitate household savings, ignore the significant negative component of the savings equation which is rooted in poverty and relies for its resolution on very long-run strategies for reducing indebtedness, increasing thrift, and promoting self-reliance among the rural population. This is the fundamental problem in the formulation of an appropriate savings strategy. It arises out of the conflict in economic theory between approaches which perceive a central role for the rate of interest as equating the demand for and the supply of loanable funds, and those approaches which assume for the rate of interest a role in relation to savings which is secondary to the role of income. In this latter case, there is an implicit distinction between borrowing for consumption and borrowing for investment purposes. Poverty leads to dissaving at low income levels. Poverty may also mean a dearth of profitable investment opportunities. It is likely to be accompanied by high rates of interest for potential lenders, deriving from risky money-lending activities in the informal sector.

In recent years information on the size and structure of 'informal' credit markets in Africa has increased, though much work still remains to be done. Informal credit arrangements cover the activities of traditional savings clubs, but also include a huge variety of non-institutional money-lenders and traders, as well as friends and relatives. Most studies confirm that interest rates charged on loans in the informal sector are significantly higher than those charged in the formal sector. The informal sector, where traders, money-lenders, friends and relatives constitute the principle sources of credit, has a large component of borrowing for 'non-productive' purposes. Borrowing is significantly linked to the timing and extent of poverty-based rural indebtedness. Few of the borrowers can meet the collateral requirements of the formal banking system. The high risks associated with this type of lending explain, partly though not entirely, the exorbitantly high rates of interest to be found in the informal sector.[3]

One of the few recent innovations in policy-making in sub-Saharan Africa has been the attempt to develop links between formal and informal financial markets, in order to increase the supply of credit to the rural sector and reduce the interest rate differential between the two markets. Much stress has been placed on the potential of indigenous savings clubs, such as the *esusu*, to develop into institutions more akin to rural banks. It may be, however, that efforts to build up local financial institutions need to be more firmly rooted in schemes to alleviate poverty. This is the view taken in the recent Economic Commission for Africa's *African Alternative Framework to Structural Adjustment Programmes*, and it is one which a long-run appraisal of policy on savings and credit tends to support.

1. Savings and Credit in the pre-Independence Era

It is unlikely nowadays that in sub-Saharan Africa the general population has a significant propensity for long-term hoarding, as distinct from short-term 'putting aside' in the absence of sufficient savings facilities.[4] But for the majority of the population in early colonial days, the principle method of saving money appears to have been hoarding. This fact was known to colonial administrations from the earliest days. Hoarding was perceived as a problem by colonial administrations because it made it difficult to estimate the amount of traditional currencies and modern currencies in circulation.[5] Colonial administrations were also aware of the extensive, though fragile, system of credit which characterized the more commercialized areas of sub-Saharan Africa. At one end of the scale, wealthy merchants provided credit for professional traders, an increasingly important activity from the mid-nineteenth century onwards with the spread of the mercantile economy. This is what Hicks, in his *Theory of Economic History*, referred to as the growth of the 'inside' market in the development of merchant capitalism, the market for credit-worthy borrowers with merchant lending to merchant. In capitalist economies it was linked to the growth of money and the legal system, with the emergence of financial intermediaries, banks and insurance contracts.

At the other end of the scale in pre-independence Africa, were the small indigenous savings and credit institutions. Groups of kinsmen or friends would club together to raise money for social purposes, often with a ceremonial aspect such as a wedding or a funeral. Members usually made a very small regular contribution to the fund and, in addition to the common purpose, could receive accumulated savings on a rotational basis. Finally, poor men might borrow from their richer neighbours, an extensive system which varied from society to society as to the detail and the demands of customary law. Land might serve as collateral, or even the borrower's own person or that of a kinsman be offered as security. Labour services could be rendered to the lender, or the product of the land handed over, until the day when the pledge was redeemed.

It was in the last decades of colonialism in Africa, with increased emphasis on economic development as a necessary adjunct to political change, that the issue of rural savings and agricultural credit attracted the attention of researchers and policy-makers. The problem was then perceived as one of encouraging small farmers to invest in improved techniques of production involving better livestock, implements, fertilizers and soil conservation methods. It was assumed that many farmers were too poor to finance necessary improvements out of their own resources, and that increased attention needed to be paid to methods of providing capital for peasant farmers. It was further noted that many peasant communities exhibited large-scale and chronic indebtedness. A significant proportion of this debt had not been incurred through borrowing for 'productive' purposes. Rather it was the consequence of such occurrences as illness or natural disaster, falling crop prices, litigation, past debt, or, in some circumstances, extravagant expenditure on ceremonies such as weddings and funerals, required by custom. Finally, it was recognized that relatively few farming households made use of commercial banks or post offices for whatever savings they might have, preferring to keep their cash at home or with a trusted friend or relative.

The availability of agricultural credit came increasingly to be seen as a problem, one which together with rural indebtedness was seen as severely limiting the scope for improvement in the standard of living in sub-Saharan Africa. Rural indebtedness was a preoccupation of the colonial administrations throughout the 1930s and 1940s. To a large degree, the recognition of widespread rural indebtedness was responsible for the neglect of the rural savings potential. Farmers were assumed to be too poor or too profligate to save. It took Polly Hill, many years later, to remind us that in African conditions, where most debt is owed locally, for every rural debtor there must be a rural creditor with surplus funds available for investment.[6]

Rural indebtedness was common in sub-Saharan Africa during the inter-war period. Falling producer prices had dramatically increased rural poverty and hence the burden of debt. In some areas, litigation added to the problems. This was largely a consequence of increasing commercialization. Private property in land ran counter to customary law and, in the absence of written records, this resulted in large numbers of expensive lawsuits which could

Table 3.1   Average expenditure of indebted and non-indebted families in Akokoaso (1930s)

	125 Indebted families			76 Non-indebted families		
	£	s	d	£	s	d
1. Food purchased	4	0	4	3	2	2
2. Clothes purchased	2	7	0	1	14	2
3. Utensils, etc.		7	8		7	1
4. School fees		11	8		2	8
5. Religious expenses		18	7		8	8
6. Public welfare	1	7	6		9	6
7. Other (palm wine, repairs, etc.)	1	4	3	1	4	3

Source: W. H. Beckett, quoted in Hancock (1942)

impoverish not only individuals but entire communities. In Akokoaso, for instance, the famous Gold Coast cocoa village surveyed in the 1930s by W. H. Beckett, the Senior Agricultural Officer, annual community debt from litigation was equivalent to £500 per year.

Beckett's work was instructive also in providing a picture of the private debt which dominated Akokoaso. About half of the farming households were described as 'indebted' with debts ranging from less than £1 to over £500. The majority of families owed between £10 and £50. Half of the private debt was owed inside the village by neighbour to neighbour. Indebted farmers were poorer on average than their non-indebted neighbours but, interestingly, the average expenditure of debt-encumbered families was greater than unencumbered ones (Table 3.1). Commenting on Beckett's data, Hancock remarked that they 'seem to suggest that Akokoaso was divided into rollicking Esaus and stingy Jacobs'. The reality was more complicated. The list of indebted households included the chiefs and elders, who were obliged to spend more money than ordinary families. Nevertheless, Hancock concluded, like Beckett, that borrowing was in large measure for 'non-productive' purposes.

The view that rural indebtedness was widespread, and that it arose largely from the side of consumption expenditure, influenced official attitudes to the financing of agricultural investment in the 1930s and 1940s. The possibility of mobilizing farmers' own savings to finance such investment received very little attention. In Britain, the Economic Advisory Committee, called upon in 1945 to report on agricultural credit in the colonies, did not discuss farmer's own savings as a source of investment funds. The Committee concluded that the main credit need of agriculturalists in the colonies was for short-term credit to finance the purchase of seed, livestock and fertilizers to meet harvesting storage and marketing costs, and to finance the hire or purchase of implements. It was argued that no general solution to this problem could be expected through the medium of banks. The solution favoured instead by the Committee, much in tune with the spirit of the times, was that of *rural cooperative credit societies.* Cooperative societies would build up funds based on a levy of producer earnings. These funds would be used as a basis for rural credit. Government finance might also be channelled to producers through the societies. Rural co-operatives had already proved successful in Ceylon, Cyprus, Palestine and Mauritius, but in Africa there was scope for much more development in this direction than had yet occurred. Cooperative credit societies were regarded as the only organizations capable of competing with local money-lenders, since they would know all members personally, would have low operating expenses and interest charges, and few formalities.

Colonial administrations took little account of the many indigenous savings and credit associations which operated in sub-Saharan Africa, which have become in recent years the focus of attention in rural savings programmes. In some instances, as documented for example by Anthony Nwabughuogu (1984) for the Igbo *esusu* (Nigeria), the colonial authorities were positively hostile to the savings clubs. The *esusu* club had created a large capitalist class which dominated social, political and economic life in Ngwaland. The clubs also had a long history of shady dealing and exploitation. A member who took no loan before joining the club would be fortunate if he received half of the money he had actually contributed.

In south-eastern Nigeria the colonial government attempted unsuccessfully to replace the *esusu* clubs with cooperative thrift societies. In the end, the administration had to be content with registration of the clubs and new rules to govern their behaviour. By 1949, 1300 clubs were registered and, according to Nwabughuogu, it was impossible for the average man to pay taxes, educate his children or invest, without the help of the village *esusu*. The *esusu* is apparently a major force in capital formation in south-eastern Nigeria to the present day.

In East Africa, the cooperative movement which dated from the 1950s arguably achieved wider support than did the West African movement. Uganda and Tanzania were regarded by the colonial administrations as highly suitable for cooperative organization, being dominated by small-scale peasant producers. The marketing function of the cooperative structure was paramount, but agricultural credit schemes were widely regarded as a major additional benefit. The Credit Union movement began in Tanzania in the 1950s, as did the cooperative Thrift and Loan societies in Uganda, though the latter were not particularly successful. In Kenya, however, the pre-independence settler government actively discouraged cooperatives.

A feature of colonial policy in relation to rural savings, credit and indebtedness, is that it was developed in the 1930s, 1940s and 1950s without any systematic study of savings behaviour in the rural economies to which it was intended to apply. Economic research was in its infancy, colonial economic research even more so. A few studies of rural budgets were made in the late colonial period by individual researchers and colonial officials. Most of these studies came to grief on the question of rural savings and there was no attempt to relate savings to changes in income, cross-sectionally or through time. In these early budget studies, no consistent patterns of savings behaviour are discernible. Some studies showed little margin between income over expenditure for rural households, others recorded a significant excess of income over expenditure. To give some examples, a study (1949) by Mitchell and Barnes (Northern Rhodesia) revealed very little saving among rural households. A similar survey by Turner and Turner showed significant unaccounted differences between income (high) and expenditure (low). The researchers in this latter case commented that 'if an informant publicly revealed the full extent of his cash savings he would speedily become the subject of demands on them from kin'. An interesting aspect of early research into rural budgets, is the way in which researchers were encouraged to treat any observed discrepancies between income and expenditure. It was considered highly unlikely that a significant proportion of the local informants could have spent less than they earned. Therefore the income figure was taken to be correct and the difference entered as 'unaccounted' on the expenditure side, so that in each case income would equal expenditure. The smaller the unaccounted item, the better the survey – scarcely an inducement for the researcher to interest himself in the extent of rural savings.[7]

The 1950s also saw the publication of a quite remarkable survey undertaken between 1950 and 1954 into the cocoa farmers of Nigeria.[8] Among other matters, the researchers (R. Galletti, D.K.S. Baldwin and I. O. Dina) investigated the income and expenditure of farming households, the facilities for borrowing money and the extent of rural indebtedness. Almost 40 years on, this massive study of peasant households, nearly 1000 closely argued pages in the published version, has scarcely been bettered for any African economy, though there are surprisingly few references to it in present-day development literature. The chapter on rural indebtedness is, in itself, a remarkable achievement. At that time, not even African members of the Cocoa Marketing Board, which had sponsored the survey, were sure of the extent to which farmers were indebted. The researchers questioned 615 families in 19 localities. Forty per cent of families were free of debt in 1951 and 42 per cent in 1952, though in some localities the number of families reporting debts could be as high as two-thirds. Detailed information was provided on the causes and purposes of borrowing. Three categories of debt were defined, that incurred for 'productive' purposes such as investment in land, implements, stock-in-trade; that incurred in providing necessities such as food, shelter, education and medical expenses; and, finally, that associated with customary ceremonies such as marriage, funerals and festivals, together with that deriving from litigation. On average, 'productive' debt accounted for 31% of outstanding debt; food, shelter and other necessities for 43%; and the category of ceremonial expenditure and litigation for 26%. In all areas the main source of loans was described as 'neighbours', (Table 3.2). The survey made no distinction between the loans from wealthier kin and neighbours and those drawn from the *esusu* funds, though the latter appeared to be particularly important in meeting the costs of celebrating festivals and funerals, fighting lawsuits or building houses. Based on Bascom's work, the survey provided a particularly detailed account of the workings of the *esusu*, stressing that the members who did not draw from the fund on any occasion received their contributions at the end of the cycle. To them, the institution would be one of thrift instead of credit.[9] Table 3.2 also indicates that the

Table 3.2   Proportions of loans outstanding borrowed from various sources in towns, market villages and rural settlements in June 1952 (357 families)

Source	% of Totals		
	Towns	Market villages	Rural settlements
Cooperative	0.3	1.6	9.8
Wholesale traders	–	–	6.4
Produce buyers	21.0	16.8	21.0
Petty traders	3.8	10.1	5.0
Neighbours	39.6	52.2	40.5
Money-lenders	24.1	3.3	12.0
Labourers	9.1	15.7	4.7
Other	1.8	–	0.6
Not known	0.3	0.3	–
Total	100.0	100.0	100.0

Source: Galletti *et al.* (1956: 543)

producer cooperatives, much favoured by the colonial administration in the 1940s, had made relatively little headway in the provision of rural credit at the time of the survey, despite booming cocoa prices. The 'failure' of the cooperative model in West African conditions is well-documented.[10]

For such a detailed piece of research it is disappointing, though not surprising in view of the reluctance of farmers to provide such information, that the Nigerian survey paid very little attention to the question of rural savings. Savings were derived simply as a residual by deducting recorded expenditure from recorded receipts. Even so, the disposition to save appeared remarkably high. The savings out of income were no less than two-fifths of the whole disposable income and not a great deal less than household expenditure. This was for the year 1951/52, which recorded an unusually high cocoa price and, it should be added, that throughout the 1950s, with buoyant producer prices, peasant farmers in West Africa appear to have had a remarkably high propensity to save.[11] One result of this in the Nigerian case was that the farming families became considerably more solvent. The survey concluded that

> if an ordinary family had used all its cash, savings and jewels to pay off the debts it would have been left with an amount of between nothing and £40 in June 1951, but with an amount of between £5 and £60 in June 1952. The general financial position of the survey families was sound at the beginning of the survey, and a good deal sounder at the end (Galletti *et al.*, 1956: 570).

The early 1950s were boom years for primary products and it may well be that peasant producers throughout sub-Saharan Africa temporarily enjoyed a reduction in indebtedness. Nevertheless, agricultural indebtedness was a serious long-run problem, as revealed for instance in the Ghana Report on Agricultural Indebtedness (1957) which described a series of attempts, going back as far as 1918, to provide better thrift and investment facilities for farmers.[12] As a result of a deputation of Africans in 1925, a cooperative credit system was instituted. By the late 1930s, instability of prices resulted in significant overdue loans. Table 3.3 below illustrates the type of loan made by the Cooperative Marketing Society in the 1930s. Loans averaged £2 per farmer, at a time when the price of cocoa per 60 lb load was less than a quarter of this amount. In the 12 years from 1944 to 1956, the Ghana Co-operative Societies issued loans of more than £2.25 million to members, and had £333,000 of outstanding debt at independence. Although the cocoa farmers of Ghana had enjoyed some ten years of relatively high cocoa prices, at independence rural indebtedness was a serious problem, with three quarters of the farmers in Southern Ghana and Ashanti indebted in one form or another. Some £3 million was owed by farmers to the cocoa purchasing companies.

To summarize: in the late colonial period, administrators were obliged to take account of widespread rural indebtedness in certain parts of sub-Saharan Africa. Paradoxically, the very poorest regions had little debt, because they contained few creditworthy borrowers. Credit was perceived as necessary to bring about the modernization of agriculture in the development process, yet much of the credit granted was 'unproductive' in the sense that it represented 'dissaving' by poorer households, attempting to maintain expenditures in the face of falling incomes. Such policies as there were for agricultural credit, savings and rural indebtedness were developed without any systematic studies which would have provided information on savings and borrowing. Official attitudes, therefore, may well have missed important aspects of savings and investment behaviour in African conditions. In short, there were, in most communities, individuals and households able and willing to save both in cash and in kind. They had the wherewithal, if they so wished, to finance their own capital expenditures on land and other farming inputs. Often they preferred instead to invest in such things as housebuilding, transport or education. Professional money-lenders,

Table 3.3   *Analysis of loans granted to farmers in the Gold Coast by produce marketing societies, 1933–4*

Number of farmers	% Total	Purpose of loan
807	45.3	Expenses of cultivation
493	21.9	Household expenses
113	7.9	Old debts
65	4.6	Purchase of land
73	4.3	Building expenses
59	3.9	Funeral expenses
67	3.7	Education expenses
58	3.0	Hospital fees
18	2.6	Redemption of mortgaged fees
10	1.1	Marriage expenses
10	1.0	Court fees
12	0.6	Church dues
3	0.1	Purchase of firearms
1788	100.0	

Source: Report of the Committee on Agricultural Indebtedness (1957) (Quaidoo Report)

traders, farmers and skilled labourers would lend to others in straitened circumstances, often to meet necessary household and ceremonial expenditures. High rates of interest reflected the risks involved in lending for consumption purposes to those at or near subsistence level. The solutions favoured by colonial administrators, which were intended to encompass both the credit and debt aspects, centred on cooperative structures which may not have been suitable for all African conditions.

2. The Mobilisation of Personal Savings

In the 1960s and early 1970s, relatively little attention was paid in sub-Saharan Africa to the issues discussed in the previous pages. Some surveys of household behaviour were undertaken in the early years of the post-colonial economy but, by and large, independent governments had other preoccupations in which the interests of farming households did not feature very prominently. The savings function was taken on by the produce marketing boards, which set producer prices at levels below the ruling international price. Despite the availability of cheap credit through the marketing boards, much-needed small-scale investment in the African agricultural system was seriously neglected, though capital was forthcoming for investment in larger projects in industry and in the infrastructure. The last decade has changed all this. The debt service problem, plus the food situation, in which a considerable proportion of the demand for cereals is now being met by imports, has focused attention on the need to increase food production through improved farm inputs. The twin objectives of rural savings mobilization and improved agricultural credit schemes are given high priority in rural development strategies at the present time. Whether today's policy-makers are any better informed than their colonial predecessors about the motivations and responses of peasant households in this most critical area, is an open question.

The FAO philosophy for Africa considers rural savings mobilization as an integral part of development strategy, one which has been neglected to date in the majority of African countries.[13] The promotion of rural savings will, it is claimed, if properly linked to effective agricultural credit, lead to increased rural productivity and income. Particular attention needs to be paid, however, to situations in rural Africa, where a formal banking system is inappropriate. Existing informal forms of organization, such as rural self-help groups with a strong savings component, might offer greater benefits.

This philosophy is widely disseminated in official statements as well as in the development literature. One might question, however, whether it has been accompanied by the type of detailed research into the savings, consumption and investment behaviour of the peasant household which a successful strategy of rural savings mobilization requires. We can take, as an example, the case studies from Nigeria quoted in the paper by Seibel and Marx (1986).[14] These case studies address the question of the development potential of indigenous savings and credit associations. The most widely supported of the studies, carried out in Anambra State (Eastern Nigeria) compared three different types of self-help organization: indigenous *esusu* savings and credit associations; cooperatives based on *esusu*; and cooperatives not based on *esusu*. The criteria used to evaluate performance were such things as the savings contribution per member per month, the number of overdue loans, the total number of business ventures undertaken per month, and the income per business venture per month. The conclusions of the study were useful in showing

1. that indigenous savings and credit associations were more effective in mobilizing personal savings and financing private consumption and investment than were cooperative societies;
2. that cooperatives based on *esusu* out-performed, in both savings and investment, cooperatives without such a base.

These results confirm what might have been expected from the colonial experience. The cooperatives were imported institutions, ill-adapted in some respects to the communities on which they were imposed by policy-makers. The latter were themselves largely ignorant of the complexities of indigenous savings and investment behaviour.

Closer examination of savings and investment behaviour, however, may lead us to question whether or not the present emphasis on local savings clubs in rural savings mobilisation programmes could, in some cases, be similarly misplaced. It is possible to construct an argument which runs as follows. 'Esusu' clubs have quite specific social roles to play in African societies in financing particular types of consumption and investment expenditure. To expect the transformation of such associations, in all circumstances, into more formal savings and investment institutions, may be unrealistic. Despite the proliferation of such associations in Africa, and their long-standing nature, they have not made a great impact on personal savings. Farmers often prefer to keep cash at home and to finance investment from their own resources where possible. Experience indicates that *esusu* frequently fail to attract the savings of the wealthier and better educated members of rural societies. Mofunanya argues, in Chapter 9 of this volume, that policy-makers have a tendency to overlook the fact that the *esusu* still fulfil primarily a social role. This has everything to do with the African concept of group responsibility for the welfare of the individual. Group spirit is central to the mutual aid and rotating credit associations of Africa. Successful savings institutions, on the other hand, fill a role which is essentially individualistic. The individual needs to provide for himself and his family. Furthermore, he may wish to accumulate financial assets. Sound management takes precedence over group spirit in a savings institution.[15]

In some respects it is interesting to compare the African *esusu* with the mutual thrift and credit societies which proliferated in Britain before 1939, which have been studied extensively by Paul Johnson.[16] In his research, Johnson shows that the poor in Britain, through their Friendly societies, co-ops, burial and savings clubs, were locked into 'mutuality conditioned by economic necessity'. As in Africa, interest rates, so important to economists, were barely recognized or even understood by those who patronized the mutual thrift and credit societies. Working class life and culture centred around these institutions, which played a critical part in the social and economic survival of working class communities.

Though economists are not, by inclination or training, disposed to discuss issues such as these, they are necessary to an understanding of savings and investment behaviour in poor societies, and especially to the complex question of the allocation of savings between different types of asset. As prosperity spreads, in both 'traditional' and 'modern' societies, it is the individualistic and independent outlets – banks, building societies and similar savings institutions – which prosper. They become the vehicle for increased thrift and capital formation. The manual workers of Britain turned away from the mutual thrift and credit associations, and towards the banks and building societies, as household incomes rose. Nevertheless, given certain conditions, the African *esusu* can be remarkably adaptive and resilient, as Nwabughuogu has shown.

Rural indebtedness is a most important consideration, since a significant proportion of savings has, historically, been diverted into the highly profitable activity of money-lending. The paper by Muser (1986) offers some valuable insights in this respect.[17] First, the mobilization of personal savings is set within the general context of policies for overcoming rural poverty. Policies aimed at increasing personal savings among the poor begin from the assumption that there is such a thing as self-help among the poor, and that it can be promoted if the necessary conditions for its achievement are investigated carefully. From this point of view, 'hoarding', even saving in kind, is a valuable quality in poor societies and not to be disparaged. It fulfils the purpose of self-help and reduces rural indebtedness for societies living close to the margin of subsistence. It safeguards against personal and family emergencies and often constitutes a favoured type of capital formation for future investments.

If this approach to traditional savings behaviour is adopted, then indigenous savings and credit institutions (and indeed the more formal banking arrangements to which such institutions may be linked) appear in a new light. First, the savings function of any banking institution is paramount for the promotion of self-help. Saving, even of small amounts, needs to be done regularly. Thrift is strengthened when saving is carried out in small groups whose members know each other. This is the hidden principle of traditional savings associations, in which social control intensifies the regularity and performance of group members' savings.

Muser argues that this philosophy, rooted firmly in an understanding of savings behaviour in traditional societies, underwrites all the more successful programmes of rural savings mobilization. It is supported by the historical experience of the first German savings banks, founded in the late eighteenth and early nineteenth centuries at a time of widespread deprivation. The motive was one of self-help to overcome poverty and relieve the poor (domestic servants, labourers and tenants) of the need to rely on private money-lenders, and to keep their nest eggs at home. Only later was lending begun, and even then restricted to personal credit only, the linking of credit to the level of personal savings being a certain guarantee against excessive demand and the inability to repay credit. Only when the institutions are fully developed (a matter of many years) should such institutions attempt to transfer surplus capital from one sector to another, or one region to another.

The success stories noted by Muser in the developing world exhibit clear parallels, he claims, with the German historical experience. All began primarily as savings clubs and were only later converted into credit unions: the Grameen Bank in Bangladesh, the Agricultural Development Bank of Nepal and the National Credit Union Federation in Korea all conform to this pattern. There may also be lessons to be learned from the progress in Africa of rural banks. For instance, rural banks were established in Ghana in the 1970s under the auspices of the Central Bank, but are essentially controlled and managed by local people. Some writers see great potential in this direction, provided that rural banks are properly administered.[18]

3. Household Savings, Credit and Structural Adjustment Programmes

Over the past ten years, more than 30 African countries have adopted structural adjustment programmes (SAPs) with the support of the IMF and the World Bank. As far as the mobilization of household savings is concerned, SAPs place the market at the centre of the stage. It must be emphasized, however, that experience has made a number of commentators less confident now than they were about the ability of such policies to deliver higher savings and to allocate credit more efficiently. Against this background, we conclude the present chapter by examining briefly the policy reforms now advocated by the World Bank, together with the 'alternative' philosophies promoted by UNCTAD and the Economic Commission for Africa.

World Bank policy recognizes the role of the government in influencing the level of national savings. This can be seen in two respects: first, in the way that governments influence incentives to save for households and corporations; and, secondly, through the government's approach to its own taxation and expenditure, which influences the level of government saving. On government saving, World Bank policy demands higher public saving through expenditure controls and increased revenue. There is a general presumption against higher taxes on producers. In particular, the World Bank advocates lowering export taxes and raising taxes on consumers. As far as private savings are concerned, the emphasis is on strengthening the formal and informal financial system. Interest rates need to rise, to reflect market conditions. Stronger bank supervision is advocated, together with more prudent lending ratios and firmer debt collection policies.

Turning specifically to the question of rural savings and credit, World Bank policy argues that parastatal agricultural credit banks have been a failure. Their problems have arisen largely from political manipulation and poor management. It is argued that they should be replaced by cooperative and commercial banks. The latter are believed to be willing to go into rural areas, given attractive interest rates and an appropriate regulatory framework. In this context, commercial banks, it is argued, should be permitted to charge interest rates which fully reflect the risks involved, and the costs incurred, when they are obliged to lend on a small scale to poor farmers who are at or near subsistence level.

As far as the informal sector is concerned, the commercial banks are urged by the World Bank to develop links with traditional associations in order to improve the latter's access to credit. The supply of credit could also be improved by policies aimed at increasing land and building registration,to provide collateral for borrowers. For the informal sector, the emphasis should be on self-help schemes, with collective effort in the form of cash and labour being used to promote development activities at the local level.

The World Bank approach is rooted firmly within a macro-economic framework; this is a feature which distinguishes it, and other approaches discussed in this concluding section, from the earlier policies outlined in this chapter. Getting the macro setting right, through the adoption of appropriate fiscal and monetary policies, is fundamental to the present-day philosophy. Financial stability is a necessary prerequisite for increased household savings. It is also essential, argues the World Bank, in order to avoid capital flight, and to encourage nationals to invest in their own stock markets. The banking system has deteriorated in many African countries in recent years and, it is claimed, governments must accept much of the blame. The CFA commercial banks, for instance, have been obliged to finance expenditures which have not met any market criteria. Commercial banks should be managed on strict business principles, with the minimum of government interference. At a later stage, when the banking system is more secure, it will be appropriate for the government to encourage a deeper and more diversified system. Flexible money and capital markets will then enable the government to use a variety of monetary instruments in order to achieve the appropriate fiscal/money mix.

Against the World Bank view may be set policies on domestic savings associated with agencies of the United Nations, principally UNCTAD and the Economic Commission for Africa. Though there is agreement with the World Bank that financial stability is essential for increased domestic savings, the UNCTAD/ECA view calls primarily for the restoration of economic growth to increase domestic savings. The key relationship is perceived as that between income and savings. Interest rates, it is claimed, have not been shown to be statistically significant, or to influence savings in a positive way:

> The absence of conclusive evidence does not mean that interest rates do not matter, but rather that their influence depends on a host of factors, including the underlying financial structure, the degree of financial stability, and a whole range of economic policies.[19]

Raising interest rates, argues UNCTAD, may simply favour short-term finance over investment finance. Funds will be directed into short-term speculative investments which promise a rapid return, rather than into productive activities.

Similar views may be found in the 1989 *African Alternative Framework to Structural Adjustment Programmes* from the ECA.[20] It is argued here that upward adjustment of interest rates in order to increase savings may simply encourage speculative activities, given the imperfections of the African capital and money markets. The AAF–SAP policy comes down very heavily against high interest rates, questioning whether the savings effect of interest rates is significant for the economy as a whole and, more particularly, whether interest rate adjustments are likely to realize the rural savings potential. Instead, it is argued, in present-day African conditions high nominal interest rates may push the economy further into recession, bringing about a total collapse of credit demand and fuelling inflation through the cost–push mechanism.[21]

The ECA/UNCTAD philosophy relies primarily on fundamental structural change in Africa to bring about increased domestic savings. There is no space in this chapter to debate the far-reaching policy measures which are advocated. They include such things as land reform to give better access to land, large-scale private and public investment in agriculture, community self-help programmes and an enhanced role for women to strengthen and diversify productive capacity in rural areas and thereby raise rural savings ratios. The creation and strengthening of appropriate rural financial institutions is also supported.

The ECA/UNCTAD documents do not make clear the behavioural assumptions on which their policy measures are based, but there does appear to be broad support for the approach, in some empirical studies at the micro level. For instance, Clive Bell points out that economic theory and associated empirical work for developing countries 'warns us not to expect too much of rates of interest'. Futhermore, evidence indicates that 'a well-functioning rural credit market may be a consequence rather than a cause of general development'; and, more specifically, that 'public investment in rural infrastructure and policies which promote agricultural output, may reduce lenders' costs and encourage entry into credit markets far more powerfully and efficaciously than a volume of regulation.'[22]

By and large, however, current policy-making, either from the World Bank or from UNCTAD/ECA, does not seem to interest itself very much in testing the micro-level underpinnings of suggested policy measures. In this respect there may be something which has been lost in comparison with policy-making in the late colonial era. Although policy at that time was not rooted in any systematic study of household savings behaviour (hence 'mistakes' such as the strong espousal of the cooperative thrift and credit societies), nevertheless the micro unit was the starting point for the formulation of policies on savings and credit. The emphasis on rural indebtedness, for instance, itself a 'delicate' topic which scarcely features at all in the present-day policy documents, took its cue in the 1940s and 1950s, not from any macro-economic study of economic performance or external indebtedness, but rather from the immediate problems of farming households themselves, closely observed by traditional leaders and field administrators. The 1989 AAF–SAP document makes references to the need to encourage thrift through the establishment of rural money and credit markets, but we need to go back to an ECA document of the early 1960s to be reminded that the emphasis on thrift as being good in itself may be meaningless to people at the margin of subsistence who rely upon the goodwill of their neighbours to see them through the most desperate of times. Regrettably, the need to take into account the motivations and responses of the rural household, considering social and cultural as well as purely economic factors, is not reflected fully in current policy-making on the mobilization of household savings in Africa.

Notes

1. D. W. Adams, 'Mobilizing household savings through rural financial markets', *Economic Development and Cultural Change*, Vol. 26, No. 3, 1978; A. Mauri, 'The potential of savings and financial innovation in Africa', *Introduction: Rural Africana*, No. 2, Fall 1978; J. D. von Pischke and Dale W. Adams, *Rural Financial Markets in Developing Countries, their Use and Abuse* (World Bank, Baltimore, 1983). A useful general survey of attempts to measure and analyse household savings behaviour in the Third World is D. W. Snyder, 'Econometric studies of household saving behaviour in developing countries', *Journal of Development Studies*, January 1974. More recent surveys can be found in M. Gersovitz, 'Saving and development', and C. Bell, 'Credit markets and interlinked transactions', in H. Chenery and T. N. Srinivasan, eds, *Handbook of Development Economics*, Vol. 1, 1988.
2. On the savings potential of informal savings clubs see, in particular, Marvin P. Miracle, Diane S. Miracle and L. Cohen, 'Informal savings mobilization in Africa', *Economic Development and Cultural Change*, Vol. 28, No. 4, 1980. See also A. I. Nwabughuogu, 'The *isusu*: an institution for capital formation among the Ngwa Ibgo', *Africa*, Vol. 54, No. 4, 1984, and UN Economic and Social Council, *Indigenous Savings Associations in Eastern Africa and the Mobilization of Domestic Savings* (UN Economic Commission for Africa, 1968).
3. A useful survey of current knowledge on informal credit markets, including the level and trends of interest rates in the informal sector, can be found in African Centre for Monetary Studies, *The Role and Structure of Interest Rates in Africa* (Association of African Central Banks, April 1985), pp. 40–55.
4. UN Economic Commission for Africa, *op. cit.*
5. A. G. Hopkins, 'The creation of a colonial monetary system: the origins of the West African Currency Board', *African Historical Studies*, Vol. 3, No. 1, 1970. Although hoarding may not be an important *long-run* form of savings in sub-Saharan Africa today, nevertheless various forms of hoarding are still common in rural areas, resulting in a high rate of currency circulating outside the banks, relative to total money supply. See Association of African Banks, *op. cit.*
6. P. Hill, *Studies in Rural Capitalism in West Africa* (Cambridge University Press, Cambridge, 1970).
7. E. L. B. Turner and V. W. Turner, 'Money economy among the Mwinilunga Ndembu: a study of some individual cash budgets' *Rhodes-Livingstone Journal*, No. 18, 1955. J. C. Mitchell and J. A. Barnes, *The Lamba Village: Report of a Social Survey*, School of African Studies, New Series, No. 24 (University of Cape Town, Cape Town, 1950). The research techniques are as described in J. C. Mitchell, 'The collection and treatment of family budgets in primitive communities as a field problem', *Rhodes-Livingstone Journal*, 1949.
8. R. Galletti, K. D. S. Baldwin and I. O. Dina, *Nigerian Cocoa Farmers, an Economic Survey of Yoruba Cocoa Farming Families* (Oxford University Press for the Nigerian Cocoa Marketing Board, Lagos, 1956).

9.   W. R. Bascom, 'The *Esusu* a credit institution of the Yoruba', *Journal of the Royal Anthropological Institute*, Vol. 82, Part I, 1952.
10. C. F. Strickland, *Report on the Introduction of Co-operative Societies into Nigeria* (Government Printer, Lagos, 1934); H. D. Seibel and U. G. Damachi, *Self-Help Organisations: Guidelines and Case Studies for Development Planners and Field Workers – A Participative Approach* (Bonn, 1982). Both quoted in H. D. Seibel . and M. Marx, 'Mobilization of Personal Savings through Co-operative Societies or Indigenous Savings and Credit Associations: Case Studies from Nigeria' in the Proceedings of the Symposium on the Mobilization of Personal Savings in Developing Countries, held under the auspices of the UN at Yaounde, Cameroon, December 1984.
11. This was the conclusion reached in B. M. Ingham, *Tropical Exports and Economic Development* (Macmillan, London, 1981).
12. Report of the Committee on Agricultural Indebtedness (Quaidoo Report), 1957.
13. UN FAO, *Savings Mobilization for Agricultural and Rural Development in Africa* Third International Symposium on the Mobilization of Personal Savings in Developing Countries held in Yaounde, Cameroon, December 1984.
14. H. D. Seibel and M. Marx, *op. cit.*
15. UN Economic Commission for Africa, *op. cit.*, p. 28.
16. Paul Johnson, *Saving and Spending, the Working Class Economy in Britain, 1870 to 1939* (Clarendon Press, Oxford, 1985).
17. A. Muser, 'Mobilization of personal savings through self-help promotion institutions', paper presented at the Third International Symposium on the Mobilization of Personal Savings in Developing Countries, UN, 1986.
18. W. Aggrey-Mensah, 'Rural banks as instruments for mobilizing savings: a case study of Ghana', Second International Symposium on the Mobilization of Personal Savings in Developing Countries, Kuala Lumpur, Malaysia, March 1982.
19. United Nations Conference on Trade and Development, 'Savings and investment in developing countries', *Trade and Development Report, 1987*, p.56.
20. E/ECA/CM, *African Alternative Framework to Structural Adjustment Programmes for Socio-Economic Recovery and Transformation*, (UN/ECA, July 1989).
21. *Ibid.,* p. 46.
22. Clive Bell, 'Credit markets and interlinked transactions', in Chenery and Srinivasan, *op. cit.*, p 826.

References

Adams, D. W. (1973). 'The case for voluntary savings mobilisation: why rural capital markets flounder', *USAID Spring Review of Small Farmer Credit,* Vol. 19.

Adams, D. W. (1978). 'Mobilizing household savings through rural financial markets', *Economic Development and Cultural Change,* Vol. 26, No. 3.

Aggrey-Mensah, W. (1982). 'Rural banks as instruments for mobilizing savings: a case study in Ghana', Second International Symposium on the Mobilization of Personal Savings in Developing Countries, Kuala Lumpur, Malaysia.

Association of African Central Banks (1985). *The Role and Structure of Interest Rates in Africa* , African Centre for Monetary Studies, Dakar, Senegal, April.

Bascom, W. R. (1952). 'The *ususu* a credit institution of the Yoruba', *Journal of the Royal Anthropological Institute,* Vol. 82, Part I.

Bottomley, A. (1975). 'Interest rate determination in underdeveloped rural areas', *American Journal of Agricultural Economics,* No. 54.

Bhjatt, V. V. & Meerman, J.(1978). 'Resource mobilization in developing countries: financial institutions and policies', *World Development,* Vol. 6, No. 1.

CEAC (1946). *Agricultural Credit in the Colonies,* Report of the Finance Sub-Committee, 46, 74, Public Records Office, London

Chalmers, R. (1893/1972). *History of Currency in the British Colonies,* Chapter 18, reprinted by the Vineyard Press, Colchester.

Chandrakar, A. (1977). *Monetization of Developing Economies,* IMF Staff Papers, Vol. 24, No. 3.

Chenery, H. and Srinivasan, T. N. (1988). *Handbook of Development Economics,* North-Holland.

Colonial Office (1946). *Memorandum on Colonial Agricultural Policy,* C0990/2 133087, Public Records Office, London.

De Lancey, M. W. (1978). 'Savings and credit institutions in rural West Africa', *Introduction: Rural Africana,* No. 2, Fall.

Economic Commission for Africa (1989). *African Alternative Framework to Structural Adjustment Programmes,* UN/ECA, July.

FAO (1986). 'Savings mobilization for agricultural and rural development in Africa', paper presented at the Third

International Symposium on the Mobilization of Personal Savings in Developimg Countries, held at Yaounde, Cameroon, 10–14 December 1984, United Nations.

Galbis, V. (1977). 'Financial intermediaries in economic growth in less developed countries: a theoretical approach', *Journal of Development Studies*, No. 13.

Garlick, P. (1971). *African Traders and Economic Development in Ghana*, Clarendon Press, Oxford.

Galletti, R., Baldwin, D.K.S. and Dina, I. O. (1956). *Nigerian Cocoa Farmers. An Economic Survey of Yoruba Cocoa Farming Families*, Oxford University Press for the Nigerian Cocoa Marketing Board.

Hart, K. (1970). 'Small scale entrepreneurs in Ghana and development planning', *Journal of Development Studies*, July.

Hancock, W. K. (1942). *Survey of British Commonwealth Affairs*, Royal Institute of International Affairs.

Haswell, M. R. (1963). *The Changing Pattern of Economic Activity in a Gambian Village*, HMSO, London.

Hicks, J. (1969). *A Theory of Economic History*, Oxford University Press, London and New York.

Hill, P. (1970). *Studies in Rural Capitalism in West Africa*, Cambridge University Press, Cambridge.

Hopkins, A. G. (1970). 'The creation of a colonial monetary system: the origins of the West African Currency Board', *African History Studies*, No. 111 (1).

Ingham, B. M. (1981). *Tropical Exports and Economic Development*, Macmillan, London.

Johnson, Paul (1985). *Saving and Spending, The Working-class Economy in Britain, 1870–1939*, Oxford University Press, Oxford.

Lewis, W. A. (1955). *The Theory of Economic Growth*, Allen & Unwin, London.

Mauri, A. (1983).'The potential for savings and financial innovation in Africa', *Savings and Development*, No. 4.

Miracle, M., Miracle, D. and Cohen, L. (1980). 'Informal savings mobilization in Africa', *Economic Development and Cultural Change*, Vol. 28, No. 4, July.

Mitchell, J. C. (1949). 'The collection and treatment of family budgets in primitive communities as a field problem', *Rhodes-Livingstone Journal*, No. 8.

Mitchell, J. C. and Barnes, J. A. (1950). *The Lamba Village: Report of a Social Survey*, School of African Studies. New Series, No. 24, University of Cape Town, Cape Town.

Muser, A. (1986). 'Mobilization of personal savings through self-help promotion institutions', paper presented at the Third International Symposium on the Mobilization of Personal Savings in Developing Countries, held at Yaounde, Cameroon, 10–14 December 1984, United Nations.

Newbury, C. W. (1972). 'Credit in early nineteenth century West Africa trade', *Journal of African History*, Vol. 13, No. 1.

Nwabughuogu, A. I. (1984). 'The *isusu*: an institution for capital formation among the Ngwa Igbo, its origin and development to 1951', *Africa*, Vol. 54, No. 4.

Ofonagoro, W. I.(1979). 'From traditional to British currency in Southern Nigeria: analysis of a currency revolution, 1880–1948', *Journal of Economic History*, September.

Olayemi, J. K. (1980). 'Food crop production by small farmers in Nigeria', in Olayside, S. O. *et al.* (eds), *Nigerian Small Farmers: Problems and Prospects in Integrated Rural Development*, Caxton Press West Africa, Ibadan.

Quaidoo Report of the Committee on Agricultural Indebtedness (1957). Government Printer, Accra.

Salami, K. A. (1986). 'Analysis of the role and operation of formal agricultural lending institutions in Ghana', Institute of European Finance, research paper, University College of North Wales.

Seers, D., and Ross, C. R. (1952). *Report on the Financial and Physical Problems of Development in the Gold Coast*, Office of the Government Statistician, Accra, July.

Seibel, H. D., and Marx, M. (1986). 'Mobilization of personal savings through cooperative societies or indigenous savings and credit associations: case studies from Nigeria', paper presented at the Third International Symposium on the Mobilization of Personal Savings in Developing Countries, held at Yaounde, Cameroon, 10–14 December 1984, United Nations.

Snyder, Donald W. (1974). 'Econometric studies of household saving behaviour in developing countries: a survey', *Journal of Development Studies*, January.

Turner, E. L .B. and Turner, V. W. (1955). 'Money economy among the Mwinilunga Ndembu: a study of some individual cash budgets', *Rhodes-Livingstone Journal*, No. 18.

United Nations, Economic and Social Council (1968). *Indigenous Savings Associations in Eastern Africa and the Mobilization of Domestic Savings*, E/CN.14/HOU/21, October.

United Nations, Department of Industrial Economic and Social Affairs (1984). *Savings for Development*, Report of the Second International Symposium on the Mobilization of Personal Savings in Developing Countries, Kuala Lumpur, Malaysia, March 1982.

United Nations Conference on Trade and Development (1987). 'Savings and investment in developing countries', *Trade and Development Report 1987*.

Von Pischke, J. D., Adams, D.W. and Donald, G. (1983). *Rural Financial Markets in Developing Countries, their Use and Abuse*, World Bank, Baltimore.

Wai, U. Tun (1957). 'Interest rates outside the organized money markets of underdeveloped countries', IMF Staff Papers, November.

Warren, J. (1977). 'Savings and the financing of investment in Ghana', in *Financing of Economic Development*, Oxford University Press, Oxford.

4 The Determinants of Savings in Ethiopia*

Asmeron Kidane

1. Introduction

One of the basic requirements for understanding a nation's potential for growth and for planning its development strategy is an evaluation of the potential for domestic saving. This can only be captured by studying consumption and saving behaviour in the aggregate economy.

Many studies have been conducted to identify the important variables that affect the consumption and saving process. The focus of this study is restricted to two important determinants of savings – income and external inflow of capital – and more emphasis will be given to the former.

Various models relating savings and income have been developed by prominent economists during the past 50 years. Foremost among these is the Keynesian Absolute Income Hypothesis (AIH). Several economists have uncovered problems relating to its relevance to the consumption and savings habits of people in the industrialized world, however, and various other saving income hypotheses have been advanced. The most important ones are: (1) the Permanent Income Hypothesis; (2) the Life Cycle Hypothesis; (3) the Relative Income Hypothesis.

Whilst most empirical studies of the above theories test their validity for industrialized Western economies, their relevance to developing countries has remained unclear. This is because insufficient work has been done and no conclusive evidence has been put forward. In this study we will restrict ourselves to two models, namely the Keynesian Absolute Income Hypothesis and Friedman's Permanent Income Hypothesis. Because of data constraints, the remaining two hypotheses will not be considered. The procedure that will be followed will be a brief description of each hypothesis followed by presentation and discussion of the empirical findings.

2. The Keynesian Absolute Income Hypothesis (AIH)

This is the most commonly applied and easily understood saving function. Specifically, it states that saving is a linear function of income. The function is expressed as

$$S = a + bY \qquad (2.1.1)$$

---

* This contribution is based on an earlier paper, presented to the IDRC Macroeconomic Network Workshop, Nairobi, December 1985.

where S and Y are saving and income respectively while a is autonomous saving and b is the marginal propensity to save. The function is easy to apply both at a micro and a macro level. But as Snyder (1974) has pointed out, the application of equation 1 at a macro level may not yield satisfactory results for developing countries because most data on saving as estimated by national income accountants are residuals. The estimated MPS will thus be biased because of errors in measuring the saving variable. This problem is widely discussed in many econometric texts (Johnston, 1984). The alternative method may be to regress aggregate consumption against aggregate income, estimate the MPC and subtract this from one so as to obtain the MPS.

Whenever the empirical saving function in 2.1.1. has low explanatory or predictive power or the MPS is statistically non-significant, the functional form may have to be modified so as to get better estimates of the current saving-income relation. Two of the commonly applied non-linear saving functions are

$$S = a' + b' \ln Y \qquad (2.1.2)$$

$$\ln S = a'' + b'' \ln Y \qquad (2.1.3)$$

Equation 2.1.2 implies that as current aggregate income rises, saving will increase at a decreasing rate. Miksell and Zinser (1973) explain such behaviour as plausible for countries in a transitional stage of economic development – namely, countries moving from a lower to a higher stage of economic development. During this stage, consumers may become familiar with the availability of various durable and non-durable consumption items and may have to finance such items from saving or by borrowing. This will lead to low MPS and APS. The above argument may well be true for developing countries with little or no restriction on the importation of such items and where there is little restriction on the individual's ability to acquire foreign exchange. This was the case for Nigeria in the late 1970s and early 1980s. The argument would not be valid for Ethiopia, however, as it is a country with low foreign exchange reserves and with strict regulation on the acquisition of hard currency and the importation of luxury items.

Equation 2.1.3 is the typical (Cobb–Douglas type) function relating saving to income and obtaining b'' where the latter is constant income elasticity of saving. The value of b'' determines the magnitude of MPS and APS. A value of b'' greater than one implies that savings may increase more than proportionately as income rises and hence MPS>APS. The opposite will be the case when b''<1.

Empirical findings of the AIH

Before we proceed with the description and analysis of the empirical findings, a brief account will be given of the source and nature of the data. The data on which this study is based come from the national income accounts as furnished by the Central Statistics Office of Ethiopia (1960–85). The data are made available on a yearly basis. Other data sources include the monthly and yearly reports of the National Bank of Ethiopia. The data on saving are based on imputation and, as a result, may not be precise. However, possible errors and omissions have been minimized by subjecting the estimates to some consistency checks such as comparison with those of other countries experiencing similar per capita real income to that of Ethiopia.

The estimated value of the MPC and the corresponding MPS using the Keynesian AIH is given by equation 2.2.1.

$$C_t = -\ 370.198^* + 1.002\ Y_t^* \qquad\qquad 2.2.1$$
$$\quad\ (100.781)\quad (.154)$$

$R^2 = .994, \qquad F = 4229, \qquad DW = 1.428, \qquad n = 26$

*Significant Coefficients.

The results show that the MPC is slightly more than unity and the corresponding MPS equals –0.002. This result is based on the 1960–85 data of the national income accounts of Ethiopia. The results imply that, during the years under study, there was almost no saving and the level of national income (which is gross domestic product at market prices) was insufficient to cover current consumption. This result is not unexpected for a country with one of the lowest per capita incomes in the world, with rampant drought and famine and ongoing internal and external rebellions. The government had no choice but to earmark a large share of the national income for defence in order to defend the territorial integrity of the country and the unity of the people.

A similar conclusion was drawn when total savings was regressed on gross domestic product at market price – Y_t.

$$S_t = 370.196 - .002\ Y_t \qquad\qquad (2.2.2)$$
$$\quad\ (100.711)\quad (.156)$$

$R^2 = .010, \qquad DW = 1.428, \qquad F = .024, \qquad n = 26$

The marginal propensity to save, which is .002, is negative and not significantly different from zero.

An attempt was made to estimate the MPC and MPS, using different functional forms, of the two types shown in equations 2.1.2 and 2.1.3. The results are presented below.[1]

$$C_t\ =\ \ 42473.160 +\ \ 5599.903\ \ln Y_t$$
$$\qquad (2391.431)\qquad (278.186)$$
$$\qquad\qquad\qquad\qquad\qquad\qquad (2.2.3)$$

$R^2 = .944, \quad DW = 0.1739, \quad F = 405.219, \quad n = 26$

$$\ln C_t =\qquad -.515 +\qquad 1.051\ \ln Y_t \qquad (2.2.4)$$
$$\qquad\qquad (.196)\qquad\quad (.023)$$

$R^2 = .989, \quad DW = 1.723, \quad F = 2136, \quad n = 26$

The MPC and MPS from the semi-logarithmic function (2.2.3) are 1.09 and –0.09 respectively, while those from the double logarithmic function (2.2.4) are 1.06 and –0.06 respectively. These results further confirm that the potential for domestic saving out of income in Ethiopia is minimal and possibly negative.

One of the determinants of saving could be a structural change in the economy. Such structural change can be minor, such as change in monetary and/or fiscal policy, change in investment policy and change in interest rate. A structural change can also be a major one such as the change in government or a total change in the whole socio-economic system. The latter is what happened in Ethiopia in 1974. During that year, there was a change in government followed by the nationalization of industrial and major commercial enterprises, banks and insurance companies, as well as nationalization and redistribution of farmland.

This major transformation of the Ethiopian economy could have an impact on aggregate consumption and saving. In an attempt to check such an impact, the 1960–85 data were classified into two parts; the first set of data which has 14 observations (1960–73) covers pre-revolution Ethiopia while the second set (1974–85), with 12 observations, covers the post-revolution period. The MPC and the MPS for each of the two periods will be estimated and any variation in the coefficients may express the effect of the structural change of the economy on the prospects for saving. The results are given in the following equation.

1960–1973 $C_t = 301.712 + .816Y_t$ (2.2.5)
                 (181.105) $(.046)$

$R^2 = .962$,   DW = 3.395,   F = 309.6,   n = 14

1974–1985 $C_t = -353.114 + 1.005Y_t$ (2.2.6)
                 (240.086) $(.028)$

$R^2 = .992$,   DW = 2.301,   F = 1309.29,   n = 12

The results show that the MPC and MPS for the 1960–73 period are .816 and 0.184 respectively while those for 1974–85 show an MPC of 1.005 and MPS of -.005. These results show that there was positive saving during the pre-revolution Ethiopia while the opposite is true during the post-revolution period. There was a significant difference between the two MPCs : the standard error of the difference is about .052.

The above results are to be expected; as a result of major structural changes in the economy, there may be a short-run decrease in savings and increase in consumption. This has been, and is, the case for developing and developed countries. The effect of structural change in the economies on savings is of particular importance to African countries where there were several changes of government, of institutions and of economic systems during the past 25 years. This situation may have resulted in uncertainty and unwillingness on the part of individuals and institutions to save and invest. The above findings suggest that a stable government and a consistent policy are necessary prerequisites for positive saving.

3. The Permanent Income Hypothesis

The preceding results are based on the Keynesian Absolute Income Hypothesis. As was stated earlier, this function has been widely applied because of the ease of estimating and interpreting the coefficients. A major challenge to the Keynesian AIH has come from Milton Friedman, who has argued that consumption and saving do not depend on current income but rather on permanent income. In its simplest form, Friedman's permanent income hypothesis can be expressed as follows:

$$S_t = b_o + b_1 Y^P + b_2 Y^T \qquad (3.1.1)$$

where Y^P and Y^T are permanent and transitory income respectively.

Permanent income is defined in terms of lifetime expectation of income. This requires knowledge of an individual's planning horizon which, in turn, depends on the economic development of the country where the individual resides and on the individual's level of income and occupation. Other things being equal, the businessman's time horizon may be longer than that of the wage earner; an educated person's time horizon may be longer than that of the uneducated.

The problem of measuring permanent income in developed countries is quite difficult. It would be more so for a developing country such as Ethiopia. The problem of collecting data is simply insurmountable and it would be difficult to identify an individual's planning horizon. The problem becomes more serious for cross-section data. Several methods have been suggested for measuring permanent income in developing countries for both cross-section and time series data. Since we will attempt to apply this method for the Ethiopian case, a brief discussion of one of the methods is given below.

The most common measures of permanent and transitory income are obtained using the procedure applied by Williamson (1968) and somewhat modified by Gupta (1975). Williamson measures permanent income by a three-year moving average. The deviation of the actual from the permanent level is then referred to as transitory income. A two-year moving average was attempted by Gupta. Thus, given Y_t as the actual income in year t, the permanent and transitory incomes will be

$$Y^P_t = \frac{Y_t + Y_{t-1}}{2} \qquad (3.1.2)$$

$$Y^T_t = Y_t - Y^P_t = \frac{Y_t - Y_{t-1}}{2} \qquad (3.1.3)$$

When we substitute 3.1.2 and 3.1.3 into 3.1.1 we can rewrite Friedman's equation as follows:

$$S_t = b_o + \frac{(b_1 + b_2)Y_t}{2} + \frac{(b_1 - b_2)Y_{t-1}}{2} \qquad (3.1.4)$$

From equation 3.1.4 one should be able to indirectly estimate b_1 and b_2 , namely the MPS out of permanent and out of transitory income, respectively.

Empirical findings of the permanent income hypothesis

The effects of transitory and permanent income on saving for the 1960–85 Ethiopian data, using 3.1.4, are given in equation 3.2.1.

$$S_t = 376.976 + .198Y_t - .215Y_{t-1} \qquad (3.2.1)$$
$$(104.729) \quad (.132) \quad (.139)$$

$$R^2 = .101, \quad DW = 1.259, \quad F = 1.237, \quad n = 26$$

The implied MPS out of permanent and transitory income based on the relations in 3.1.6 and 3.1.7 are –.017 and .313 respectively. Even though the explanatory power of the equation is low and the coefficients of equation 3.2.1 are only significant at 50 per cent, they can give some approximate indication of the effect of transitory and permanent income on saving. The results show that saving out of permanent income is negative and that out of transitory is positive. This suggests that saving out of permanent income is much less significant than that out of transitory income. This is despite the assumption that an individual's or an institution's planning horizon is limited to two years.

Further tests were conducted to see if there is a change in the relative importance of permanent over transitory income as a result of the structural change in the economy. Again two different saving equations were estimated – one for the period before the Ethiopian revolution (1960–73) and the other for the period after the revolution (1974–85). The results are given below:

$$1960\text{–}73 \quad S_t = -359.347 + .480Y - .302Y_{t-1} \qquad (3.2.2)$$
$$(210.493) \quad (.419) \quad (.449)$$

$$R^2 = .602, \quad DW = 2.596, \quad F = 7.565, \quad n = 14$$

$$1974\text{--}85 \quad S_t \quad = \quad 382.315 \quad + \quad .170Y \quad - \quad .190Y_{t-1} \qquad (3.2.3)$$
$$(215.023) \qquad (.097) \qquad (.101)$$

$R^2 = .125, \quad DW = 2.0596, \quad F = 1.788, \quad n = 12$

From the two preceding equations, the implied MPS out of permanent and transitory incomes is given in Table 4.1.

Table 4.1   Implied MPS out of permanent and transitory incomes

Period	MPS from permanent income	MPS from transitory income
1960–73	.178	.302
1974–85	–.020	.085

Once again the results in Table 4.1 suggest that, during the two periods, positive saving (where applicable) has probably come from transitory income rather than from permanent income. Again, these results seem to be consistent with the results obtained from the Keynesian Absolute Income hypothesis. This is because the implied MPS out of transitory and permanent income seems to be higher during the 1960–73 rather than the 1974–85 period. In other words, the permanent income hypothesis suggests that there is little or no prospect for saving after the popular revolution. Such results could be similar to those of other countries undergoing profound structural changes. Again, it should be emphasized that the estimated MPS values out of permanent and transitory incomes should not be taken at their face values. They are indirectly estimated from equations 3.2.1, 3.2.2 and 3.2.3, whose coefficients were not significant. They are presented here to check on the relative importance of transitory and permanent incomes.

4. A Simultaneous Equation Model for Estimating Saving Function

All of the preceding discussion considers the determinants of savings using a single equation approach. It may be useful to apply a simultaneous equation approach to study the determinants of savings. Macroeconomic variables are often interrelated and to try to study the determinants of savings via a single equation approach would not be sound from the point of view of economic theory. In addition, the statistical drawbacks inherent in the application of a single equation to a situation that requires a simultaneous equation model are obvious to economists, especially those interested in macro modelling.

There are not many models that try to analyse the determinants of savings in developing countries via a simultaneous equation approach. A relatively recent simultaneous equation model applicable to a typical developing country is the one developed by Leff and Sato (1973). As the model is quite clear and most of the data it requires are available from the national income accounts, we will summarize it and, in the process, discuss its relevance to the Ethiopian setting.

The model starts by defining four commonly used identities, namely

$$
\begin{array}{llll}
Y & = & C + I + X - M & \qquad (4.1.1) \\
I & = & S + F & \qquad (4.1.2) \\
S & = & Y - C & \qquad (4.1.3) \\
F & = & M - X = I - S & \qquad (4.1.4)
\end{array}
$$

where Y, C, M, X, F and S are income (GDP), consumption, imports, exports, capital inflow and saving respectively.

Leff and Sato assume that saving is a process of capital formation or asset accumulation, and thus saving is said to be related to the demand for assets. For a given level of desired saving (S') and actual previous saving (S_{t-1}), the discrepancy between these two levels is multiplied by the coefficient K to give the change in saving in this period. Given a as a ratio of desired assets to income we have

$$a = \frac{A'}{Y} = \frac{dA'}{dY} = \frac{S'}{dY}$$

$$dS_t = K(S' - S_{t-1}) \tag{4.1.5}$$

$$S_t = S_{t-1} + K(S' - S_{t-1}) \tag{4.1.6}$$

$$S_t = S_{t-1} - KS_{t-1} + KS' \tag{4.1.7}$$

Based on equations 4.1.5 and 4.1.6, one can rewrite equation 4.1.7 in terms of observed values and obtain the following equation :

$$S_t = (1-K)S_{t-1} + Ka \, dY \tag{4.1.8}$$

Equation 4.1.8 is based on simultaneous equation relations and can be readily estimated from observed data. The following information can be extracted from the coefficients of equation 4.1.8.
1. The coefficient of S_{t-1} captures both the ratchet effect and the effect of lagged saving on income.
2. The coefficient of dY should show income responsiveness of savings and life cycle effects.
3. One should be able to estimate K and discuss its value in detail. Once K is obtained then a, the desired asset income ratio, can be obtained and this, in turn, can give some indication of the need for saving in developing countries.

Empirical findings of the simultaneous equation model

Equation 4.2.1 shows Two Stage Least Square results of the reduced form equations in 4.1.8.

$$S_t = \begin{array}{cccc} 41.462 + & .404S_{t-1} + & .279dY \\ (149.215) & (.298) & (.122) \end{array} \tag{4.2.1}$$

$R^2 = .368, \quad DW = 2.505, \quad F = 2.622, \quad n = 25$

While the coefficient of lagged savings is not significant, that of the first difference in income (dY) seems to be significant and has the expected sign. The adjustment coefficient (one minus lagged savings coefficient) is .596 which seems to be quite high for Ethiopia. This would imply a relatively fast adjustment of the actual to the desired asset values. This result does not seem to be reliable because the adjustment process is directly related to the magnitude of saving as well as the stage of economic progress of the country. Countries like Taiwan, Philippines and Costa Rica, which are on a relatively higher level of economic growth than Ethiopia, have an adjustment coefficient of .228, .172 and .249 respectively. (Leff and Sato, 1973: 1223).

The coefficient of dY, which is 0.279, is rather low compared to similar studies for Taiwan, Philippines and Costa Rica. For these three countries the estimated coefficients are 0.779, 0.677 and 0.819 respectively. Thus, even though the coefficient is significant it still shows an income inelastic response of saving. Again this result is consistent with those obtained from the Keynes and Friedman equations.

A comparison was also made between 1960–73 and 1974–85 to see if there is a change in the asset adjustment coefficient and the saving-income relation using equation 4.1.8. The results are summarized in equations 4.2.2 and 4.2.3.

$$1960–1973 \qquad S_t = 128.026 + .417S_{t-1} + .239dY \qquad\qquad (4.2.2)$$
$$ (103.209) \quad (.203) \qquad (.122)$$

$$R^2 = .219, \quad DW = 2.02, \quad F = 2.982, \quad n = 13$$

$$1974–1985 \qquad S_t = 92.743 + .305S_{t-1} + .836dY \qquad\qquad (4.2.3)$$
$$ (148.392) \quad (.287) \qquad (.507)$$

$$R^2 = .349, \quad DW = 2.219, \quad F = 2.687, \quad n = 12$$

While equation 4.2.2 shows significant coefficients for both the lagged saving and the first difference in income, equation 4.2.3 does not.

In spite of this, a comparison was made and the following observations are made.
1. Faster asset adjustment process during pre-1973 than post-1974.
2. Less inelastic saving–income relation during post-1974 than pre-1973.

The above comparisons were performed after checking that the coefficients of equation 4.2.3 were not significantly different from zero. The above results are further consistency checks showing that a major structural change in the socio-economic system results in uncertainty and an inelastic income–saving relation.

5. Foreign Capital Inflow and Saving

Some development economists argue that foreign capital inflow, especially loans and grants, may have a negative impact on domestic saving. The relation between these two variables has been considered by Griffin (1970), Papanek (1972) and Suckling (1975). The issue here is whether foreign capital inflow is a complement or a substitute for domestic saving. Some argue that foreign capital inflow may have a negative impact on domestic saving because it may replace the latter. As Suckling has pointed out, such a displacement may be crucial in the private sector because foreign capital inflow from developed countries along with the experience and know-how of entrepreneurs could have a discriminatory effect on domestic savers. There are also others who state that savings and capital inflows tend to complement each other.

Papanek argues that rather than studying the relation between domestic saving and foreign capital inflow, the two should be treated as explanatory variables.[2]

Since our objective is to try to isolate the determination of saving, a linear regression equation showing the relation between domestic saving and capital inflow (L_t) was estimated for two periods, 1960–85 and 1960–73. Similar estimates could not be obtained for the post-revolutionary period (1974–85) because data on capital inflow were only available for eight years. The results are given below:

$$1960–73 \qquad S_t = 460.537 - .162L_t \qquad\qquad (5.1.1)$$
$$ (141.772) \quad (.293)$$
$$R^2 = .18, \quad DW = .803, \quad F = .305, \quad n = 17$$

$$1960–85 \qquad S_t = 449.712 - .087L_t \qquad\qquad (5.1.2)$$
$$ (174.415) \quad (.365)$$
$$R^2 = .005, \quad DW = .783, \quad F = .056, \quad n = 12$$

Equation 5.1.1 and 5.1.2 seem to have very low explanatory power and non-significant coefficients. Thus there seems to be little relation between domestic saving and foreign capital inflows. But one could still consider the direction of the relation between the two variables and there seems to be an inverse relation between them. This is true for the entire period under consideration as well as the period preceding the 1974 revolution.

Finally, an attempt was also made to check the impacts of income and foreign capital inflow on domestic savings for the two periods 1960–73 and 1960–85. The results are shown in equation 5.1.3 and 5.1.4.

1960–85 $S_t = 391.413 - .171L_t + .014Y_t$ (5.1.3)
             (191.878) (.300)   (.027)

        $R^2 = .034,   DW = .807,   F = .278,   n = 19$

1960–73 $S_t = 106.666 - .088L_t + .131Y_t^*$ (5.1.4)
             (278.425) (.311)   (.055)

        $R^2 = .240, DW = 1.093, F = 2.828, n = 14$

It seems that neither income nor capital inflow have a high effect on saving for both periods under consideration. But when the two periods are compared, equation 5.1.4 seems to have higher explanatory power than 5.1.3. Moreover, for the period 1960–73, income seems to have effect on savings while this is not so for the entire period. Both equations show a negative relation between saving and capital inflow.

6. Conclusions

The above results suggest that the prospects for domestic savings in Ethiopia are poor. Aggregate saving may even have a negative value after the 1974 revolution. This suggests that, as a result of basic structural changes in the economy, the magnitude of saving is now much lower. The above conclusion was drawn when the Ethiopian data were applied to the Keynesian Absolute Income Hypothesis and to Friedman's permanent income hypothesis, and after the application of the Leff and Sato simultaneous equation model of the determinants of savings.

The findings also suggest a country must reach a higher stage of economic development before any domestic savings can be generated. This will take one to the oft-mentioned vicious circle of poverty. Another point that needs to be emphasized is that a stable government and a conducive savings–investment policy is a necessary prerequisite for generating domestic saving.

One of the reasons for a low or negative income savings relation could be a relatively high expenditure on defence by the government. This may seem to be unfortunate, but it had to be done if the Ethiopian government was to maintain the territorial integrity of the country and the unity of its people. After all, the latter is also another important prerequisite for a higher level of economic growth and subsequent higher level of domestic saving.

A very low MPS was obtained for Israel by Leff and Sato (1973), as well as by Chenery and Carter (1973). The latter reported that the MPS for Israel took place despite the rapid economic growth of that country. The economic rationale that Leff and Sato gave for Israel's low MPS is as follows (1973: 1224):

Israel's difficult security situation and heavy defence expenditure, viewed in the context of a separable utility function in which the future utility is a function of both savings and current expenditure on national security.

A similar conclusion could also be drawn for Ethiopia. Finally, the effect of foreign capital inflow on domestic saving was not significant even though the signs tended to suggest that there may be an inverse relation between the two. Another explanation for the non-significant capital inflow saving relation is that most of the outside capital inflow tends to go to the government sector which in turn uses such inflow to finance basic infrastructures such as highways, education, health and other social services. The impact of such inflow on domestic saving could only be felt in the long run.

Finally, the effect of both income and capital inflow on domestic saving was not found to be substantial. These two explanatory variables explained only 24 per cent of the variation in domestic savings when the 1960–74 data were applied. Out of the two explanatory variables, income seems to be the more important. It would appear that domestic saving can be generated only after a substantial growth in income, by a conducive saving–investment policy and a stable government.

Acknowledgement

This research was conducted thanks to a grant received from the IDRC (3-83-0099). The author wishes to express his gratitude to the Centre and especially to Messrs J.Fine and S.Kiggundu for their encouragement. Special thanks also go to Professor John Harris of the African Studies Centre, Boston University, for his comments and suggestions. Any errors or omissions are, however, the sole responsibility of the author.

Notes

1. Similar estimates could not be made for the saving function as some of the values of total savings are negative.
2. The relation between economic growth on the one hand and capital inflow on the other was regressed and the result was

$$Y_G = .061 + .003S_t - .0001L_t \text{ with } R^2 = .067$$

Thus, Papanek's argument does not seem to hold for Ethiopia.

References

Central Statistics Office of Ethiopia (1960–85). *Statistical Abstract*, Addis Ababa.

Chenery, H. B. and Carter, N. G.(1973). 'Foreign assistance and development performance', *American Economic Review*, Vol. 63, No. 2, pp. 459–69.

Griffin, K. (1970). 'Foreign capital, domestic savings and economic development', *Bulletin of Oxford Institute of Economics and Statistics*, Vol. 32, No. 2, pp. 99–112.

Gupta, K. L. (1975).'Personal saving in developing nations, further evidence', *Economic Record*, Vol. 46, No. 2, pp. 243–9.

Johnston, J. (1984). *Econometric Methods*, McGraw Hill, London.

Leff, N. and Sato, K. (1974). 'A simultaneous equation model of savings in developing countries', *Journal of Political Economy*, Vol. 83, No. 6, pp. 1217–1228.

Miksell, R. F. and Zinser, J. (1973). 'The nature of the saving function in developing countries: a survey of theoretical and empirical literature', *Journal of Economic Literature*, Vol 11, No. 1, pp. 1–27.

Papanek, G. L. (1972). 'The effect of aid and other resource transfers on saving and growth', *Economic Journal*, Vol. 82, No. 3, pp. 934–5.

Snyder, D. (1974). 'Econometric studies of household saving behaviour in developing countries'. *Journal of Development Studies*, Vol. 10, No. 2, pp. 139–53.

Suckling, J. (1975). 'Foreign investment and domestic saving in South Africa', *South African Journal of Economics*, Vol. 43, No. 3, pp. 315–32.

Williamson, J. G. (1968). 'Personal saving in developing nations: an intertemporal cross-section from Asia', *Economic Record*, Vol. 44, No. 2, pp. 194–210.

5 Mobilization of Public & Private Resources in Kenya from 1964 to 1987

S. O. Kwasa

From the time of attaining independence from Britain in 1963/4, Kenya has experienced high economic growth rates, punctuated by periodic contractions and crises. In the period 1963–73 it achieved continuous growth. This was a time when restrictions on African farmers were removed, transfer of land from settlers to Kenyans was effected and high-yield crops and livestock were introduced. The oil crisis of the mid-1970s brought a setback but the economy recovered quickly and took advantage of *karafuu* (clove) and coffee booms in 1977 to grow rapidly in the latter part of the decade. This was followed by a new recession due to the oil price increase and the drought of 1983–84, when the growth rate of per capita income became negative. In the next three years a recovery set in, as a result partly of higher prices for agricultural exports and partly of new government policies, based on the Sessional Paper No. 1 of 1986 'Economic Management for Renewed Growth', which set out a policy framework towards the year 2000 as the basis of the Sixth National Development Plan (SNDP).

Table 5.1   Kenya economic indicators 1981–87 (current prices)

	1981	1982	1983	1984	1985	1985–1987
Growth rates (%)						
Gross domestic product (GDP)	6.0	2.9	3.2	0.9	4.4	5.7
(Agriculture)	6.0	4.7	4.5	−3.3	3.5	4.8
(Industry)	4.4	−0.6	2.3	1.7	5.0	5.2
Gross national income (GNY)	−1.6	−1.6	1.3	−0.6	0.2	11.6
(GNY) per capita	−5.4	−5.1	−2.6	−0.6	−3.6	7.4
Money supply	13.3	16.1	4.9	12.9	6.7	32.5
Domestic credit	24.2	29.2	0.1	10.9	13.0	28.6
Consumer price index	12.6	22.3	14.5	9.1	10.7	5.7
Percentage of GDP (%)						
Consumption	80.6	82.2	79.9	81.4	10.6	75.5
Gross domestic investment	28.4	22.4	21.1	21.8	25.7	23.8
Gross national savings	17.3	24.8	18.9	28.2	14.8	18.0
Budget deficit (FY)	9.5	6.7	3.1	4.3	4.4	4.0

Sources: Central Statistical Office, *Economic Survey*, various issues 1981–7; Central Statistical Office, *Statistical Abstracts*, various issues 1980–7

85

The key economic indicators based on growth rates in Table 5.1 show a gradual decline in GDP growth from 6.0 per cent in 1981 to 0.9 per cent in 1984, and a recovery to 5.7 per cent by 1985. The decline was partly a result of the oil crisis, followed by the drought of that period. The recovery must be attributed, among other things, to the reviews of economic policies which followed those two negative developments. From 1985 up to 1987 there was a more encouraging recovery in every economic indicator including the consumer price index.[1]

Looking more widely at the Kenyan economy over the years from 1964, it is possible to conclude that the general performance has been satisfactory. But one aspect which raises several unanswered questions is the area of savings. Perhaps the question was best put in the 1987 budget speech by the Minister of Finance: 'Kenyans save enough but we do not invest our savings productively enough to generate rapid growth. Why?' The remaining section of this chapter will attempt to answer that question as it relates directly to the issue of the saving capacity of the public and private sectors in Kenya.

1. The Main Determinants of Savings

This section considers possible determinants of aggregate savings in Kenya. The possibilities include income, wealth, interest rates, price levels, demographic factors (such as age structure and size of the household), changes in economic and political conditions and changes in the international economy. This can be used as a guide only, to the factors in Kenya which are likely to respond to the drive for resource mobilization for a faster rate of economic development.

Income
Table 5.2 gives the time series data for Gross Domestic Product (GDP) and aggregate resources available for investment and consumption, including resources generated from the external sector. Both sets of data are adjusted to 1976 prices. The data show a consistent growth in real terms. Saving in the Kenyan economy grew steadily and, as a proportion of GDP, varied between 21.2 per cent in 1983 at the peak, and 16.0 per cent in 1985 at the lowest point. The average annual GDP growth rate of about 4.2 per cent has been effective in sustaining an average saving rate of 20 per cent for the period of the study.

Wealth
In so far as the Kenya economy is concerned, what little evidence there is on the relationship between wealth and saving seems to indicate a positive relationship.

Rate of Interest
Interest rates in Kenya are a significant determinant of saving in the formal monetary sector of the economy, but in the subsistence sector the effect of interest rates on saving is small. The savings data observable in Table 5.2, column 3, refer to the formal monetary sector of the Kenyan economy. The subsistence sector was not included.

Inflation
Inflation in Kenya, despite its erosive effect on the economy, has tended to increase saving, albeit in monetary terms. In Kenya this effect was particularly noticeable during the two boom periods 1978–88 (*karafuu* boom) and 1982–3 (coffee boom). In both periods the level of inflation rose and so did saving. Quite a substantial amount of that saving was transferred into real estate by the indigenous Kenyans, while so-called Kenyan 'paper citizens' moved large quantities of that saving to foreign banks, especially in Canada, the USA and Europe

Table 5.2   Growth of GDP, consumption and savings as a ratio of GDP (Kenya)

Year	GDP* (KShs m) (1)	Total resources available for investment & consumption (KShs m) (2)	Savings (as a ratio of GDP) (3)
1964	766	339	16.6
1965	801	444	17.5
1966	879	486	19.8
1967	930	517	18.9
1968	999	585	19.3
1969	1071	684	20.3
1970	1137	737	19.7
1971	1179	816	19.3
1972	1250	999	19.1
1973	1207	940	19.8
1974	1305	1084	16.9
1975	1332	1091	18.1
1976	1412	1124	20.4
1977	1624	1345	17.2
1978	1692	1381	18.4
1979	1749	1446	17.3
1980	1828	1477	19.2
1981	1870	1509	19.3
1982	1898	1517	21.1
1983	1956	1569	21.2
1984	1974	1583	16.0
1985	2204	1553	16.0

* in constant 1976 prices

Source: Central Statistical Office, Statistical Abstracts, 1977–86

but also in India, Pakistan, Bangladesh and Australia. This had a negative effect on Kenya's economic growth rate. Another source of drainage of savings from the domestic circular flow was the outflow to neighbouring countries. Because of economic problems in neighbouring countries, the Kenyan shilling became a hard, sought-after currency in the region. Consequently, many speculators and merchants found it a convenient currency to hold both as a store of value and as a medium of exchange in neighbouring countries' market transactions. The difference between domestic credit and money supply, to which reference has been made, may be explained partially at least by the above phenomenon.

Population structure

In the last 25 years or so Kenya has experienced a significant change in its population structure. A rapid increase has occurred in the youngest age group (0–15 years) and in the oldest (55 years and above). Increased 'dependency' in the population may well have caused a significant erosion of the savings of the age-group 16–54 years, which is the group that earns the larger portion of the household income. This phenomenon could have affected the level of Kenyan saving capacity to a considerable extent.

Rural–urban income distribution

The findings of an earlier study by the present author are relevant.[2] In Kenya, while urban monetary incomes have remained higher than rural monetary incomes, savings (from formal and informal incomes) have remained higher in the rural sector than in the urban sector, on an individual household basis. On the other hand, the distribution of credits still favours the urban sector. In Kenya up to 85 per cent of commercial bank loans were disbursed in urban centres and only 15 per cent in the rural sector. Informal saving is significant in the rural households, and more efforts towards mobilization of resources could be focused there.

Economic and socio-political conditions

Socio-political and economic conditions which may have affected significantly the level of domestic saving in Kenya have included foreign exchange laws and regulations, political stability and a general eco-social milieu conducive to 'the good life'.

Kenya's foreign exchange laws and regulations have remained the most lenient in the whole of Africa to the flight of capital, with the possible exception of Botswana. Their mildness and sensitive application even to the law-breakers have stemmed, to a certain extent, the flight of capital to foreign banks but, by the same token, they have left considerable room for expatriation of capital, profit and other incomes earned and remitted legally.

The political stability that Kenya has sustained since independence has also contributed to attracting capital and retaining profits of foreign companies for re-investment internally.

Lastly, the general economic and social milieu within the country seems to build a certain confidence that has enabled the economy to remain attractive to domestic and foreign investors. All these factors have generated and maintained the level of confidence Kenya requires to sustain its growth of capital stock through re-investment of domestic profits and a measure of foreign capital inflow.

The external sector

In Kenya, there is very little literature on the link between the changes in the international price level and domestic saving. We have already made references to the *karafuu* and coffee booms of the 1970s and early 1980s. The favourable commodity prices of those years undoubtedly had some positive effects on saving. But the international rate of interest in both periods was on the upward trend. This neutralized some of the gains from higher commodity prices.

2. Public Sector Savings

The two sources of public sector savings in Kenya are direct government savings and savings by public corporations (parastatals). Both feature prominently in supplementing the private sector as sources of mobilizable resources for economic development. Their roles have changed with time since 1964, with public and semi-public corporations increasing their saving capacity as they gradually increased their profit margins and remitted larger dividends to the Treasury.

Government saving

The relations between the Kenya government's tax revenue and her total expenditure are shown in Table 5.3 below. The figures are adjusted to constant 1976 prices. Column 7 shows the difference between total tax revenue and total government consumption. Between 1964 and 1973 it was in deficit, with the exception of the fiscal year 1966/7 when it showed a surplus of K£6 million. But between 1973 and 1985 it was in credit, with the not very significant exception of the 1976/7 fiscal year when it showed a deficit of K£1 million. Columns 3 and 6 (total government tax revenue and total government expenditure as percentages of GDP) tell the story. Column 8 shows the ratio of government saving to GDP. From 1964 to 1972 that ratio was negative but from 1973 to 1985 it was positive, averaging 3.2 per cent per year over this period. The overall average saving ratio of the government sector excluding the parastatal corporations was therefore approximately 1.25

Table 5.3   Growth of Kenya's GDP, government revenue and expenditure

(1)	(2)	(3)	(4)	(5)	(6)	(7)	(8)
Fiscal year	GDP (K£m)	Tot. tax revenue (K£m)	Govt exp. (K£m)	Govt rev. as a % of GDP	Govt exp. as a % of GDP	Tax rev. minus govt exp.	Saving as a % of GDP
1964/65	766	102	110	13.3	24.4	-8	-1.04
1965/66	801	108	113	13.5	14.1	-5	-0.6
1966/67	879	127	212	14.4	13.8	6	-0.7
1967/68	903	134	137	14.4	14.7	-3	-0.3
1968/69	999	140	159	14.0	15.9	-19	-1.9
1969/70	1071	160	176	14.9	16.4	-16	-1.5
1970/71	1137	192	194	16.9	17.1	-2	-0.2
1971/72	1179	201	210	17.0	17.8	-9	-0.8
1972/73	1250	202	215	16.1	17.2	-13	-1.04
1973/74	1201	214	205	17.8	17.1	9	0.7
1974/75	1304	243	234	18.6	17.9	9	0.6
1975/76	1332	240	237	18.0	17.8	3	0.2
1976/77	1411	243	244	17.2	17.3	-1	-0.07
1977/78	1624	349	299	21.5	18.4	50	14.3
1978/79	1692	337	330	19.9	19.5	7	2.1
1979/80	1750	378	350	21.6	20.0	38	1.6
1980/81	1828	406	358	22.2	19.6	48	1.8
1981/82	1870	409	351	21.9	18.8	42	2.2
1982/83	1898	391	363	20.6	19.1	28	1.5
1983/84	1956	416	385	21.3	19.7	31	1.6
1984/85	1974	404	375	20.5	19.0	29	1.4

Sources: Central Statistical Office, Statistical Abstracts, 1965–87 and Economic Surveys, 1964–86

per cent of GDP per year for the whole period 1964–85. It may, therefore, be concluded that, given its tax buoyancy, the government sector in Kenya has the capacity to save and to generate resources for development.

Public corporation savings

In most countries, public corporations (parastatal companies) have acquired the reputation of being over-protected, monopolistic and inefficient. Kenya's public corporations have been described in the same way. A study by IDS (Nairobi) in 1982 concluded that 'parastatal firms tend to be large, capital intensive, import intensive and almost exclusively oriented towards a protected overpriced local market.'[3]

The study implied that parastatal companies depend heavily on government subsidies. They are, therefore, unlikely to generate significant savings which can be mobilized in the process of economic development. On the other hand, two studies by Barbara Grosh on Kenya's agricultural and industrial parastatals concluded that public corporations in Kenya are more efficient than they are generally portrayed.[4] In both papers Grosh has concluded that Kenya's public corporations' performance is quite satisfactory and their profit margins are, on the average, quite competitive with those of private corporations. Consequently, their capacity to generate mobilizable savings is comparable to that of their private counterparts.

The research outcome of this study seems to confirm Grosh's conclusion and at the same time provides some possible explanations for the IDS contrary conclusion. The study revealed that there are two types of public corporation in Kenya. First, there are those which were formed to provide essential services. Profit is not the prime objective of this category of parastatal corporation and they may operate at levels below their cost effectiveness. In this category are such parastatals as Kenya Airways, Kenya Railways, Nyayo Bus Corporation and others. The second category includes those parastatals which operate as private profit-oriented companies. These include Kenya Posts and Telecommunications, National Bank of Kenya, Kenya Commercial Bank, Kenya Re-Insurance Corporation, Kenya National Assurance Company and others. The corporations in the latter group usually realize fairly large profits, a share of which goes as dividends to the government. Kenya Posts and Telecommunication and Kenya Ports Authority, for example, have been making considerable profits. Government banks and insurance companies have also been in the forefront as sources of large dividends for the government.

The combined outcome of these two categories of public corporation, to which Grosh's study refers, provides a positive result. The IDS study, on the other hand, concentrated only on the semi-agricultural parastatals which are mainly of the first category. The present study, however, goes further than both these studies. It seeks to determine the performance capacity of parastatals by way of analysing their aggregate productivity and capacity to generate savings which can be mobilized for further economic development. This analysis also traces the trend of savings in the public corporation sector.

Two measures of performance in industrial, agricultural and service parastatals are used. The first measure is the domestic factor cost ratio (DFCR). It is the ratio of domestic factor costs to value added. A DFCR which is less than one implies that there is more value added than resources are consumed. Such a situation implies that the firms make efficient use of resources. A DFCR which is greater than one implies that more resources are consumed in domestic production than the value that is added by local production. In such a case domestic production by a public corporation would reduce resources rather than increase domestic savings, and it would have been better to import the products instead of producing them locally. The second measure of performance is the financial rate of return of public corporations (FRR). This is a measure of total returns to capital which includes interest, costs and profits divided by the replacement cost of capital.

Table 5.4   Measures of performance of Kenya's public corporations (agricultural, industrial and services)

	DFCR	FRR
Industrial corporations *		
Minimum	.30	-4.8%
Maximum	7.21	122.6%
Average	1.14	21.2%
Number of firms = 30		
Service companies		
Minimum	.52	-25.8%
Maximum	4.48	20.1%
Average	1.89	1.2%
Number of firms = 8		
Agricultural and marketing corporations		
Minimum	1.02	-1.1%
Maximum	1.78	38.1%
Average	1.42	5.1%
Number of firms = 15		
Total public corporations		
Average	1.12	10.7%
Number of firms = 53		

*includes mining and oil exploration company shares acquired by the government

The outcome of these two measures is shown in Table 5.4. On the DFCR measure Kenya's parastatals are shown to be somewhat inefficient (average DFCR = 1.12). Among these parastatals, industrial corporations did much better (DFCR of 1.14) than the agricultural and service parastatals (1.42 and 1.89 respectively). On the FRR measure, the average rate of return to parastatals was 10.7 per cent which was as close as can be expected to that of private corporations (14.8 per cent). The least profitable parastatal sub-sector (services with average of 1.2 per cent) still had a positive FRR despite the minimum negative value of 25.8 per cent.

3. Private Sector Saving

The savings pattern of the Kenyan economy shown in Table 5.2 fluctuated between 16 and 26 per cent of the GDP. The table also shows resources available for investment, but these included foreign resources whereas our interest in this chapter is the domestic resources which emanate from government and private saving. The private savings which are shown in column 3 of Table 5.2 is therefore of more interest to us, because it represents purely domestic saving without any additions from the foreign sector.

A more detailed study of Kenyan savings data further suggests that private sector savings originate from three main sources: (1) financial institutions, (2) non-financial corporations and (3) private households' and individuals' savings.

Financial institutions include banks of all types, insurance companies, building societies, savings and loan or mortgage societies, cooperative unions and other loan-dispensing corporations. They constitute the main sources of savings in the private sector and account for approximately 40 per cent of the total private sector savings in Kenya.

The second most important source of saving in the private sector is the private corporations which are not of the financial category. These private corporations contribute approximately 36 per cent of the total savings in the private sector, almost as much as the financial institutions. But their significance lies more especially in the increasing role they play. This study shows that their share has continued to increase, unlike that of the financial institutions which tends either to decrease or to remain constant with time. If this pattern continues, by the next decade they will replace financial institutions as the major source of private saving.

The least significant contributor to private sector saving is the household and the individual sector. We use the word 'household' to mean any self-contained unit with a complete budgeting function and include in it the individual and all other units which are not effectively registered and recognized as companies. Informal sector enterprises fall under this household categorization. It should be noted that this sector deposits a proportion of its savings in financial institutions. This means that such savings are reflected in the financial institutions' savings accounts and not in the household sector.

Government saving was negative during the periods 1964–9 and 1980–5. If other countries' fiscal histories are anything to go by, then we can safely assume that this trend (negative government saving) will continue and may even increase in the future. On the other hand, private sector saving capacity, which has shown some stability at 16 per cent of GDP, is likely to counteract these effects. It is most likely to continue to generate the investible surpluses required for mobilization and growth. The continued generation of a small measure of surplus resources for investment is therefore a realizable possibility if the economy sustains its present level of performance. The main question, however, is whether such generated resources will be sufficient to provide the volume required under the APPER programme of stabilization of the economy, and to forestall the increasing burden of external debt. This chapter's response to that question is a pessimistic one. Despite the economic performance of the Kenyan economy, which appears encouraging in comparison with other African and Third World countries, the prospects for a significant increase in the investible surplus do not appear good, at least within the next decade or so.

4. Conclusions

This chapter has outlined the structure and trend of growth of domestic mobilizable resources within the Kenyan economy. It concludes that the Kenyan economy has shown significant fluctuations in its savings performance. These fluctuations moved within the range of 16 to 22 per cent of GDP between the years 1964 and 1987. The government sector, despite the encouraging performance of its public corporations, has tended to fall into deficit in the 1980s. This trend is predicted as likely to continue and even to increase as the target year 2000 approaches.

The private sector, on the other hand, has performed consistently, with its saving capacity as a ratio of GDP remaining at an average level of 15 per cent throughout the study period. As compared with the government sector, which reached a deficit level of 0.8 per cent of the GDP in the early 1980s, the strength of the saving capacity of the private sector might still be able to uphold the economy's performance for a brief period of time. But this short spell of time cannot be relied upon to enable the economy to attain the level of performance required to generate the saving required under the APPER programme. Kenya, like other Third World countries, will face the shortfall of saving necessary for achieving that APPER objective.

The aggregate growth of resources required for the attainment of APPER objectives can be considered to be in the range of 10 to 15 per cent of GDP every year, with some leeway for fluctuations. Those fluctuations will depend, among other things, on the nature and performance of the nation's agricultural and industrial sectors. The financial sector will tend to lean heavily on agriculture and manufacturing to boost its capacity to mobilize savings. The impetus for growth in the financial sector will depend heavily on agricultural and industrial performance.

Other agents of growth in the financial sector include the financial institutions. These too have shown a high capacity to respond to an improvement in the economic performance of the key agricultural and industrial sectors. All in all, the performance of the Kenyan economy, despite its commendable record, shows signs of underlying constraints that are likely to reduce its capacity to grow at the rate envisaged by the requirements of the APPER programme. In this respect, Kenya seems to display the same difficulties as other African countries. The attainment of the APPER objectives, therefore, remains optimistic if the resources required for its launching have to emanate from internal sources. A review of the strategy will be necessary in order to achieve the objectives of the programme.

Notes

1.   The disturbing element was the increase in the money supply between 1985 and 1987, (32.5 per cent), and the increase in domestic credit (28.6 per cent). Money may have filtered out of the country or was being hoarded for black market speculations.
2.   See S.O. Kwasa, 'Rural-Urban Remittances and Economic Growth with Inflation', Kenyan Economic Association Discussion Paper, 1985.
3.   IDS. *Occasional Paper No. 39*, 'Parastatal Development Agencies and Their Relationship with the Private Sector', Nairobi: 1982.
4.   B. Grosh, 'A Brief Look at the Performance of Agricultural Parastatals in Kenya Since Independence'; 'Performance of Manufacturing Firms in Kenya: Parastatals vs. Private. With Implications for Privatization', mimeo, Institute for Development Studies, University of Nairobi.

6 Mobilization of Domestic Financial Resources in Uganda: Commercial Banks versus the Uganda Cooperative Savings and Credit Union

Germina Ssemogerere

Introduction

The purpose of this chapter is to appraise the potential of commercial banks, as compared with the Uganda Cooperative Savings and Credit Union, in mobilizing domestic savings for investment in Uganda. The issues identified suggest policies which might be implemented in order to intensify mobilization efforts and alleviate the current liquidity crisis in Uganda.

It is widely acknowledged that within the financial sector in Uganda there is an acute shortage of domestic financial resources for productive investment. The statistics which identify Uganda's shortage of saving are scanty, but the little information which is available indicates that gross national saving was only 15 per cent of disposable income in the 1970s. It had declined to 4 per cent by 1981, and only showed slight improvement to 7.5 per cent in the 1982/3 fiscal year.[1] This compares with the recommended 25 per cent for the recovery and development of African economies.[2] Unfortunately, after 1983 there is no published time series on gross national saving but, given that real GDP in constant 1966 prices was virtually stagnant over the 1980s, it is unlikely that gross national saving would have increased much. It has remained very low.[3]

Looking at the near future, the Rehabilitation and Development Plan 1987/8–1990/1 estimated that, in 1987 constant prices, Uganda Shs million 31,347 would be required to fund the domestic portion of planned capital expenditure. By 1989/90, at the peak of implementing the Plan, the estimated amount required to fund the domestic portion is Uganda Shs million 63,784, a doubling of the first figure, to be achieved in just over a year. Failing to raise these sums means that foreign resources mobilized for the Plan will remain under-utilized.[4] The low level of gross national saving, therefore, constitutes a serious constraint on development.

The qualitative dimensions of the crisis

Since the early 1980s evidence has mounted that, of the total committed external assistance, less than half gets utilized on time. One of the main reasons for under-utilization is the shortage of matching domestic resources, especially working capital. This is directly connected to a shortage of liquidity in the financial sector.

It is widely argued in Uganda that working capital constraints reflect a shortage of liquidity within the financial sector and a scarcity of commercial bank funds, since some firms appear to have difficulty borrowing even where there is no credit-worthiness problem. The commercial banking sector has . . . been operating above the lending ratio of 70 percent required by the Bank of Uganda . . . with certain banks reaching lending ratios of over 100 percent from time to time; the Uganda Commercial Bank has generally shown the highest lending ratios, reflecting its heavy involvement in financing local cover for IDA funds. The main causes of the shortage of liquidity are low domestic savings and the large share of domestic credit that is tied up in crop financing (about 30 percent of total borrowing during peak months).[5]

Proposals have been made to rationalize crop finance and reduce it by about 70 per cent of its current level during the peak season. But this reduction (to 21 per cent of total borrowing) would release only an extra 9 per cent of domestic credit, an increase which would still be too small to relax the liquidity squeeze in the economy.

> According to an earlier review of the same liquidity problem . . . of the various problems which . . . development banks face, the most important is the serious shortage of local funds to support and permit full utilization of external funds . . . while the institutions . . . tend to ascribe this problem to an unnecessarily conservative stance . . . of the commercial banks and especially to an overriding preference to short-term lending, the root cause of the problem lies elsewhere.
>
> As long as the aggregate savings base remains low and the deposit base of the banks is so restricted relative to the demands placed upon it, it would be futile to pressure the commercial banks to lengthen significantly the maturity of their lending.[6]

The currency reform of May 1987, by imposing a 30 per cent compulsory conversion tax on all transactions, including all bank accounts, aggravated the liquidity crisis within the financial sector. The Ministry of Industry and Technology, the Uganda Commercial Bank, and the business community, contended that the conversion

> had greatly constrained the ability of commercial banks to extend loan facilities to the private sector and the ability of the firms to raise local cover required to pick up foreign exchange allocation.[7]

1. Methodology to Study Domestic Resource Mobilization in the Light of Uganda's Data Limitations

The determinants of savings

One method is to evaluate the relative importance of the determinants of savings and how they can be influenced by policies to intensify the mobilization of effort and channel the resources into productive investment. The principle determinants in the literature are: income, wealth, interest rates, the price level and the demographic structure.[8] This method requires consistent time-series data, from a relatively stable economic and political environment, from which one can compute credible coefficients showing the relative importance of each variable in explaining savings behaviour, and then use these coefficients to predict and suggest policies to influence future behaviour.

The economic and political environment in Uganda has been too unstable to produce credible time series. There have been civil wars in 1966, 1971, 1979 and continuous civil strife over the 1980–8 period. Because the time-series data are unavailable or, when available, are inaccurate, inconsistent, or riddled with gaps,[9] this chapter cannot compute behavioural coefficients of the determinants of savings.

The sectoral sources of savings

A second method is to study the sectoral sources of total savings: households, business, government, and the foreign sector, noting how savings move between these sectors and how to channel them into productive investment.[10]

Data limitations in Uganda also preclude a systematic evaluation of the sources of savings:

> when an attempt is made to identify which sector/groups are undertaking the savings as a prelude to discussing policies to increase its volume, the data are almost non-existent. It is also difficult statistically to identify the channels through which savings are made.[11]

The report quoted specifically refers to households, business and government.

For the foreign sector, lack of consistent data is unfortunate because this sector contributes about half of government's recurrent revenue. Coffee, the leading export, is heavily taxed: the export duty takes at least 50 per cent of the international price in local currency. It would have been interesting to assess which policy incentives are most likely to revive this sector as the leading source of savings, but data limitations rule this out, too.[12]

Financial intermediaries

A third approach to the problem of domestic resource mobilization is to study the institutions that collect the savings; this is based on the growing recognition in the literature that the building of a suitable institution, even among the very poor in rural areas – the self-help *esusu* of West Africa or the pawnbroking system in Sri Lanka – can provide the starting point to mobilize savings to overcome poverty.[13]

Two types of financial intermediaries have been selected for study in this chapter: banks, and the Cooperative Savings and Credit Union. Some hitherto unpublished materials on these institutions contain very relevant policy suggestions that deserve to be brought into wider discussion. On the commercial banks, the materials include: (1) the proceedings of a seminar on banking in Third-World countries; (2) a report on the proposed Agricultural Development Bank;[14] (3) the proceedings of a seminar on financial programming;[15](4) 'The role of financial institutions in promoting real sector development', in the Report of the Real Sector Committee;[16] (5) and current monetary survey data from background documentation for the budget.[17]

On the Cooperative Savings and Credit Union, the unpublished materials include: (1) Report of the National Cooperative Survey Project;[18] (ii) The Cooperative Societies Act 1970: Proposed Amendments; (iii) research into a sample of 26 societies, undertaken in preparing the present study.

A key reason for choosing to contrast the commercial banks with the Cooperative Savings and Credit Union is that the Ugandan economy is not integrated but segmented into distinct sectors: the formal monetized sector; the informal intermediate sector; and the non-monetary, largely rural, sector. Given this segmentation, it is necessary to examine a variety of institutions that span the whole spectrum of resource mobilization problems in the economy with respect to the distinct groups of savers, their characteristics and requirements. The commercial banks will be shown to address themselves to the formal monetized sector while the Savings and Credit Union is tilted towards the informal, the non-monetized sectors.

2. The Structure of the Ugandan Economy

The structure of the Ugandan economy from the standpoint of domestic resource mobilization requirements, can be divided into the following sectors: non-monetary economy, monetized agriculture, productive non-agricultural monetary sector, commerce and trade, and general government.

The non-monetary economy

T. Killick defines the extent of monetization of economic activity 'as indicated by the ratio of monetary GNP to non-monetary or subsistence GNP'.[19] For our purpose, it is more useful to measure the ratio of the non-monetary to the total GDP as an indicator of the extent of policy effort required to monetize the economy.

Monetization is important: the spread in the use of money increases the efficiency of exchange; the increased efficiency stimulates specialization and raises real output from which financial savings can be collected. There is also evidence that too many rural communities in the rich agricultural zones of the country produce a marketable surplus which they barter or save in kind. Monetization would replace savings in kind and improve the allocation of these savings.

Table 6.1, row 1 indicates that well over 30 per cent of Uganda's economy is non-monetary. This sector produces the bulk of food for domestic consumption and constructs owner-occupied dwellings for the rural population, which constitutes 80 per cent of the total population. Potentially, the non-monetary sector is a significant source of domestic savings since it produces a surplus which it barters with the other sectors: what is required is to educate the population to use the money and financial institutions so that the surplus, now in kind, can be monetized and mobilized for productive investment.

It is to be noted in Table 6.2, row 1 that the non-monetary economy receives no loans and advances from commercial banks.

Monetary agriculture

Monetary agriculture, whose relative importance is indicated in row 2, Table 6.1, comprises agricultural activities scattered on smallholder plots of about one and a half acres to five acres, using family labour, supplemented at the peak of the planting and harvest seasons by hired labour, paid in cash and in kind. Except for tea estates and a few modern ranches, there is hardly any large-scale commercial farming in the country. Monetary agriculture grows the cash crops for export and the marketed food crops for local consumption.

There is a need for a financial institution to reach the myriad of small, scattered farmers. The institution has to identify which of the activities on the small farms – land clearance, weeding, harvesting and so on – constitutes the most binding constraint on

Table 6.1   Major sectors of the Ugandan economy (percentage share in real GDP at factor cost, in constant 1966 prices)

Sector	1980	1985	1987
1. Non-monetary economy	39	35	35
2. Monetary agriculture	20	21	19
3. Productive monetary sectors*	10	11	12
4. Commerce	·8	9	8
5. General government	14	14	14
6. Misc.services and rents	9	10	12
	100	100	100

Source: Calculated From Republic of Uganda, Background to 1988–1989 (Ministry of Planning and Economic Development, Kampala, July 1988)

* The productive monetary sectors, excluding monetary agriculture, are: cotton ginning, coffee curing and sugar manufacture; forestry, fishing and hunting; mining and quarrying; manufacture of food products; miscellaneous manufacturing; electricity; transport and communication; and construction.

raising agricultural productivity, for the constraint has to be lifted in order to increase earnings above subsistence, at which point savings can be mobilized. This same institution must also be able to collect the small, scattered savings during the marketing season.[20]

In Table 6.2 monetary agriculture hardly receives any loans and advances (see row 2), to enable it to improve upon productivity, and then save from the higher incomes. The Agricultural Development Bank, planned to finance smallholder farmers in particular, has yet to be established.[21]

Table 6.2   Structure of commercial bank loans and advances to the private sector (as % of total commercial bank lending)

Sector	1980	1985	1987
1. Non-monetary economy	0.00	0.00	0.00
2. Monetary agriculture	0.09	0.06	0.11
3. Productive non-agricultural monetary sectors[1]	0.21	0.25	0.33
4. Trade, commerce and crop finance[2]	65.00	71.00	64.00

Source: Calculated from Republic of Uganda, Background to the Budget 1988–1989 (Ministry of Planning and Economic Development, Kampala, July 1988)

1. The productive monetary sectors include: transport, manufacturing, building and construction. The rest of the sectors classified in row 3 of Table 6.1 could not be identified in row 3 of Table 6.2.

2. The unclassified private sectors, whose proportion of total commercial bank loans and advances are not shown in Table 6.2 are simply defined as 'others, including balancing items' in Background to the Budget, Table 15.

The informal sector

Ugandan statistics in Table 6.1 do not cover the informal sector, nor can we relate it to credit flows in Table 6.2. But educated guesses put its activities around almost 40 per cent of total GDP. This sector partly explains how civil servants on mediocre salaries survive. It also includes a large section of smuggling on the parallel market.[22]

The informal sector spans the rural and urban zones of the economy. In the rural areas, it is annexed to monetary agriculture; its activities are financed from surplus agricultural incomes, especially local produce sold at uncontrolled market prices that adjust to inflation. Activities include crafts, cottage industries, small businesses and transport.

In towns, many civil servants and other regular employees in the private sector augment their small money incomes from informal activities such as market gardening, chicken pens, repair shops, sewing, retailing and fabricating household goods from scrap metal. These activities thrive on the fringes of major towns where land prices are lower and building regulations less stringent, and at less supervised border outlets.

The financial institutions to mobilize savings from the informal sector need to be located at the road junctions in the rural areas and at the peripheries of major towns and border outlets where these businesses thrive. The institutions need highly flexible procedures to cater for the frequent deposits and withdrawals that finance the informal economic opportunities which are passed on, mostly by word of mouth. The staff need to be familiar with the trustworthiness of their clients, as many clients would neither have collateral nor understand formal accounting procedures. Given the size of this sector and the way it permeates the economy, plus its reputed resilience to shocks such as heavy taxation or political upheavals, the resource mobilization effort cannot succeed unless institutions are created to cater for its needs.[23] We shall examine the Savings and Credit Union from this standpoint.

Productive monetary sectors

The non-agricultural productive monetary sector consists of manufacturing, construction and transport, which add up to 10–12 per cent of GDP in Table 6.1.

The sector needs a massive injection of domestic financial resources: first, to provide local cover with which to purchase foreign exchange needed to import capital equipment and spare parts to replace and maintain the aged plant and equipment that were neglected during the civil wars; second, to import raw materials, since many businesses in this sector are import-intensive; third, to provide working capital until the businesses can accumulate their own retained earnings.

A number of factors, however, prevent the desired injection of financial resources.

1. To date, many businesses cannot borrow because of the ownership disputes that arose from the expropriation of Asians and arbitrary reallocation of their properties in the early 1970s.[24]

2. In the wake of the currency devaluations of 1981 onwards, and also because of rapid inflation, there is a need to revalue properties in order to bank them for collateral. Many businesses, both private and parastatals, have difficulty agreeing on valuation since the choice of valuation methods depends on the purpose. The departed Asians want valuation for compensation or repossessing the property; the existing occupants want valuation for purchase, bank loans or compensation for improvements made since 1972.[25]

3. Even credit-worthy businesses often cannot borrow because of the liquidity squeeze in the financial sector. Table 6.2 indicates that the private enterprises in this sector receive only a negligible amount of commercial bank loans and advances.

Thus, although constituting a small part of the economy, on the available evidence this sector will be a net borrower rather than a saver in the near future; a massive mobilization of domestic savings is required if it is to revive.

Commerce and other tertiary activities

While this sector constitutes at most 10 per cent of the economy (row 4 of Table 6.1) it is the most favoured for commercial bank lending because of the quick returns in an unstable environment: it takes over 60 per cent of commercial bank loans and advances to the private sector (row 4 of Table 6.2).

There is considerable dispute as to whether this sector is sufficiently taxed in the form of duties on imported consumer goods and sales taxes on locally produced goods. The taxability needs to be carefully assessed before we can predict the potential contribution of this sector to domestic resource mobilization.

The government sector

Coffee export duty is the single most important source of recurrent revenue, constituting over 50 per cent. This duty claims at least half of the international price of coffee, leaving at most 30 per cent of the price to the farmer, the rest covering processing and marketing charges.

The general opinion in Uganda is that the excessive tax on coffee is counter-productive. Late pay to the farmers, of the meagre 30 per cent of the international price, eroded by inflation and converted at the low official exchange rate (another tax), dampen producer incentive and lead to poor husbandry or complete abandonment of coffee shambas in favour of food crops whose prices are not controlled.

While food production is welcome, foreign exchange is also needed to buy imported inputs and build infrastructure to boost overall agricultural productivity: the excessive taxation of exports, therefore, remains an ill-advised policy.[26]

What government needs is overall tax reform to (1) broaden the tax base by collecting more consumption and sales taxes to add to the export duty; (2) change anti-smuggling policies and collect more customs duty, instead of the current practice that seals off border trade; (3) revive the productive sectors so that they can yield excise taxes; and (4) increase overall efficiency of tax collection. These issues require full analysis of fiscal policy and the flow of financial savings from the government sector, which data limitations have placed beyond the scope of this chapter.[27]

Conclusions on the structure of the Ugandan economy and domestic resource mobilization: a market segmentation view

1. This chapter advances the view that commercial banks are more suited to mobilize savings from the formal, non-agricultural monetary segments: productive monetary sectors; trade, commerce and crop finance (as defined in Table 6.1) and general government. Except for trade and commerce, however, there is a serious liquidity squeeze in the formal sector. This scarcity of credit is an indicator of the serious efforts necessary for the commercial banks to mobilize savings and to channel them into productive investment. This chapter examines commercial banks from this standpoint.
2. The informal sector is even larger than the formal sector, at most 40 per cent of total GDP. This chapter argues that existing formal commercial banks are ill-suited to mobilize domestic savings from this sector. The Uganda Savings and Credit Cooperative Union will be examined, especially the characteristics of this institution that are well suited to finance informal activities.
3. The non-monetary sector is large, over 30 per cent of total GDP, and it has not decreased over the past 10 years. The rural population depends largely on this sector. It can yield domestic savings because the economic agents in it are not subsisting, but do produce a marketable surplus, which they barter or sell for cash. The challenge before Uganda is to devise a new type of institution to monetize this sector and mobilize its savings. Original field work is needed to identify the most promising channels for monetization and for savings mobilization before it will be possible, at some future date, to set out appropriate policies for this sector.

3. The Commercial Banks and Domestic Resource Mobilization for the Formal Monetary Economy

The structure of commercial banks

The structure consists of the commercial banks listed, according to relative importance in terms of branches, in Table 6.3. The Uganda Commercial Bank (UCB) is the largest of the commercial banks, 'accounting for about half of the total assets of the commercial banks and for more than two thirds of the total number of branches.'[28]

The Cooperative Bank is fully owned by the Cooperative Movement. It was supposed to give loans and technical assistance to farmers and to function as a farmers' bank through the Cooperative Movement. However, it started a purely commercial section to make quick profits to tide itself over long-term loans from the Cooperative Movement, and currently functions as a commercial bank.

The expatriate banks used to dominate commercial banking with 79 per cent of the branches and 189 mobile units prior to 1972. But the expulsion of its Asian staff and the acquisition of private businesses by the government forced these banks to sell their branches to UCB; they have not expanded since then.[29]

Since 'banking statistics do not cover transactions taking place on "unorganized" money markets in rural areas due to lack of sufficient banking facilities', it is reasonable to argue that commercial banks largely cater for the formal monetary economy.[30]

Table 6.3   The relative importance of commercial banks by number of branches

	(1)	(2)	(3)
	1984 branches	1988* branches	Ownership
Uganda Commercial Bank	51	65	100% Gov't
Uganda Cooperative Bank	11	14	100% Coop
Barclays Bank	4	4	49% foreign
Bank of Baroda	3	3	49% foreign
Libyan Arab Uganda Bank	3	3	49% foreign
Grindlays Bank	1	1	49% foreign
Standard Chartered	1	2	100% foreign
Gold Trust	1	3	new
Nile Bank	–	1	new
	75	96	

* New branches since 1984 were reported to me in telephone conversations

Other financial institutions and their relationship to commercial banks

The other financial institutions include the Bank of Uganda (the Central Bank), two development banks, insurance companies, the Housing Finance Company, The Social Security Fund, the Post Office Savings Bank, the newly created and fast growing building societies, the Savings and Credit Cooperative Union, and the Centenary Rural Development Trust.

The East African Development Bank, with headquarters in Kampala, serves three countries: Kenya, Tanzania and Uganda. The Uganda Development Bank is fully government-owned and is the main institution through which project development assistance is channelled. These development institutions should assist commercial bank customers with credit to obtain goods involving aid in foreign exchange. In turn, development bank customers should be assisted by commercial banks to obtain working capital. But, currently, the development banks are confined to conservative fixed investment, especially that involving foreign exchange. The link with the commercial banks is weak.[31]

The Bank of Uganda should be supportive and development-oriented, assisting the commercial banks to improve the quality of their infrastructure by running training courses for staff, for example. It should also assess and supervise performance for clearly defined economic objectives. Currently supervision tends to be confined to credit.

The Post Office Savings Bank used to have 61 branches and 37 sub-branches throughout the country. It was well suited to collecting small, scattered deposits at low cost. But inflation, war looting and damage reduced its total savings deposits to only 1 per cent of total deposits in the country by 1982.

It can be argued that the other financial institutions should behave in a complementary fashion by collecting deposits and supervising loans from small customers, then banking with the commercial banks. This would reduce operating expenses for a given volume of resources mobilized in the economy. But there are serious limitations to most of these institutions.

The Centenary Rural Development Trust, a savings and credit institution, is operating three branches in Kampala, Masaka and Kabale, and six liaison offices which it intends to turn into branches at Fort Portal, Mbarara, Hoima, Mbzale, Arua and Jinja. The Trust, started by the Catholic Church, was supposed to open a branch in every parish. But stringent supervision requirements per branch, monitored by the Bank of Uganda, have resulted in a slow spread of branches. Insecurity also forced the Trust to restrict most commercial loans to Kampala until February 1986.

Among the insurance companies, the National Insurance Corporation, which is the largest, is wholly owned by government and accounts for 70 per cent of insurance business in the country.[32] Unfortunately, no published data are available to appraise the domestic resource mobilization efforts of the insurance business and many insurance policies have been rendered valueless by inflation.

The Housing Finance Company and the building societies, though becoming more active, are still too small to make a difference to resource mobilization and are also under-capitalized. The Social Security Fund is dormant. The Uganda Cooperative Savings and Credit Union is the other large financial institution on which some data are available; its operations are discussed later in this chapter.

The potential and problems of commercial banks in the mobilization of domestic financial resources for the formal sector

Two sets of statistics indicate that Uganda is 'underbanked': (1) the size of the non-monetary economy (see Table 6.1, row 1) which is over 30 per cent of total GDP; and (2) the currency circulating in the hands of the public in the monetary sector which is close to 50 per cent of 'broad money' (see Table 6.4, column 3).[33]

Table 6.4   Monetary survey (Ugandan shillings, millions)

	(1) Broad money (M$_2$)	(2) Currency in circulation	(3) Currency in circulation as % of broad money
1978	9,580	3,518	37
1979	13,166	4,641	35
1980	17,436	6,243	36
1981	30,848	10,344	34
1982	38,512	12,835	37
1983	54,423	18,920	35
1984	116,292	43,930	38
1985	261,960	105,040	40
1986	724,160	357,600	49
1987	1,854,000	904,000	49

Sources: Republic of Uganda. Ministry of Planning and Economic Development, *Background to the Budget* 1985–6 and 1987–8 (Kampala, June 1985 and July 1988)
Note: The last row is reported in new money; two zeros were added to make the figures comparable to those in the old money before the currency reform of May 1987.

The low branch density

Prior to 1972, when expatriate banks dominated commercial banking, there were 290 branches, one branch per 34,000 people. The expropriation of Asians reduced the branches to only 74 by 1983. In 1984, in order to encourage commercial banks to open more branches in rural areas, the government decided to grant a Corporate Tax exemption for two years to any commercial bank which opens at least two branches in a year outside Kampala, Jinja, Entebbe and Mbale, beginning 1 July 1984.

The response has come mainly from UCB, opening 14 branches, and the Cooperative Bank, opening three branches between 1984 and 1988. The current density ratio (96 branches) is one branch per 145,833, given a population of 14 million people. Unless other incentives are legislated, the burden of opening new branches will have to be born by UCB

– but too many UCB branches might produce an unintended publicly owned monopoly of commercial banking where, because of lack of competition, customers have to seek services rather than the banks looking for business.

Efficiency of services to customers
There are several measures commercial banks could take, or are just beginning to adopt, to render more efficient services to attract customers. Three such measures are discussed here for illustration: the first of these is *the reduction of frauds and forgeries.* Historically, the banking system has tended to blame these crimes on incomplete investigations by the police, which prevent prosecution of offenders; inadequate legal provisions to punish the prosecuted; and the participation of some lawyers in such 'sidelines'.

While the above faults cannot be proved 100 per cent absent in all cases, the legal opinion suggests lack of vigilance from the banks themselves in giving proper training to their staff who are better placed than, and should assist, the police to investigate frauds and forgeries.

> Prosecutors could be more vigorous and better trained . . . from institutions like banks, much more should be expected; and before any suspect is surrendered to the Police, the investigations by the bank and the Police should be complete and the case for prosecution should virtually be ready for trial. A victim in the position of banks should take the initiative in the investigations and supply its technical man where the Police may be lacking.[34]

The banks are also blamed for not reporting fraudulent lawyers to the Legal Disciplinary Committee which would take punitive action.

There is also delay by the banks, and reluctance by the public, to introduce and accept more convenient means of payments, cheques for example, because of forgeries: this in part explains the high cash ratio in circulation relative to the total money supply (see Table 6.4, column 3). Inevitably, the neglect of frauds and forgeries results in an erosion of confidence in the banks by the public.

The *attitude of bank employees* is another aspect of service efficiency to which banks should pay attention. In general, in Uganda, the customer is the one to seek out poorly advertised services instead of the bank seeking out customers. There is no enquiries desk at the front of most commercial banks. There are no specialized service desks for student customers, say, or smallholders. In Uganda, banking personnel tend to be polite to the educated and rich (hoping for tips!) and give a cold, sometimes rude, reception to the less educated or those with small accounts. Special attention should be paid to promoting competition, forcing the banks to look for customers.

Hours of business should also be revised. Banking hours had been 8.30 a.m. to 12.30 p.m., Monday to Friday, until 1988 when they were lengthened to 2.00 p.m. This still leaves cash earned in the afternoons and at weekends unbanked.

Reasons for short banking hours include the manual system of bookkeeping and the colonial tradition of devoting the morning to the few 'credit-worthy' customers, followed by a leisurely afternoon.[35] Simplified and low-cost computerized technology would lengthen the customer hours and increase overall efficiency.[36]

Mobilization: extension services and variety of accounts
The limited competition among banks for customers means that there is hardly any attempt to mobilize a variety of services and 'evangelize' the public to save.

Existing literature suggests that Africans save, not necessarily out of increased incomes, but because they have specific objectives: building a home, meeting marriage expenses and so on.[37] A wide variety of deposits is needed to suit different customer targets and preferences. As variety increases, extension services, say at local county administration centres or through schools or hospitals, are needed to explain to the public the benefits of each service and the procedures to open and maintain each type of account. A customer who introduces, teaches, and manages to attract new customers should be rewarded for the mobilization effort, and explanatory pamphlets should be available to customers who want to recruit others.

The various accounts mentioned below have been proposed but either not adopted by commercial banks or, if adopted, not accompanied by the publicity and extension services necessary to mobilize the public to utilize them:

1. *Term deposit account:* where a customer deposits for one year, with no withdrawals. Interest is accredited at the end of the year to reduce administrative costs on small deposits.
2. *Reinvestment plan:* where a customer deposits a sum for a specific period, during which time the interest is added to the principal so that she/he earns interest on interest.
3. *Recurring deposits:* where the customer invests a fixed sum for, say, one year and interest accrues from the time of the first deposit, to attract large deposits.
4. *Perennial pension fund:* where the customer deposits a fixed amount for any 7 years, per year, at the end of which the bank pays him monthly sums (twice as large as the deposits, or more) to take care of major expenses in old age.
5. *Specific benefit scheme:* where a customer stands to win a prize after depositing for, say, 7–10 years.
6. *Loan-linked saving:* where a customer can borrow a multiple of savings if the deposit account has been maintained for some time – a practice followed in the Uganda Savings and Credit Union, where loans can be one and a quarter times the amount of deposits.
7. *Special scheme for school children:* to induce parents to save and to teach students to save.
8. *Door-to-door passbooks:* to collect savings from customers who do not want to leave their work to go to the bank.[38]

Reducing the rate of inflation

Providing a variety of accounts with different term-structures of interest rates would change the commercial banks' deposit structure, which is heavily weighted in favour of demand deposits, and against time and saving deposits.

A comparison of nominal interest rates on commercial bank deposits and advances (Table 6.5), and the available indices of domestic inflation (Table 6.6), suggests that real interest rates are sharply negative. Whereas the negative lending rates favour the borrower, the negative deposit rates discourage savings. In order for commercial banks to match their short-term deposits to lending, they make loans which favour the tertiary sector. This takes over

Table 6.5   *Commercial banks: structure of nominal interest rates (per cent)*

	Oct 1981	Dec 1982	Dec 1983	Dec 1984	Dec 1985	Dec 1986	1987/8
Deposit rates							
1. Demand deposits	————optional————			5.0	5.0	10.0	7.0
2. Saving deposits	8.0	9.0	13.0	18.0	18.0	28.0	28–32.0
3. Time deposits (min 1yr.)	12.0	13.0	17.0	20.0	20.0	30.0	22.0
Lending rates							
4. Agriculture	13.0	14.0	18.0	24.0	24.0	38.0	32–35.0
5. Export and manufacturing	14.0	15.0	19.0	24.0	24.0	38.0	
6. Commerce	15.0			25.0	25.0	40.0	
7. Unsecured	17.0	(20.0)	(22.0)	26.0	26.0	42.0	

Source: Republic of Uganda: *Background to the Budget* 1988–9 (Ministry of Planning and Economic Development, Kampala, July 1988)

Table 6.6   Indices of inflation and the structure of commercial bank deposits

1978	(1) The GDP Deflator[1] 1981=100	(2) Kampala Cost of living Index,[2] Low Income,Group Sept.1981=100	(3) Kampala Cost of living Index,[2] Middle Income, Group Apr.1981=100	(4) Demand Deposits (Shs.M)	(5) Time[3] saving Deposits (Shs.M)	(6) Total nominal Deposits (Shs.M)	(7) Demand deposit as % of total deposits	(8) The Real value of Total Deposits
1981 April	–		100	–				
1981 Sept	–	100	–					
1981 Dec	100	88	163	14,260	6,244	20,504	70	20,504
1982	176	138	220	16,940	8,736	25,676	66	14,588
1983	246	170	267	24,620	10,800	35,420	70	14,399
1984	375	275	538	49,950	17,630	67,580	74	18,021
1985	836	933	1093	120,580	36,340	156,920	77	18,183
1986	2171	2316	4691	260,940	105,620	366,560	71	16,884
1987[4]	5485	6419	12313	74,700	20,100	94,800	79	1,370

Source: Republic of Uganda, Ministry of Planning and Economic Development. Background to the Budget 1985–86–89 (Kampala: June 1985 and July 1988)

1. The GDP Deflator is derived by dividing GDP figures in current prices by GDP figures in constant 1966 prices, and setting the inflation rate to 1981 = 100
2. These are the available indices, with a weight of 41 per cent for food in the Middle Income Index, and 70 per cent for food in the Low Income Index. December Data of the weighted average are taken in each case.
3. Time deposits are not reported separately; they are a very small proportion of total deposits.
4. Figures for 1987 are in new Uganda Shs. after the currency reform of May 1987, with two zeros added to compare them to old Shs. The result shows a drastic decline in total deposits, and a simultaneous increase in the ratio of demand to total deposits. This suggests that the currency reform worsened the liquidity squeeze. Since the ratio of currency in circulation to broad money remained the same in 1987 as in 1986, i.e. 49 per cent (Table 6.4 column 3), the 30 per cent conversion tax squeezed more the money deposited in the banking system, especially time deposits.

60 per cent of total commercial bank loans and advances to the private sector (Table 6.2, row 4). Because these loans are short-term and quick to recover, the interest rates charged to the borrowers, though negative, are higher than the lending rates in the productive sectors. This discourages the flow of credit into production.

It does not solve the problem to argue that interest rates should be adjusted upwards until they become positive. What is required is cooperation between the monetary authorities and the banks to effect a drastic reduction in the rate of inflation.

4. The Cooperative Savings and Credit Union and Domestic Resource Mobilization for the Informal Sector

The structure of the cooperative movement in Uganda

The Uganda Cooperative Movement is extensive, covering a wide range of economic activities, and dating back to the 1950s, but with rapid growth and diversification of activities in the 1980s (Table 6.7).

The Movement is organized around Primary Societies, which individual members join at the parish level. These numbered 4833 in 1986. The Societies formed 31 active District Unions in 1984.[39] The Unions are linked to six National Cooperative Organizations and to the Uganda Cooperative Alliance, an Apex Society.

The Cooperative Movement is dominated by coffee and cotton marketing (Table 6.7). The farmers sell these crops to the Cooperative Societies which, in turn, sell to the District Unions for processing. There is some competition against the Primary Societies and District Unions by private buyers and processors. But, once processed, the output is sold to the Coffee and Lint Marketing Boards which have the monopoly for export.

Table 6.7   Categories of cooperative societies and relative importance by end of 1983

	(1) Category	(2) Number of societies in category	(3) Category's number of societies % of total	(4) Sample of each category in the survey (%)
1.	Marketing coffee/cotton	2,922	66.8	10
2.	Saving and credit	373	8.5	12
3.	Multi-purpose	285	6.5	15
4.	Consumer	220	5.0	13
5.	Transport	204	4.7	14
6.	Livestock	127	2.9	15
7.	Marketing tobacco	57	1.3	19
8.	Hides and skins	52	1.2	31
9.	Farm/vegetables	48	1.1	35
10.	Fishing	37	0.8	11
11.	Dairy	35	0.8	26
12.	Marketing tea	11	0.3	27
	Total	4,371	100	

Source: Republic of Uganda, Ministry of Cooperatives and Marketing, Planning Unit, Report of the National Cooperative Survey Project (August 1985)

The Cooperative Movement does not function as an autonomous business enterprise, as originally intended by the 1946 Cooperative Ordinance. The Ordinance, similar to that of colonial India and Ceylon, envisaged a model for the development of the cooperative ideal: a voluntary body with open membership and run on sound business principles. The Ordinance was modified in 1951, 1952 and 1953 to reflect local conditions and to prepare for independence.

In 1970, however, after an Ad Hoc Committee of Enquiry chaired by Shafiq Arain, the Ordinance was amended into the Cooperative Act (1970) which gives government extensive powers to tightly control cooperatives and interfere directly in the affairs of the cooperatives. The Registrar of Cooperatives, who is also the Commissioner or head of the Cooperative Department, under the Minister of Cooperatives and Marketing, has extensive powers to register, cancel or suspend cooperatives. He also elects district Cooperative Officers and appoints or approves the appointment of the General Manager, the Internal Auditor and the Accountant of each District Cooperative Union.[40]

There are proposals to amend the Cooperative Act to delete most of the direct powers of the Ministers; but since the powers of the Registrar, under the Minister, remain largely intact, the deletions will not be substantive.

A Cooperative Development Council is proposed, with two members appointed by the Minister, the Registrar or his representative, and four members appointed by the Uganda Cooperative Alliance. The Registrar is supposed to consult with the Council on significant matters affecting the Cooperative Movement. If the results of the consultations are not overruled by the Minister, the Council may turn out to be the institution to modify government control.

However, some of the most offensive provisions of the 1970 Act remain unaltered in the amendments. For example,

> No registered society shall pay a dividend or bonus or distribute any part of its accumulated funds without the prior written consent of the Registrar. . . .

Usually consent is delayed, sometimes for as long as a year. This is a disincentive for societies to make or declare surpluses which become depleted by inflation by the time they are distributed. Another offensive provision is that the estimates of revenue and expenditure of each society must receive the approval of the Registrar before they are submitted to the Annual General Meeting. This deprives the societies of autonomy to allocate their resources.

Added to the direct government interference are the price regulations of cotton and coffee which are set annually and announced by the Minister of Finance in the Budget speech. More recently other price guidelines were also set by the Produce Marketing Board for crops in which the government needs to meet its export barter commitments, such as maize, beans or soybeans.

Price regulations and direct government interference, therefore, leave the cooperatives little room in which to function as autonomous business enterprises. In particular, the mobilization of domestic savings by the coffee and cotton marketing cooperatives, the largest single category of cooperatives in Table 6.7, is limited severely by the low prices of these crops and by delayed payments to the farmers.

The Uganda Cooperative Savings and Credit Union and domestic resource mobilization

The Uganda Cooperative Savings and Credit Union was chosen as the basis of a study of the role of cooperatives in domestic resource mobilization. The choice was based on the following considerations:

1.   The Union had the second largest number of registered societies (Table 6.7).

Table 6.8   Comparative performance criteria of the five largest categories of Cooperative Societies by end of 1983

Performance criterion	(1) Cotton coffee marketing	(2) Credit and saving	(3) Multi purpose	(4) Consumers	(5) Transport
1. Average membership number per Society	417	685	53	391	39
2. Active members %	80	82	91	97	100
3. Usable audits %	68	72	35	31	28
4. Dormant societies %	16	19	19	59	50*
5. Operating surplus %	52	74	86	89	25
6. Net margin before taxes	–	11	16	20	18
7. Credit rating, good %	8	20	77	56	75*
8. Societies surveyed, number	288	43	43	29	28
9. Societies surveyed %	7.1	23	15	13	14

Source: Republic of Uganda, Ministry of Cooperatives and Marketing, Planning Unit, Report of the National Cooperative Survey Project (August 1985)

* The Societies with the highest dormancy rate (row 4) also have a good credit rating (row 7) as the poor performers in the category are dormant.

2. By performance criteria (Table 6.8), the Union had the largest average membership per society (row 1, column 2). Although 18 per cent of the members are not active (row 2), the society has the largest number of usable audits, 72 per cent, of all cooperative societies (row 3), which shows an active accounting system. Although 19 per cent of the societies are dormant (row 4) the Union ranks third in operating surplus (74 per cent, row 5). The net margin before taxes is only 11 per cent (row 6) and the credit rating is only 20 per cent (row 7), but these poor performance criteria are due to circumstances not entirely within the Union's control, to be discussed below. On the whole, this is a large and active Union.

3. By 1983, the Union had an infrastructure of 18 zonal offices in the country, each with a staff of two. This is second only to the UCB in number of branches. The Union is, therefore, attempting to serve a wide public.

4. The Union was started in the 1960s by the Catholic Church as a set of Thrift Societies in the Cooperative Saving and Credit movement; one of the main objectives was to mobilize domestic savings, the subject of this volume. [41] It was formalized in 1972 by government into the national association of the then 20 Savings and Credit Societies, which numbered 373 by 1983. The government, through the Department of Cooperative Development, provided inspection, audit and staff to complement the services of the Union's field staff. Unfortunately, it is this involvement which became too restrictive under the 1970 Cooperative Act. But the fact that the Union is not marketing cotton and coffee gives it a little more autonomy from the interference of the Ministry.

5. The Union was started to serve low-income civil servants and rural dwellers who operate in the informal sector, already identified as the largest and most resilient sector of the economy.

The organizational structure of the Savings and Credit Cooperative Union

Individual members join the Primary Societies at the parish level. At their Annual General Meeting they elect a management committee to represent them at the Union level and on its sub-committees. A Secretary/Manager heads the Union and runs its daily functions with the support of staff employees. This Manager is appointed by the Minister, together with the Auditor and the Accountant. To reduce administrative costs, in 1983 the Union divided itself into 18 zones.

The zonal 7 committees are local sub-committees of the Union, elected at the zonal get-together meetings of the elected chairpersons, secretaries and treasurers of all Primary Societies in the zone. The zones serve as a communication link between the Union and the Primary Societies. The functions of the zonal committees are:
1. to draft the zonal budget and to ensure that the zone is self-financing;
2. to ensure participation of each society in the Union activities, which would be difficult if each society were directly contacted by the Union headquarters;
3. to determine the training needs and arrange courses for societies;
4. to collect pertinent statistical data for planning and implementation of projects;
5. to plan zonal development strategies and projects;
6. to ensure that Union services are equitably shared among the societies.

Functions of the Cooperative Savings and Credit Union and domestic resource mobilization at Union level

The Central Fund

The Cooperative Savings and Credit Union administers a Central Fund which was started in 1975 for inter-societal lending. Each society buys shares in the Fund on becoming a member (column 1, Table 6.9). Subsequently, the society contributes 10 per cent of its monthly savings into the Fund (column 2) on which it earns 10 per cent interest annually. Although the Fund has grown rapidly, it still mobilizes only a small amount of domestic savings, compared to the commercial banks, because societal membership of the Fund is voluntary. Societies deposit as and when they can.

The funds are loaned out to the member societies at 20 per cent interest charge. The Union retains the margin between 10–20 per cent interest to run inter-societal services. Although small, the intention of the Union is to make the Fund the Central Bank of the Societies.

Table 6.9   The Central Fund: Zonal contributions per year to the Savings and Credit Union, Uganda Shillings (millions)

	(1) Shares	(2) Deposits	(3) Loans
1980	0.3	11.4	5.3
1981	0.4	21.7	15.4
1982	0.5	27.8	14.9
1983	0.8	34.5	19.7
1984	2.8	41.2	23.6
1985	5.4	51.4	31.4
1986	10.8	74.2	69.7
1987*	25.9	174.0	83.7

Source: Uganda Savings and Credit Union (Kampala, June 1988)
* Data for 1987 was converted to old Shillings by adding two zeros

Since most of the Savings and Credit Societies do not have any tangible security to offer, they cannot obtain loans from the banks.[42]

The Fund, therefore, caters for a segment of society which cannot obtain loans from the formal sector: as this objective is popularized, contributions to resources mobilized by the Fund should grow.

The Risk Management Programme

In 1974, the Union established a group insurance to cover members' loans and savings. In the case of disability or death, the programme pays the loan without touching the savings or personal property of the member. The programme also augments the members' savings, depending at what age he/she dies.

However, the importance of risk management, especially for small loans in the informal sector, cannot be underrated: its absence deters lending even in the formal sector. Witness the reluctance of commercial banks to lend to smallholder farmers and small businesses, which prompted government to consider the Credit Guarantee Scheme.[43]

Table 6. 10   Risk Management Fund

Year	(1) No.of societies participating	(2) Premiums collected Uganda Shs	(3) Claims settled Uganda Shs	(4) Balance (res.) Uganda Shs
1980	283	12,246	3,006	+9,240
1981	100	13,690	28,157	−5,227
1982	152	18,961	21,456	−7,722
1983	189	23,451	26,006	−10,267
1984	296	30,927	23,886	−4,126
1985	363	37,564	34,529	−1,091
1986	373	104,669	41,005	+62,578
1987	222	330,640	179,452	+213,768

Source: Uganda Cooperative Savings and Credit Union, Reg. No. 2725 (Kampala, June 1988)

The Education Fund

In 1975 the Union set up an education fund to train ordinary members in cooperative principles, committee members in leadership and management, and employees in accounting, auditing, credit handling and management of operations. Table 6.11 shows the number of courses offered per year and the total participation.

Domestic resource mobilization requires an extension service to teach the public and employees the importance of mobilization institutions and how they operate. This extension service is lacking in the traditional commercial banks: merely opening up more branches cannot ensure more banking unless the public is trained to appreciate and use the institutions. The future problem is how to sustain the courses as education is expensive and has previously been largely funded by foreign grants.

Other Union programmes associated with domestic resource mobilization

A *Mixed Saving Programme* was started in 1983 to operate like traditional banking where deposits can be withdrawn on demand. A *Supplies Department* offers loans in kind for essential commodities like farm inputs, implements and building materials, which the Union buys in bulk at lower prices. The Union's mark-up also generates revenue which it

Table 6.11   Education facility

Year	(1) Number of courses	(2) Total participation
1980	12	720
1981	10	1,250
1982	15	6,805
1983	28	11,630
1984	17*	8,219
1985	8*	4,160
1986	33	12,860
1987	123	45,644

Source: Uganda Cooperative Savings and Credit Union, Reg.No.2725 (Kampala, June 1988)
* Some courses were kept up even under extreme insecurity in 1984 and 1985

uses to extend services to members. Plans are under way to expand this department to provide production inputs to farmers.

The Union's *Projects Department* runs a carpentry workshop at Kisubi, seven miles from Kampala, which sells furniture to the general public to raise revenue. USAID has also given a US$5.5 million loan for the Uganda Rural Recovery Economic Programme, under which a brick and tile making pilot project in the war-ravaged Luwero Triangle has started, supervised by the Union. Cooperative members pay 20 per cent of the cost for bricks, receiving the rest as a loan in kind. They can also obtain furniture from the carpentry project to meet other housing needs. The Projects Department's policy is to encourage savings in kind for particular targets.

Functions of the Cooperative Savings and Credit Union and domestic resource mobilization at the primary societal level

A 5 per cent sample of Primary Societies was drawn from the Union files to compute indicators of resource mobilization. The following picture might exaggerate the performance record, as the best societies had the most complete records. But this is the only societal record we could obtain, short of a fieldwork survey.

Table 6.12   Seven-year growth trend of the Savings and Credit Cooperative Movement (sample of 25 Societies or 5 per cent of total number of Societies in the Movement)[1]

	No. of members of 25 Societies (1)	Shares (2)	Deposits in Uganda Shillings (m) (3)	Loans[2] in Uganda Shillings (m) (4)
1980	19,938	1.5	82.2	63.1
1981	22,098	1.6	110,7	83.6
1982	23,755	2.0	131.8	113.2
1983	25,047	3.8	184.4	153.9
1984	25,557	10.1	298.7	227.9
1985	27,590	30.4	503.9	344.6
1986	27,495	106.1	1105.7	934.0
% Inc.	37.9	6970	1345	1480

Source: Uganda Cooperative Savings and Credit Union (Kampala, June 1988)
1. The 25 Societies samples were drawn from Central (9), Western (3), Southern (3), Eastern (3), national level (7).
2. Figures are on cumulative basis.

Domestic resource mobilization

Table 6.12, columns 2 and 3 show rapid growth in shares and member deposits. Because data could not be obtained for 1987, it is not known how currency reform affected these societies. The 5 per cent sample of mobilized domestic resources is equal to 3–5 per cent of the total domestic deposits by the whole commercial banking sector. The societies, therefore, are a significant source of savings.

Reasons for joining the Primary Society

Access to credit (Table 6.13, column 3) is the principal reason given for members to join the Primary Society. The Cooperative Savings and Credit Union is thus motivating this segment of the economy to save in order to get credit which it could not obtain from the formal sector.[44] A loan can be obtained without collateral, based on 'only the known character, honesty and industry of a borrower, together with his income prospects'.[45] Despite lack of collateral, loan delinquency rates are quite low (Table 6.13, column 7). Some delinquency is caused by factors beyond the members' control:

> It has been observed as a common phenomenon that when employers are paying salaries and wages to employees, deductions . . . to societies are not remitted. In some Ministries and institutions it has taken more than six months before any remittance is made.
> . . . the practice of not remitting members' money deducted from their salaries to the Savings and Credit Societies is endangering the services of the Movement.[46]

In rural societies where members are growing crops whose prices and marketing are not strictly controlled (unlike cotton and coffee), the seasonal income enables immediate payment to the savings and credit system.

> Without traditional banking institutions in rural areas, this money remained untapped and the introduction of savings and credit societies has become an answer by committing this money to the banking stream.[47]

Given the seasonal incomes, rural delinquency rates are even lower. This speaks well of the societies, since in the beginning

> the government was not encouraging rural savings and credit societies as their success was doubtful. The first rural ones were founded at church centres because of the trust and leadership potential people expected of priests and churchmen.[48]

Of the current 650 societies, 410 are rural. The strong rural bias is also shown in Table 6.14, column 2: over 50 per cent of the membership is rural in most societies.

The reluctance to mobilize and allocate financial resources to segments of the economy which have no collateral, or are rural-based, is founded either on prejudice or on institutional administrative rigidities. It is argued in this chapter that domestic resource mobilization policies should be based on a market segmentation perspective, in order to build appropriate institutions and attitudes for the different segments of the economy.

The second main reason given for joining a Primary Society is *saving facilities.* Table 6.13 reveals that saving facilities are valued in their own right whether they offer dividends or not (ranked low in column 4) or whether they offer insurance benefits (column 5). This suggests that the low-income earner is a 'target saver' who needs a facility to accumulate savings for a particular objective and is less interested in considerations such as dividends. Financial institutions, therefore, should provide a variety of saving instruments for particular objectives as part of their domestic resource mobilization strategy.

Table 6.13 cites *convenience* as the third most important reason for joining the Savings and Credit Society. This is consistent with our earlier suggestion that the financial

Table 6.13   Priority reasons for joining credit & saving society

Society	(1) convenient	(2) Savings facilities	(3) Access to credit	(4) Dividends
Keti Falawo	3	4	5	1
Kimembe	3	4	5	1
Kitagwenda	4	5	3	2
Kyazanga	5	3	4	2
COOPDEPT	2	3	4	1
Lint Marketing	4	3	5	2
Mapeersa	3	4	5	
Buddo	3	4	5	1
CULCOM	4		5	2
Busoga TRS	3	4	5	1
Extelcoms	3	4	5	
U.E.B.Jinja	3	4	5	1
N.I.C.	3	4	5	
Mukono	4	3	5	2
AGRIDEPT	3	4	5	
Mengo TRS	3	4	5	
Wanehewa	1	5	4	
Rubaya	3	4	5	2
M.I.B.	3	4	5	2
Rubindi	3	4	5	
Rwenkuba	3	4	5	1
Nytil	3	4	5	1
U.C.B.	3	4	5	2
Mpigi D.A.	3	4	5	1
Kyaggwe	3	4	5	1
Kampala Savings	3	4	5	1
Total rating	81	98	125	27

Society	(5) Insurance benefits	(6) Others	(7) % loan delinquency	(8) Interest rate of loan
Keti Falawo	2		2	24
Kimembe	2		3	24
Kitagwenda	1		1	24
Kyazanga	1		4	24
COOPDEPT	5		0.5	24
Lint Marketing	1		0.5	26
Mapeera	1	2	3	18
Buddo	2		4	20
CULCOM	3	1	0.5	20
Busoga TRS	2		0.8	22
Extelcoms	2	1	0.3	25
U.E.B.Jinja	2		1	24
N.I.C.	1	2	1	23
Mukono	1		3	24
AGRIDEPT	2	1	1	20
Mengo TRS	2	1	0.7	24
Wenehews	2	3	1	21
Rubaya	1		3	24
M.I.B.	1		2	23
Rubindi	2	1	2	24
Rwenkuba		2	3	23
Nytil	2		1	20
U.C.B.	1		0.2	20
Mpigi D.A.	2		3	25
Kyaggwe	2		–	–
Kampala Savings		2	2	25
	43	16		

Source: Uganda Cooperative Savings and Credit Union (Kampala, June 1988)

Note: Information from files on a 5 per cent sample of 26 Saving and Credit Societies in the Cooperative Union. Ratings: 1 = lowest; 2 = low; 3 = middle; 4 = high; 5 = highest.

Table 6.14 Type of society, location and primary source of income of members

Society	Savings	Loans	Location %		Primary source of income of members (%)			
			(1) Urban	(2) Rural	(3) Farming	(4) Own business	(5) Daily pay	(6) Regular Employees
Keti Falawo	6,008,432	2,136,107	30	70		100		
Kilembe	135,492,318	55,815,243	10	90				100
Kitagwenda	4,571,057	1,620,710		100	100			
COOPDEPT	235,710,445	174,972,459	50	50				100
Kyanzanga	90,224,669	74,717,592	100		90	5	3	2
Lint Marketing	30,510,377	23,991,121	50	50				100
Mapeera	151,923,704	164,564,173	20	70	5	70	5	20
Buddo	50,194,422	35,236,294		100	3	27	10	60
CULCOM	35,505,043	22,829,817	50	50				100
Busoga TRS	12,747,015	15,063,756	10	90				100
Extelcoms	14,108,880	10,739,651	100					100
UEB	33,363,205	27,025,982	20	80				100
N.I.C.	20,702,091	16,646,145	100					100
Mukono	87,074,297	79,523,748	15	85		85	5	10
AGRIDEPT	189,292,881	153,741,161	50	50				100
Mengo Teachers	889,673,467	710,155,048	20	80				100
Wanehewa	56,435,290	46,578,702	100					100
Rubaya	29,255,886	24,946,974		100	90	3		7
MIB	45,791,178	34,514,455	100					100
Rubindi	47,609,645	41,319,249		100	100			
Rwenkuba	12,477,169	12,913,517		100	100			
Nytil	96,929,065	93,875,043	100					100
UEB	72,535,316	68,456,398	70	30				100
Mpigi DA	40,930,230	38,270,373	5	95				100
Kyaggwe DA	16,748,652	16,517,902	3	97				100
Kampala Savings	109,083,508	159,081,000	100			20		80

Source: Uganda Cooperative Savings and Credit Union (Kampala, June 1988)
Note: Information from files on a 5 per cent sample of 26 Savings and Credit Societies in the Cooperative Union

Table 6.15   Purpose of Loan (%)

Society	Cumulative Savings 1980–1986 Shs.	Cumulative Loan 1980–1986 Shs.	(1) Agric.	(2) Live-Stock	(3) Medical	(4) Trad-ing	(5) Educ.	(6) Home Imp.	(7) Build-ing	(8) Land	(9) Personal	(10) Others
Keti Falawo	6,008,432	2,136,107	25	3	7	35	28	10	5		15	10
Kilemhe	135,492,318	55,815,243	27	1	12	15	30	15		5	10	
Kitagwenda	4,571,057	1,620,710			10	10	30	3		10	4	7
Kyazanga	90,224,660	74,717,592	55		5	5	15		5		3	10
COOPDEPT	235,710,445	174,972,459			15	12.5	25	15	1	2	30	14
Lint Marketing	30,510,377	23,991,121			3		16	21.5	2	4	30	
Maneera	151,923,704	164,564,173	2	5	8	40	30	3		2	6	15
Buddo	50,194,422	35,236,294		4	1	10	26	5	8	1	29	30
CULCOM	35,595,943	22,839,817			2		7	10	7		50	10
Busoga TRS	12,747,015	15,063,756	3			12	48	8			18	10
Extelcom	14,108,880	10,739,651			12	3	10	25			40	17
UEBJinje	33,363,205	27,925,982		3	9	8.3	22	20			20	12
NIC	20,702,091	16,646,145					40	30		3	15	
Mukono	87,974,297	70,523,748			6	50	20	20			10	5
AGRIDEPT	189,292,881	153,741,161	7	3	1.7		18	36			25	
Mengo TRS	889,673,467	710,155,048	7.9			32	20	20	9	6	3.4	10
Wanehewa	56,435,290	46,578,702			5	7	18	40			20	
Rubaya	29,255,886	34,514,455			10	5	10	6			9	
MIB							50	3	7		25	
Rubindi	47,609,645	41,319,249	60	5	10	10	10				5	
Rwenkuba	12,477,169	12,913,517	60			30	10					
Nytil	96,929,065	93,875,043			2	12	28	34		3	21	3
UCB	71,535,316	68,456,398		10		9	13	42	6	2	15	5
Mpigi DA	40,930,230	38,270,373	8		12		30	15	5	15	10	
Kyaggwe DA	109,083,508	159,081,000	15	4	10	20	27	15	2	13	20	
Kampala Savings							40	5		4	2	

Source: Uganda Cooperative Savings and Credit Union (Kampala, June 1988)
Note: Information from files on a 5 per cent sample of 26 Savings and Credit Societies in the Cooperative Union.

institutions to serve the informal sector must be located conveniently, with flexible hours so that customers can walk in and out informally. In Sri Lanka, for example, the pawnbroker is open in the evenings and at weekends when the poor have time off their work to arrange for loans.[49]

The fourth and last reason given is the *interest rate on loans.* Given the high rate of inflation, the real interest rates corresponding to the nominal rates in Uganda are sharply negative. The societies surveyed, however, all charged interest rates in 1986 which were lower than the lending rates of the commercial banks. This would suggest an optional allocation of financial resources by the societies. However, most commercial bank loans go to the tertiary sector, whereas the societies lend to productive sectors.

Production loans for the informal sector

It turns out that most loans go to the productive sectors or to acquire productive inputs: agriculture, livestock, investment in human capital (medical and education), home building and improvement and the purchase of land. Of the 26 societies surveyed, 19 allocated more than 50 per cent of their loans to productive activities. Less than 50 per cent of loans were for trading, personal and other purposes. Six societies did not trade at all. The credit allocation is the exact opposite of that in Table 6.2, where over 60 per cent of the loans go to the tertiary sectors.

Out of the loans given by the Savings and Credit Union, 60 per cent are put into agriculture, 29 per cent into trade, 15 per cent into education and 5 per cent into housing. The allocation pattern of the 5 per cent sample of the societies surveyed, therefore, is consistent with that of the Union as a whole. Given that agriculture and the informal sector produce the bulk of GDP, government has to lower the rate of inflation, rather than raise interest rates, to enable these sectors to borrow for production instead of trading.

5. Conclusion and Policy Recommendations

The Uganda economy is facing a serious liquidity shortage to finance production. The economy is under-banked, with a large non-monetary sector and half of the money supply held as cash in the hands of the public.

The commercial banks pay too low an interest rate on deposits relative to the rate of inflation. The instruments of saving are also too few and inadequately publicized. Competition is limited and relatively little effort is made to look for customers. The single government incentive, to make commercial banks open more branches, is increasing UCB's monopoly position. Other conveniences to customers like hours of business or control of frauds and forgeries are limited. This chapter suggests that government should devise policies to encourage competition within commercial banking, both local and foreign-owned, especially competition that would increase savings needed to finance production.

The Ugandan economy is segmented. However competitive commercial banks become, they are less suited to serve the informal sector, where the Cooperative Savings and Credit Union is better suited to mobilize savings. Its deposit instruments are suited to the lower-income target savers. The possibility of loans in kind, without collateral, the convenience of service, with branches in the rural areas, the lower interest rate on loans, all attract savers who intend to borrow for productive investment. Extension service through the Cooperative Movement educates the savers and builds up trust.

However, the Cooperative Savings and Credit Union has some serious problems which need to be addressed by policy. Its Central Fund, education facilities and risk management programme are all meagre and need capitalization. To achieve this, two sources of member funds need immediate government action: deductions by employers should be remitted immediately; and producer prices paid for crops need to cover the cost of production plus a reasonable profit margin to permit savings. Finally, excessive control as embodied in the Cooperative Societies Act, needs to be relaxed to allow cooperatives to function as business enterprises.

Notes

1. IBRD (1985).
2. Estimates of the required financing for Africa's recovery for the period 1986–90 are given by the United Nations (1986). See also, in this volume, Frimpong-Ansah, Chapter 1.
3. See Table 6.1 below
4. Republic of Uganda, Rehabilitation and Development Plan, March 1987.
5. IBRD (September 1986).
6. IBRD (June 1985).
7   The Chartered Institute of Bankers (August 1987). See also note 4, Table 6.6 below.
8. S. Ghatak (1981). Reviews of this literature are also given by Frimpong-Ansah (1987) and USAID/AFR/DP (1987).
9. The *Statistical Abstract* (which used to be an annual publication of official statistics) was last put out in 1972. Data on disposable income, gross national savings and gross investment are unavailable on a continuous basis after 1983. Many data compiled by departments of the same government ministry are often inconsistent. For example, figures from the Coffee Marketing Board (a parastatal) on the production of coffee, Uganda's major export which contributes over 90 per cent of exports earnings, differ markedly from production figures in the Ministry of Cooperatives and Marketing, the parent ministry of the Board. In fact, only the data on marketed output of coffee, not production, are available, because the last agricultural census to provide figures on production was carried out in 1963/5 and the next one is not planned until 1990. An extended discussion of Uganda's statistics is given by B. Kiregyer, 'Data inadequacy in the Ugandan economy', in G. Ssemogerere (ed.) (1987).
10. This approach is described by V. V. Bhatt (1986).
11. IBRD (June 1985).
12. The export sector was the first major source of national savings which formed the Stabilization Fund, from which the government financed the Uganda Development Corporation enterprises and built a wide range of infrastructural projects in the 1950s. It was also a source of household savings under Governor Sir Andrew Cohen's administration, which paid reasonable producer prices to the farmers from which they built permanent homes, established a cooperative infrastructure, and educated their children: the remnants of these activities still stand today.
13. Bhatt (1986), Ingham and Mofunanya (1988), and Bauman and Houtman (1988).
14. Bank of Uganda and the Chartered Institute of Bankers (1983 and 1985).
15. International Monetary Fund Institute (1985).
16. Bank of Uganda and the Chartered Institute of Bankers (1965).
17. Republic of Uganda (various issues).
18. Republic of Uganda, Ministry of Cooperatives and Marketing, Planning Unit (1965).
19. T. Killick (1981).
20. D. Hunt (1972).
21. Bank of Uganda (1985).
22. R.H. Green (August 1981), p. 4.
23. *Ibid.*
24. IBRD (September 1986).
25. W. G. Egadu, 'Valuation of properties after the float of the Uganda shilling: the accountant's view', and P. S. Sagala, 'Valuation of properties after the float of the Uganda shilling: the surveyor's view'. Both papers were presented in Bank of Uganda and the Chartered Institute of Bankers (July 1983).
26. Uganda National Coffee Association, (1986) and the Institute of Development Studies (1988).
27. 'Data base for Uganda's monetary statistics', in International Monetary Fund Institute (1985).
28. G. V. Ramamurthy 'Domestic resource mobilization for economic development', in Bank of Uganda and Chartered Institute of Bankers (July 1983).
29. *Ibid.*
30. *Ibid.*
31. The desirable links between commercial banks and other financial institutions were indicated in the Report

on the Proposed Agricultural Development Bank. These proposals are hitherto unpublished and not implemented. See Bank of Uganda and the Chartered Institute of Bankers (1985).

32. G. V. Ramamurthy 'Deposit mobilization for economic development', in Bank of Uganda and the Chartered Institute of Bankers (July 1983).

33. The Governor of the Bank of Uganda put total commercial bank deposits as 43 per cent of the money supply in November 1988, *New Vision*, Vol.4 , No. 28, 9 February 1988. This means that 57 per cent of the money supply was held as cash in the hands of the public. In February 1989 the figure is said to be falling to 45 per cent.

34. J. B. Byamugisha, 'Frauds and forgeries in banking: the lawyer's view', in Bank of Uganda and the Chartered Institute of Bankers (July 1983). Mr. Byamugisha is a former Chairman of the Uganda Law Society and at the time he was Chairman of the Disciplinary Committee.

35. Gershenberg (April 1972).

36. The rejection of sophisticated impersonal practices, like punch-in cash points in developed countries, is well taken: but this does not constitute an excuse for delayed adaptation of simplified computerization to speed up and extend services to customers. R. H. Kaijuka, 'The suitability or otherwise of transplanting sophisticated European banking systems on to the developing economies', in Bank of Uganda and Chartered Institute of Bankers (July 1983).

37. Warton Econometrics (July 1987) and Frimpong-Ansah (January 1987).

38. These suggestions were made in 1983 by the then Director of Development Finance, Bank of Uganda, G. V. Ramamurthy. Bank of Uganda and the Chartered Institute of Bankers (July 1983).

39. Republic of Uganda, Ministry of Cooperatives and Marketing, Planning Unit, National Cooperative Survey Project (August 1985).

40. This legislation was part of a series of measures under Obote's Move to the Left, 1969, which tightened government control over the economy using the argument of enhancing 'the common man's ownership and control of the means of production'. G. Ssemogerere, 'Uganda's economic policy: basic considerations and options', in G. Ssemogerere (ed.) (1987).

41. There are some Savings and Credit Cooperative Societies which were registered under the 1946 Ordinance, e.g., Tekubanyoni in Masaka District; but at that time they were called Thrift Societies.

42. *We Speak of Cooperation,* 63rd International Cooperative Day (6 July 1985) publication (Uganda Cooperative Alliance, Kampala, 1985), p. 17.

43. Bank of Uganda, *Credit Guarantee Scheme* (1984).

44. The Governor of the Bank of Uganda has also suggested to the banks in the formal sector that they link credit facilities to the deposit record of each customer. *New Vision,* Vol. 4, No. 28, February 1989.

45. *Bye-laws of the Cooperative Savings and Credit Society Ltd.,* p.8

46. Uganda Cooperative Savings and Credit Union, Reg. No. 2725 (Kampala, June 1988), p.7.

47   *Ibid.,* p. 2.

48. *Ibid.,* pp. 1–2.

49. Bauman and Houghtman (October 1988).

References

Bank of Uganda and the Chartered Institute of Bankers (July 1983). *Banking in Third World Countries.* Proceedings of a seminar.

Bank of Uganda and the Chartered Institute of Bankers (1985).Report of the Real Sector Committee.

Bank of Uganda and the Chartered Institute of Bankers (1985). Report on the Proposed Agricultural Development Bank.

Bauman, F. J. A. and Houtman, R.(October 1988).'Pawnbroking as an instrument of rural banking in the Third World', *Economic Development and Cultural Change,* Vol. 27, No. 1.

Bhatt, V. V. (June 1986). 'Improving the financial structure in developing countries', *Finance and Development,* Vol. 23, No. 2.

Bosa, R.. G. (1969). 'The financing of small-scale enterprises in Uganda', Makerere Institute of Social Research, Occasional Paper No. 3, Oxford University Press, Nairobi, Kenya.

Chartered Institute of Bankers (August 1987). Summary Report on Financing of the Economic Recovery Programme of Uganda.

Frimpong-Ansah, J. H. (1987). *Domestic Resource Mobilisation in Africa,* Consultant's Working File, African Development Bank, Abidjan, Côte D'Ivoire.

Gershenberg, I. (April 1972). 'Banking in Uganda since independence', *Economic Development and Cultural Change,* Vol. 20, No. 3.

Ghatak, S (1981). *Monetary Economics in Developing Countries,* Macmillan, London.

Green, R. H. (August 1981). 'Magendo in the political economy of Uganda: pathology, parallel system or dominant mode of production?', Discussion Paper 164, University of Sussex, Institute of Development Studies, Brighton.

Hunt, D. (1972). 'Agricultural cooperative credit schemes', *East African Journal of Rural Development*, Vol. 5, Nos 1 & 2.

Ingham, B. and Mofunanya, B. E. (September 1988). 'The mobilization of rural savings in West Africa', paper presented at the Third World History and Development Conference, London University, School of Oriental and African Studies, London.

IBRD (June 1985). *Uganda: Progress Towards Recovery and Prospects for Development.*

IBRD (September 1986). *Uganda: Industrial Sector Memo*, Industrial Development and Finance Division, Eastern and Southern African Project Development.

International Monetary Fund Institute (1985). *Proceedings of a Seminar on Financial Programming*, Bank of Uganda and the Chartered Institute of Bankers, Kampala.

Killick, T. (1981). *Policy Economics: A Textbook of Applied Economics on Developing Countries*, Heinemann Educational Books, London.

Kiyonga, C. W. C. B. (July 1988). *Budget Speech,* Government Printer, Entebbe.

Obote, A. M. (1984). *The National Will for Recovery and Development: Budget Speech.* Government Printer, Entebbe.

Republic of Uganda, Ministry of Cooperatives and Marketing, Planning Unit (August 1985). Report on the National Cooperative Survey Project.

Republic of Uganda (March 1987). *Rehabilitation and Development Plan 1987/88 – 1990/91*, Vol. 2, Ministry of Planning and Economic Development, Kampala.

Republic of Uganda (1986 and 1988). *Background to the Budget*, Government Printer, Entebbe.

Ssemogerere, G. (ed.) (1987). *Economic Policy and Development,* Proceedings of a Seminar Organized by the Institute of Statistics and Applied Economics, Makerere University and the Konrad Adenauer Foundation, West Germany.

Steel, D. (1976). 'The theory of the dual economy and African entrepreneurship in Kenya', *Journal of Development Studies*, Vol. 22, No. 1.

Uganda Cooperative Savings and Credit Union (June 1988). Reg. No. 2725, Kampala.

United Nations (February 1986). *Financing Africa's Recovery,* Report and Recommendations of the Advisory Group on Financial Flows for Africa.

Warton Econometrics and Louis Berger Inc. (July 1987). *The Role of the African Financial Sector in Development,* USAID/AFR/DP.

7 Interest Rates, Financial Savings & Macro-economic Adjustment in Malawi [*]

**C. Chipeta &
M. L. C. Mkandawire**

1. Introduction

The purpose of this chapter is to assess the appropriateness of Malawi's strategy for increasing domestic savings which lays emphasis on the role of positive real interest rates. Periodically since the mid-1970s, Malawi has increased significantly the level of short-term nominal rates of interest, with bank rate rising from 7 to 14 per cent between 1977 and 1987. This chapter investigates the relative significance of positive real interest rates in influencing financial savings in Malawi and, on the basis of the results of this investigation, suggests appropriate strategies for stimulating financial savings in the economy of Malawi.

The chapter is presented in five parts. The second part covers past trends in savings and investment. The third part considers how savings and investment are related to the country's macro-economic adjustment problems. The determinants of savings are investigated in the fourth part and the institutional constraints are discussed in the fifth part. Some conclusions and recommendations are then offered.

2. Trends in Savings and Investment

During the 1960s domestic savings were negligible in Malawi and virtually all capital expenditure was financed by foreign savings. Gross domestic savings were 4 per cent of GDP in 1960 (World Bank, 1985). Gross national savings were also small. Between 1967 and 1969, for example, they financed only 8 per cent of total investment. The early 1970s witnessed large increases in both central government and private sector savings and the ratio of gross domestic savings to GDP increased to 14.9 per cent in 1979 (World Bank, 1985) whilst the ratio of gross national savings to total investment increased to 50 per cent. Because recurrent expenditures of government were restrained, surpluses emerged from 1972–3 to finance part of the development programme. Stimulated by a rapid expansion in incomes, private sector savings rose to reach 90 per cent of private sector investment in 1979. As domestic savings increased, the share of foreign financing to total investment fell from 92 per cent in 1967 to 50 per cent in 1979 (Malawi Government, 1983).

[*] The authors are grateful to the International Development Research Council for providing the financial assistance to complete the background research for this chapter.

Since 1979 the upward trends in savings and investment rates have been reversed. Gross domestic savings fell from 14.9 per cent of GDP in 1979 to 11.4 per cent in 1980 and 8.4 per cent in 1986. The share of gross fixed investment declined from 30.9 per cent of GDP in 1978 to 11.6 per cent in 1987, again below the rate achieved earlier (Malawi Government, 1988). In the 1970s private corporations and statutory bodies were major investors, but since 1980 the government has been the largest investor, as the financial condition of both the parastatals and the major private corporations has deteriorated, reducing their ability to generate funds for investment. Capital formation has fallen with the completion of major infrastructure investment projects such as the new capital and airport. Transport difficulties have artificially inflated total investment levels in some years (1975, 1978, 1982 and especially 1983), leading to involuntary stock-building as the country was unable to ship out exports. Import stocks may also have been higher than under normal circumstances because of uncertainties in transport.

Data on the sectoral distribution of investment are only available up to 1979. These show a rising share of investment going to agriculture (most of this was for the expansion of tobacco hectarage and the development of one new sugar estate and factory), electricity and water, and construction. The share of manufacturing and transport and communications fell during this period, with other sectors remaining about the same. These changes in sectoral shares reflect a shift from the construction of the road network to the building of the new capital and the start of the airport at Lilongwe, and the shift from privately financed electricity and water.

Estimates of capital needs during 1987–91 have been based on a target rate of growth of GDP of 4 per cent per annum and an assumed average incremental capital-output ratio of 3.5. At current market prices, investment rises from K320.3 million in 1987 to K507.3 million in 1991, or from 14.5 per cent to 16.1 per cent of GDP. On the other hand, domestic savings are projected to increase from K276.2 million in 1987 to K367.3 million in 1991. As a percentage of GDP, the savings ratio declines from 12.9 per cent in 1987 to 12.0 per cent in 1991 which implies that a large proportion of total investment will have to be financed from external resources. The estimated amount of resources that will have to be mobilized externally to finance investment requirements over the five-year period is K422.6 million in nominal terms. At constant 1978 prices, the resource gap amounts to K129.6 million, implying that about K30 million in real terms would be needed each year to meet the country's total investment requirements (Malawi Government, 1986).

This implies that the economy will continue to rely heavily on external sources of finance. Considering the adverse repercussions of foreign commercial borrowing and likely limitations on the availability of foreign concessionary funding, there is a pressing need for measures to be taken to increase the level of domestic savings. The main weapon that has so far been used to increase savings in the economy is upward adjustment of interest rates. Whether savings have responded positively to these adjustments in interest rates has not been investigated systematically.

3. The Macro-economic Adjustment Problem

The national expenditure identity – real variables

The adverse trends in savings and investment noted above are worrying for a number of reasons. Among other things, the decline in the domestic savings rate has implied that the deficit or financing gap has increased. This gap is projected to rise further in the medium term and will necessitate higher levels of foreign borrowing. External borrowing improves capital inflows, import capacity and the level of economic activity in the short run. But, in the long run, it gives rise to interest payments and other external debt service obligations which might impose a strain on limited foreign exchange reserves.

The expenditure deficit or gap can be decomposed into its private and public sector components. By definition, the *ex post* value of the deficit in the foreign sector is equal to the combined deficits of the private sector and the public sector, and can be expressed as:

(i) $(M - X + R)$ $=$ $(Ip - Sp)$ $+$ $(Ig + G - T)$
Foreign sector   private sector   public sector
deficit/surplus   deficit/surplus   deficit/surplus

where M = imports of goods and non-factor services; X = exports of goods and non-factor services; R = net factor payments; Ip = real capital formation by the private sector; Sp = savings by households and business firms; Ig = real capital formation by the public sector; G = consumption expenditures by the public sector which are equal to total government expenditures (Eg) minus real capital formation (Ig); and T = tax and non-tax revenues.

The above equation implies that if there is excess domestic investment over savings, the financing gap leads to excess imports over exports of goods and services which are financed by net capital inflows and/or a run down of foreign reserves. The public sector deficit can, alternatively, be financed by central bank money creation. When the current account deficit is smaller compared to the previous year, the reduction in the resource inflows will have to be apportioned somehow between the private and public sectors. In this way, adjustments in the foreign sector have corresponding adjustments in the domestic sector, and vice versa. In any given year, should the current account deficit be smaller than the fiscal deficit, the balance will have to be met by a private sector surplus and/or deficit financing by the central bank (Sharpley, 1986).

Malawian data relating to the national expenditure identity are readily available, as are data on the current account deficit of the balance of payments. In contrast, there are no data on the private sector deficit/surplus. This has been derived as a residual and is shown in Table 7.1. That table indicates that the resource inflows arising from current account deficits have been split between private and government sectors in Malawi, with the exception of 1984 when the private sector had a surplus. As shown in Table 7.1, the current account deficit rose from K35.0 million in 1971 to K208.2 million in 1980. During the same period, investment also rose, both absolutely and relative to GDP. Thus, the rising resource inflows did not finance increased private and public consumption, but investment for which there was a shortage of domestic saving.

The components of the foreign sector balance for the period 1978–86 show that an increasing share of the current account deficits after 1979 has been devoted to net factor payments for foreign dividends, external debt service payments and remittances of earnings by expatriates. The burden of these payments was partially offset during 1982–4 by debt relief received from the country's principal creditors. Because of the heavy demands made by these payments on limited foreign exchange reserves, imports have had to be curtailed.

In the most recent past, the debt service ratio has increased sharply to over 40 per cent. The value of exports has also risen substantially. Nevertheless, because of higher levels of other external payments and low levels of capital inflows, the overall balance of payments has been in deficit every year since 1978 except in 1980 and 1984 when improvements in the terms of trade and export of carry-over stocks of agricultural products made a difference, and in 1987 due to buoyant tobacco export earnings and a drawdown on the World Bank structural adjustment loan late in the year. These trends underscore the need to raise national savings relative to investment in order to improve the balance of payments.[1]

Table 7.1   National expenditure identity (K m)

	Foreign sector Deficit/surplus (M– X+R)		=	Private sector Deficit/surplus (Ip– Sp)	+	Government sector Deficit/surplus (Ig + G – T)
1967	–	9.8 –		0.5		+(–) 9.3
1968	–	20.9 –		7.2		+(–) 13.7
1969	–	23.2		10.1		+(–) 13.1
1970	–	29.0 –		3.5		+(–) 25.5
1971	–	35.0		– 13.1		+(–) 21.9
1972	–	46.2		– 17.6		+(–) 28.6
1973	–	31.5 –		7.0		+(–) 24.5
1974	–	34.4 –		12.1		+(–) 22.3
1975	–	73.2 –		37.7		+(–) 35.5
1976	–	64.2 –		30.8		+(–) 33.4
1977	–	51.7		– 23.3		+(–) 28.4
1978		– 142.5 –		88.9		+(–) 53.6
1979	–	205.8 –		136.2		+(–) 69.6
1980	–	208.2 –		130.2		+(–) 78.0
1981	–	119.5 –		6.3		+(–) 113.2
1982		– 131.3 –		64.4		+(–) 66.9
1983	–	169.4 –		44.1		+(–) 125.3
1984		– 15.7		+121.5		+(–) 137.2
1985		– 182.9 –		66.5		+(–) 116.4

Source: Reserve Bank of Malawi, *Financial and Economic Review*, various issues
Note: Private sector deficit/surplus includes parastatals sector. Government refers to Central Government only.

The money supply identity: financial variables

The unsatisfactory level of national savings noted above has meant that part of the domestic financing of the budget deficit has been through monetary creation. As a source of finance, money creation by the central bank for use by the public sector has become increasingly important, especially during the period after 1979 (see Table 7.2). This has had two undesirable consequences. First, it has created excess demand pressures in the economy, some of which have spilled over into imports. Second, by creating excess demand pressures it has contributed to the high rate of inflation in the economy.

The money supply also has its foreign, private and public sector components. The three components are: the banking system's net foreign assets (NFA), domestic credit claims on the private sector (DCp) and net domestic credit claims on government and the rest of the public sector (DCg). From these, the annual change in the money supply (Ms) can be written as follows:

(ii) $dMs = dNFA + dDCp + dDCg$

where the net change in foreign assets is the outcome of the overall balance of payments and reflects both the current account $(M - X+R)$ and capital account (dK) transactions, i.e. $dNFA = (M - X+R) + dK$. The data presented in Table 7.2 illustrate these components of the money supply identity for Malawi.

The aggregate identity

The deceleration in the rate of saving and hence investment after 1979 contributed to the recession which gripped the economy between 1980 and 1982. Although the investment rate has picked up since then, the average annual rate of economic growth of 3.5. per cent

Table 7.2   Changes in broad money, net foreign assets and domestic credit * (K m)

	Changes in broad money = (dMs)	Changes in net foreign asset + (dNFA)	Changes in net Claims on public sector (dDCg)	Changes in claims on private sector– (dDCp)	Changes in other items (net) (dOI))
1966	4.3	− 4.8	+ 1.1	+ 8.3	− 0.3
1967	3.4	− 0.4	+ 2.4	+ 2.2	− 0.7
1968	2.0	+ 1.4	+ 3.5	(−) 4.0	+ 1.1
1969	4.5	0.0	+ 4.3	+ 0.1	− 0.1
1970	4.9	+ 6.4	+ 5.0	− 5.6	− 0.9
1971	5.1	+ 0.5	+ 8.7	− 2.4	− 1.7
1972	6.3	+ 4.0	0.5	+ 6.6	− 4.8
1973	17.5	+ 25.4	(−) 2.7	− 3.2	− 2.0
1974	26.9	+ 13.5	16.5	+ 4.4	− 7.5
1975	4.5	− 42.2	6.7	+ 45.1	− 5.1
1976	5.7	− 45.9	20.4	16.4	+ 3.2
1977	24.6	− 35.1	11.2	− 20.7	− 1.0
1978	10.5	− 19.8	34.5	17.7	− 21.9
1979	11.5	− 71.2	48.6	34.5	− 0.4
1980	33.2	+ 6.6	11.6	31.9	− 16.9
1981	40.5	− 34.9	9.4	78.0	− 12.0
1982	33.5	− 46.7	27.2	46.0	+ 7.0
1983	8.7	− 54.0	35.7	33.0	− 6.0
1984	90.8	+ 90.5	(−)26.4	31.4	− 4.8
1985	0.1	− 104.7	(−)15.7	91.1	+ 29.4

Source: Reserve Bank of Malawi, Financial and Economic Review, various issues

* Changes in broad money = Changes in net foreign assets + Changes in net claims on public sector + Changes in claims on private sector − Changes in other items (net)

Note: Net foreign assets are made up of net official reserves and net foreign assets of commercial banks. Other items refer to capital items, minus buildings and equipment of the banking system in the consolidated balance sheet.

is only slightly more than half the average annual rate of economic growth attained in the decade before 1980. The unsatisfactory rate of economic growth has slowed down the expansion of gainful employment and demand for goods and services, thus making it difficult to further reduce poverty and inequality in income distribution.

From the point of view of external adjustment, the unsatisfactory performance of agriculture and industry, especially in the early 1980s, led to a reduction in the rate of growth of exports and import substitutes and hence created strain in the current account of the balance of payments. From the standpoint of internal adjustment, the unsatisfactory rate of economic growth led to a reduction in the rate of growth of tax revenues. As government spending commitments rose more sharply, the overall budget deficit as a proportion of GDP rose markedly. Through measures taken to restrain the growth of expenditure and to raise additional revenues, the fiscal gap has declined in relative terms but is still set at a high level.

With a slight rearrangement of terms, the national expenditure and the money supply identities can be combined to form an aggregate identity that succinctly highlights the link between real and financial variables.

This can be expressed as:

(iii) $(Sp - Ip) + (T - G - Ig) + dK = dMs - dDCp - dDCg$

private sector savings	public sector savings	balance of payments capital	broad money	private sector credit	public sector credit

In this format, explicit mention is not made of imports, exports and net factor payments, but an analysis of the foreign sector real variables (current account deficit) is implicit in the aggregate identity (see Table 7.3). The above identity forms a powerful tool for analysing the adjustment problem and for policy formulation. In Malawi, the unsatisfactory savings performance has been attributed to public sector deficits, negative real rates of interest and the unsatisfactory rate of economic growth. The causes of government budgetary deficits have already been explained. The measures that have been adopted to reduce that deficit will be explained below. The deficits incurred by parastatal bodies were associated with weak management and unremunerative prices for their products and services. Both problems are being tackled. As a result, the financial performance of some of these organizations is improving.

Table 7.3   The aggregate identity* (K m)

	Private sector savings	Government sector savings	Balance of payments capital	Broad money supply	Private sector credit	Public sector credit	
	(Sp – Ip)	T – G – Ig	K	Ms	DCpr	DCpu	Ol
1966	5.4	(–) 11.2		28.7	11.2	5.3	0.8
1967	8.9	(–) 9.3	13.5	32.1	13.6	7.5	1.5
1968	15.1	(–) 13.7	21.0	34.1	17.1	3.5	5.0
1969	13.1	(–) 13.1	21.7	38.6	21.4	3.6	0.5
1970	31.9	(–) 25.5	36.2	43.5	26.4	(– 2.0)	1.3
1971	22.4	(–) 21.9	27.0	43.6	35.1	(– 4.4)	3.0
1972	32.5	(–) 28.6	50.1	54.9	35.6	2.2	7.8
1973	49.9	(–) 24.5	56.9	72.4	32.9	(– 1.0)	9.0
1974	35.8	(–) 22.3	49.9	99.3	49.4	3.4	17.3
1975	– 6.7	(–) 35.5	31.0	103.8	56.1	40.5	22.5
1976	– 12.5	(–) 33.4	10.3	98.1	76.5	64.9	19.2
1977	65.5	(–) 20.4	06.0	122.7	87.7	44.2	20.0
1978	33.8	(–) 53.6	122.7	133.2	122.2	61.9	41.9
1979	– 1.6	(–) 69.6	134.6	144.7	170.8	96.4	42.3
1980	84.6	(–) 78.0	214.8	177.9	102.4	128.3	59.2
1981	78.3	(–)113.2	84.6	318.4	191.8	206.3	71.2
1982	20.2	(–) 66.9	64.9	251.9	219.0	252.3	44.2
1983	71.3	(–)125.3	45.9	260.5	254.7	285.3	70.3
1984	227.7	(–)137.2	73.4	351.3	228.3	326.7	75.1
1985	11.7	(–)116.4	83.7	351.4	212.6	405.8	43.7

*Private sector savings + Government sector savings + Balance of payments capital = Broad money supply – Private sector credit – Public sector credit
Source: Reserve Bank of Malawi, Financial and Economic Review, various issues

The macro performance of the Malawi economy declined specifically in the 1980s (Table 7.4). Since savings are a positive function of income, a decline in the rate of growth of income has implied a reduction in the growth of savings as well. The immediate causes of the decline in economic growth were unsatisfactory weather, untimely delivery of inputs caused by transport bottlenecks and shortage of foreign exchange, and an escalation in input costs. But there were also long-term causes at work such as inadequate allocation of development and recurrent resources to productive sectors by the public sector, especially smallholder agriculture where expansion in output was low, weaknesses in economic planning and management, and inadequate price incentives. Most of these problems are being resolved, but rates of economic growth have remained unsatisfactory.

Table 7.4   Major macro-economic indicators

	1973–8	1979–84
GDP growth (% p.a.)	6.2	1.5
Export growth (% p.a.)	6.1[1]	0.4
Import growth (% p.a.)	3.7[1]	– 12.7
Current account of balance of payments GDP (%)	– 10.9	– 14.1
Average debt service ratio (%)	12.6	24.8
Growth in consumption per capita(% p.a.)	0.8	– 2.5
Budget deficit/GDP (%)	10.2	12.3
Gross domestic savings/GDP (%)	17.4	14.1[2]
Gross fixed capital formation/GDP (%)	23.2	18.4[3]

Source: Department of Economic Planning and Development and World Bank

1. Refer to 1970–9 which is considered more representative.
2. These figures are inflated by involuntary stock-building from transport difficulties.
3 By 1984, the ratio was down to 13.1 per cent.

To reverse weak economic performance and increasing internal and external financial imbalances, Malawi has undertaken a series of stabilization programmes since 1979 supported by IMF stand-by arrangements and an extended fund facility. These stabilization programmes have aimed at bringing the financial position of the public sector to a manageable position, while reinvigorating the private sector economy, stimulating growth and reversing the overall deficit on external account. The country has also undertaken a number of structural adjustment measures designed to make more efficient use of resources and to ensure that positive growth of per capita income could be re-established and sustained. These have been supported by four structural adjustment programmes financed by the World Bank.

An important part of the stabilization programmes has been the effort to reduce the fiscal imbalance. In this respect, a number of measures have been taken to raise additional revenue. At the same time, measures have been adopted to restrain the growth of government expenditure. These have included the establishment of a monitoring system to provide early warning of deviation from targets and so enable prompt corrective action to be taken. It had been hoped that increased availability of private sector credit resources and improvements in incentives would stimulate recovery in the growth of real GDP (IMF, 1983). Apart from the usual ceiling on domestic credit expansion, restraints on foreign borrowing and exchange rate adjustment, another important aspect of the stabilization programmes has been the effort to increase domestic savings and to promote efficient allocation of bank credit and financial intermediation. In this regard, Malawi has periodically adjusted interest rates upwards. The structural adjustment measures were broad-based and aimed at diversifying production and exports, improving the performance of productive sectors, strengthening key development institutions including statutory bodies, and improving the mobilization and allocation of resources in the public sector. Strengthening producer incentives and liberalizing primary product marketing constitute other major policies.

Through the implementation of the measures explained above, the overall budget deficit declined from 12.5 per cent of GDP in 1980/1 to 6.4 per cent in 1984/5. In 1985/6, the overall budget deficit was 6.0 per cent of GDP. It then changed slightly in 1987/8 to 6.5 per cent. In real terms, the larger part of the deficit has been financed domestically.

The rise in the investment rate has been accompanied by an increase in the domestic savings rate, as a result of the measures that have been explained above. However, both investment and savings rates remain below the high levels achieved in the earlier period. Owing to rising import costs, unfavourable export prices, high freight costs and foreign debt service payments, the balance of payments was usually in deficit from 1978; only in 1980, 1984 and 1987 were small surpluses recorded.

The succeeding phases of the adjustment programme are intended to consolidate and expand gains made under the earlier phases, address remaining structural weaknesses, and help to sustain growth of per capita income. The programme will encourage productivity, diversify the export base and promote exports, strengthen the government's capability to formulate and carry out policies, and further improve the performance of development institutions (World Bank, 1984).

4. The Volume and Determinants of Financial Savings

Aggregate savings

In the national accounts of Malawi, saving is a double residual. It is defined as the difference between gross domestic product and total consumption, which is itself the residual expenditure category. For the purpose of a sectoral analysis of savings, these residual figures are likely to be highly unsatisfactory. This is particularly true in the case of household savings which are yet again a residual, this time between domestic savings and the savings of the public sector and companies. In examining savings, the main interest is precisely in these areas where the national accounts are least satisfactory. The World Bank, therefore, attempted an alternative analysis. A partial flow-of-funds analysis was carried out, making use of readily available information on capital flows between sectors of the economy, such as the balance sheets of government, the financial institutions and the main parastatal bodies. The results, which are summarized in Table 7.5, indicate a number of important trends.

Domestic savings as a percentage of GDP peaked in the mid-1970s and then began falling. The fall in domestic savings can be related to the 1979–82 recession which depressed private incomes. The contribution of foreign savings to total savings has been increasing, exceeding domestic savings in 1979/80 and 1980/1, before falling back in the next two years.

The major source of domestic savings has been the private sector which during 1972–84 accounted for 80 per cent of the total (ADB/ECA, 1987). Private companies have consistently supplied more than half of total domestic savings. The household sector has also been a significant source of savings. In fact, it is the only sector that has shown a consistent surplus (savings greater than investment), although the share of saving coming from this sector has been quite erratic.

The ability of government to save is related to the relationship between revenue and expenditure. As a percentage of GDP, the overall budget deficit rose sharply towards the end of 1970s and has since remained high. Expenditure has risen sharply for a number of reasons, including increases in prices, themselves due to currency devaluation, increases in transport costs, deficit financing, increases in the cost of imports and the rising cost of servicing the foreign debt. Revenue has increased more slowly than expenditure. The actual income and foreign trade tax bases are rather narrow despite the high tax base elasticities (ADB/ECA, 1987). The consumption tax base is particularly narrow, the main focus being on cigarettes and liquor.

The direct contribution of the parastatal sector to domestic savings has been constrained

Table 7.5   Savings (K m)

	FY74	FY75	FY76	FY77	FY78
Government	1.7 –	1.3	3.0	2.9	13.4
Parastatals	13.9	17.6	15.7	29.5	24.4
Private companies *	31.0	57.5	59.7	54.7	72.5
Financial institutions	6.5	7.3	8.8	7.8	9.6
Households *	19.1	21.0	9.1	62.0	22.6
Total domestic	72.2	102.9	57.1	101.1	142.5
(% of GDP)	(19.8)	(22.3)	(18.3)	(16.5)	(19.6)
Foreign	21.0	27.4	65.9	44.1	33.7
(% of GDP)	(6.0)	(5.9)	(12.4)	(7.2)	(4.6)
Total savings	90.0	130.3	163.0	145.2	176.2
(% of GDP)	(25.0)	(28.2)	(30.8)	(23.7)	(24.2)

Savings	FY79	FY80	FY81	FY82	FY83
Government	10.0	24.9	15.3 –	3.7 –	10.9
Parastatals	7.2	1.7	3.5	13.7	6.4
Private companies *	68.3	51.6	81.0	09.1	121.0
Financial institutions	12.0	13.6	– 1.6	20.7	– 6.4
Household *	26.7	17.1	27.3	24.9	51.5
Total domestic	132.2	108.9	125.5	144.7	161.6
(% of GDP)	(16.5)	(13.1)	(12.4)	(12.4)	(11.8)
Foreign	109.7	167.7	151.4	97.7	75.6
(% of GDP)	(13.7)	(20.2)	(15.0)	(8.4)	(5.5)
Total savings	241.9	276.6	276.9	242.4	237.2
(% of GDP)	(30.2)	(33.2)	(27.4)	(20.8)	(27.4)

Source: World Bank
Note: Because different sources were used and some of the data remained tenuous, the figures differ from the investment figures by 5.20 per cent, so the conclusions are subject to possible data error.
* Estimated by investment plus net acquisition of financial assets

by losses incurred as a result of management inefficiency, over-extension of their activities, inappropriate pricing of their products and services, and weak financial control. Indirectly, parastatal entities have adversely affected savings to the extent that they have required government financial assistance to cover their own deficits.

In view of weaknesses in the official savings data, Harawa (1981) used savings data estimated as the difference between gross national disposable income and private consumption in his study of the savings function. Fitting a Keynesian savings function to data on current gross national disposable income, he found a positive association between savings and income.[2] In order to improve the predictive powers of his equation, Harawa took into account factors such as inflation and real interest rates as explanatory variables. For changes in prices, he used the GDP deflator, with 1980 as the base year, and for real rates of interest, the Treasury Bill rate, the commercial bank savings deposit rate and the time deposit rate, all separately. The inclusion of these variables did not improve the predictive powers of his equation as all their regression coefficients were insignificant at conventional levels of significance. Besides, they were all negative. The insignificance of the price variable was not explained in the study. The insignificance of the interest rate variables was attributed to the low level of penetration of financial intermediaries into the rural sector* and the fact that interest rates are not market determined, but controlled, and offer little incentive to save as they are negative most of the time. Net capital inflows were not included as an explanatory variable in this study.

In a more recent study of the determinants of savings by the African Development Bank and the Economic Commission for Africa, Malawi was included in the sample of 12 countries (ADB/ECA, 1987). The determinants considered were levels of income (GDP), external capital flows, the nominal rate of interest on deposits, exports and total tax revenues. Income and export levels were found to be positively associated with savings in Malawi and the results were statistically significant. Tax revenue was found to be negatively associated with savings. The result, which was statistically significant, is consistent with the finding by the World Bank of a negative correlation between tax revenue and private savings. According to the World Bank study, for each one per cent increase in tax revenue, there is a 2.8 per cent fall in private savings (World Bank, 1985).

The ADB/ECA study failed to find a significant association between savings and external capital inflows, and between savings and the nominal rate of interest. In respect of external capital inflows, the association was positive, indicating that savings and net capital inflows are complementary. In respect of the nominal rate of interest, the association was negative. The national accounting concept of savings which was used included non-financial variables that are not influenced by interest rates.

In the present study we are presenting the result of that part of our work that made use of data on real private savings (S) and real gross national disposable income (Yd).[3] Data on these two variables, as well as on real time deposit rates (R), real net capital inflows (NCI) and the GDP deflator (D) are shown in Table 7.6. Nominal values of the variables have been deflated using the GDP deflator.

Table 7.6   Real private savings (S), real gross national disposable income (Yd), real time deposit rates (R), real net capital inflows (NCI) and the GDP deflator

Year	S (Km)	Yd (Km)	R (%)	NCI (Km)	D (%)
1967	74.3	528.9	4.1	35.8 –	0.3
1968	65.6	527.7 –	0.3	53.2	4.8
1969	140.7	620.6	2.5	53.8	2.0
1970	133.1	573.0	1.8	83.6	7.4
1971	132.1	673.3 –	3.8	56.8	9.7
1972	143.1	670.5	– 1.6	79.4	7.2
1973	177.0	760.2	5.7	118.3 –	0.2
1974	198.4	802.9	– 10.5	80.0	17.9
1975	201.2	858.3	– 3.0	47.6	8.8
1976	134.4	862.2 –	1.1	25.8	8.7
1977	198.8	890.0 –	5.7		14.0
1978	266.2	983.2	5.9		1.5
1979	237.0	1072.9	4.9		3.7
1980	227.1	858.4	– 5.8	214.8	17.6
1981	219.8	835.7	– 4.8	72.7	16.3
1982	203.2	862.2	1.2	51.0	9.4
1983	202.5	894.5	1.1	32.4	11.5
1984	211.2	944.9 –	0.9	45.5	13.8
1985	219.9	1035.5	6.7	48.4	7.1

Source: Reserve Bank of Malawi and International Monetary Fund

Regressing S as the dependent variable on Yd, R, NCI, and D as the explanatory variables yielded the following equation:

(1) S = $-$ 57.06   +   0.25 Yd +   0.85R   +   0.28 NCI + 1.84 D
$\quad\quad\quad$ ($-$ 1.9)$\quad\quad$ (4.5)$\quad\quad\quad$ (0.27)$\quad\quad$ (2.4)$\quad\quad\quad$ (0.69)

$\quad\quad$ $R^2 = 0.82$ F = 21.53   DW = 1.93

where R^2 is the coefficient of determination adjusted for degress of freedom, F is the F ratio and DW is the Durbin–Watson statistic. The figures in brackets below regression coefficients are t ratios.

On the basis of the F test, the regression as a whole is significant at both the 5 per cent and 1 per cent levels of significance. The constant has the expected negative sign and is significant at the 5 per cent level. The Yd regression coefficient is positive and significant at both 5 per cent and 1 per cent levels of significance. This coefficient is the marginal propensity to save and is consistent with the finding of the Harawa study referred to above. The interest rate coefficent is positive but not significant at conventional levels. Real time deposit rates were included in the study because most of the financial savings are in deposits. The net capital inflows coefficient is positive, implying that these inflows complement private sector savings. The coefficient itself is significant at the 5 per cent level. The regression coefficient for the GDP deflator is positive but insignificant. The Durbin-Watson test for auto-correlation failed to yield evidence of positive or negative first order auto-correlation.

From the above, we conclude that real private savings in Malawi are positively and significantly influenced by the level of real current income and real net capital inflows. They are also positively influenced by real interest rates.[4]

Business savings

Time series data on financial savings have been grouped into business savings and household savings according to criteria put forward by the Reserve Bank (Reserve Bank, 1985). Of the household savings, it is believed that savings deposits at commercial banks are accounted for mainly by higher income urban households, and that savings deposits at the Post Office Savings Bank are mainly attributable to low income urban and rural households.

Table 7.7   Real change in time deposits (STD), real gross business profits (P), real time deposit rates (R) and change in the number of commercial bank branches (B)

	STD (K'000)	P (K'000)	R (%)	B
1973	4,094	130,905	5.7	1
1974	7,128	162,771	$-$ 10.5	1
1975	6,912	155,214	$-$ 3.0	1
1976	4,002	167,983	$-$ 1.1	$-$ 1
1977	15,623	181,930	$-$ 5.7	0
1978	33,978	148,048	5.9	1
1979	6,065	137,764	4.9	0
1980	18,009	150,000	$-$ 5.8	0
1981	735	71,883	$-$ 4.8	0
1982	12,655	121,069	1.2	11
1983	12,375	68,335	1.1	$-$ 1

Sources: Reserve Bank of Malawi, International Monetary Fund and National Statistical Office

In order to determine the factors that influence the level of business savings in Malawi, the change in real time deposits shown in Table 7.7 was regressed on real gross business profits, real time deposit rates and change in the number of branches of commercial banks. The estimated equation is:

$$(2) \quad S_{TB} = 1345.9 + 0.07P + 503.6R + 213.15B$$
$$\phantom{(2) \quad S_{TB} = } (0.11) \quad (0.81) \quad (0.81) \quad (0.22)$$

$$R^2 = 0.23; \quad F = 0.38$$

On the basis of the F test, the regression equation as a whole is not significant at either the 5 per cent or 1 per cent levels. On the basis of the t test, the constant and the regression coefficients are not significant at similar levels. However, all the regression coefficients are positive.

Household savings

Data on the real financial savings of high-income urban households and low-income urban and rural households are shown below in Tables 7.8 and 7.9 respectively. Data in Table 7.8 were deflated with the high-income retail price index for Blantyre, while those in Table 7.9 were deflated with the low-income retail price index for Blantyre. Both indices have a longer history than the composite retail price index. The financial savings function for the high-income household was estimated as:

$$(3) \quad S_{SB} = 110.17 + 0.04 \quad Yh + 57.77 \ R - 6.43B$$
$$\phantom{(3) \quad S_{SB} = } (0.06) \quad (0.63) \quad (0.64) \quad (0.06)$$

$$R^2 = 0.16; \quad F = 0.29$$

On the basis of the F test, the regression equation as a whole is not significant at acceptable levels. The regression coefficients for real urban wage income and the real savings deposit rate are positive but they are not significant. The savings rate implied by the Yh coefficient is consistent with the World Bank finding (World Bank, 1985). The regression coefficient for the change in the number of bank branches is negative and insignificant.

For low-income urban and rural households, the financial savings function was estimated as:

$$(4) \quad S_{P0} = -22.27 + 0.037Y1 - 57.51R - 10.56B$$
$$\phantom{(4) \quad S_{P0} = } (-0.02) \quad (1.55) \quad (-0.91) \quad (-0.26)$$

$$R^2 = 0.09; \quad F = 1.46 ; \quad DW = 1.47$$

On the basis of the F test, the regression equation as a whole is not significant at the 5 per cent or 1 per cent level. None of the regression coefficients is significant at the same levels of significance.

5. Institutional Constraints

At the top of the country's financial system is the central bank, the *Reserve Bank of Malawi*. This bank took over Malawi's share of the assets and liabilities of the Bank of Rhodesia and Nyasaland. It began operating in June 1965 and is wholly owned by the Malawi government. It performs the normal functions of a central bank, including direct lending to the government, statutory bodies and commercial banks, but not to the non-bank private sector.

Table 7.8   Changes in real commercial bank savings deposits (SCB), changes in real high urban wage income(Yh), real savings deposit rates (R_D) and changes in the number of commercial bank branches (B)

Year	S_{CB} K'000	Yh* (K'000)	R_D (%)	B
1970	742.0	10,948.0	– 4.9	2
1971	924.3	11,643.6	– 4.0	– 10
1972	1973.3	34,186.7	0.1	2
1973	5815.0	36,999.2	1.6	1
1974	– 1385.0	34,234.3	– 11.6	1
1975	2102.1	26,414.3	– 13.0	1
1976	– 870.5	28,935.5	– 5.9	0
1977	354.7	24,430.2	– 6.6	0
1978	600.9	31,853.8	– 7.1	1
1979	2007.9	30,993.9	– 7.7	0
1980	464.5	31,141.4	– 14.1	0
1981	393.7	29,699.2	– 1.5	0
1982	1060.1	28,880.0	– 0.7	14
1983	294.2	29,993.6	0.2	– 1
1984	243.5	31,908.7	3.4	0
1985	659.8	30,658.8	– 6.3	0

Sources: Reserve Bank of Malawi and Department of Economic Planning and Development
* Includes income earned in all sectors except manufacturing, construction, agriculture and mining.

Table 7.9   Changes in real post office savings bank deposits (SPO), changes in real low urban and rural wage income (Y1), real savings deposit rates (R) and changes in the number of post office branches (B)

Year	S (K'000)	Y1* (K'000)	R %	B
1970	771.0	15,219.0	– 4.9	5
1971	1094.1	16,731.9	– 3.9	7
1972	688.7	32,344.3	0.4	16
1973	1871.0	38,661.3	– 1.2	5
1974	2629.1	44,614.4	– 9.99	20
1975	605.1	42,171.3	10.0	0
1976	429.8	25,532.4	1.1	11
1977	341.5	27,836.6	1.2	8
1978	2195.5	41,394.2	– 2.9	4
1979	573.0	38,805.9	– 3.8	2
1980	1443.6	44,290.3	8.7	11
1981	1390.3	41,691.6	– 0.8	5
1982	2001.0	48,399.6	– 0.8	2
1983	3298.3	40,058.3	– 4.6	2
1984	2549.2	33,159.3	– 7.7	0

Source: Reserve Bank of Malawi and the Post Office
* Includes income earned in manufacturing, construction, agriculture and mining, and migrants' remittances.

Acting on behalf of the Ministry of Finance, the Reserve Bank of Malawi prescribes minimum deposit rates. Until 22 July 1987, the Reserve Bank also prescribed prime lending rates.[5] An important consideration in determining interest rates is the interest cost of the domestic public debt which is relatively large. As at 31 December 1986, central government domestic debt stood at K651 million, comprising resident holdings of local registered stocks and treasury bills as well as Reserve Bank loans and advances. In essence, this means that not all interest rates are freely market-determined. Under financial repression, these deposit interest rates do not reflect the opportunity cost of money; nor do lending rates, which are based on controlled deposit rates, perform their allocative function efficiently.

In nominal terms, savings deposit rates stood at 10.7 per cent at all financial institutions except credit unions, where they were 5 per cent per annum until 22 July 1987. In real terms, these rates were negative in 1985. Short-term rates were at 11.5 per cent while investment deposit rates were 12.7 per cent per year. Both these were negative in 1985 as inflation, measured by the retail price index rate, reached 15.1 per cent. Even fixed-time deposit rates, ranging from 12.7 per cent to 15.7 per cent, were negative in real terms. Prime lending rates ranged from 13.5 per cent to 16 per cent per annum. Both deposit and lending rates had been negative on several occasions in the past.

Beyond setting interest rates, the Reserve Bank of Malawi has no direct role in promoting savings. It does not determine the savings deposit instruments used by commercial banks and other financial institutions. Nor does it directly promote the establishment and development of other financial institutions. It only regulates their operations. By taking a more active role in institutional development in the financial sector, the Reserve Bank of Malawi might assist in increasing savings mobilization (Bhatt, 1986).

There are two commercial banks in the country, the *Commercial Bank of Malawi* and the *National Bank of Malawi*, which is the larger of the two. Both provide the normal commercial banking services. The two commercial banks account for most of the financialized savings in the country. At the end of 1983, for example, they held a total of K165 million in the form of time and savings deposits of the private sector and statutory bodies. The Post Office Savings Bank held K41.4 million in savings deposits at the end of the same year, while the New Building Society had K15.5 million in fixed investment and savings deposits (Reserve Bank, 1985). Savings and credit cooperatives barely had K1 million in share deposits at about the same time (USAID, 1983).

The dominance of the commercial banks is due to the provision of a larger range of deposit instruments: savings, short-term (7 days and 30 days), and time deposits (from 3 months to 12 months), and a wider network of savings infrastructure which, in 1985, stood at 26 branches, 209 static agencies and 106 mobile agencies. These facilities have grown steadily in number since 1967 when there were 10 branches, 29 static agencies and 54 mobile agencies, respectively. In 1970, the comparative numbers were 17, 32 and 124 respectively. Mobile and static agencies provide both deposit and deposit withdrawal facilities. Branches provide, in addition, lending and other financial services. But despite these and other advantages like security, safety, provision of accident insurance cover and a sound image, commercial banks are not keen to extend their mobile agency network to mobilise savings.

Until 22 July 1987, when the interest rate allowed on fixed deposits of more than three years' maturity was 15.7 per cent per year and the minimum overdraft rate was 16 per cent per year, giving a minimum spread of only 0.25 per cent, commercial banks considered that deposits were too costly. Therefore, they discouraged customers from depositing their money for a fixed period of more than one year at 13.25 per cent. As at 31 March 1987, the Commercial Bank of Malawi, for example, had a total of K103,238,514.90 customers' deposits. Some 27 per cent was held in current accounts, 23 per cent in short-term deposits,

13 per cent in savings accounts, 29 per cent in time deposits maturing in up to 12 months, and only 7 per cent was held in time deposits maturing over periods longer than 13 months.

From 23 July 1987, the interest rate on fixed deposits held for over three years was raised to 17.75 per cent, while commercial banks fixed the prime overdraft rate at 20 per cent, giving a minimum spread of 2.25 per cent. After deregulation, commercial banks considered that money was still costly to them. As a result, they were not keen to encourage customers to deposit their money for a fixed period of more than 6 months at 15.75 per cent. At this rate of interest, the minimum spread increased to 4.25 per cent assuming a lending rate of 20 per cent.

The commercial banks were encouraged to follow the above course of action by the willingness of the central bank to lend them money at a relatively low bank rate. In practice, commercial bank borrowing from the central bank is negligible. This rate was 11 per cent before the July 1987 increase in interest rates. From July 1987 to April 1988 it was 14 per cent. Both rates were lower than the fixed deposit rates (three years and over) of 15.75 per cent and 17.75 per cent, respectively, before and after the interest rate increases. The problem partly had to do with the sectoral distribution of loans and advances and the rates at which those loans and advances were lent out. Until 1975, the commercial banks lent most of their resources on short term to the distribution sector for the purpose of financing trade. The mid-1970s witnessed rapid expansion of estate tobacco production for which commercial banks were requested to provide seasonal as well as long-term finance. By 1983, 52.5 per cent of all bank portfolios were held in the agricultural sector. Starting from March 1980, loans to estate maize and tobacco growers were granted at concessional rates of interest whose maximum, until 22 July 1987, was 15 per cent, or one percentage point below the prime overdraft rate of 16 per cent per annum. From July 1987 to April 1988, the applicable rate of interest was 18 per cent. It was then changed back to 16 per cent.

To the extent that the estate maize and tobacco lending rate was below the over three years deposit rate while most of the portfolio was held in these crops, commercial banks' average interest margins continued to be squeezed. That is why they were not willing to accept deposits at higher rates of interest. The amount of savings that commercial banks mobilize, plus borrowing from the central bank, though this is negligible, may be enough to meet the credit needs of large-scale business enterprises. But if, in addition, they had to lend to small-scale and medium-scale business enterprises, they would not be adequate. At present the two commercial banks do not lend much money to small- and medium-scale business entities because (1) they find it costly to deal with a large number of customers who each borrow small sums of money; (2) they consider small- and medium-scale business entities to be risky, especially as they may have no track record; (3) they do not lend start-up capital; and (4) for historical reasons, small and medium-scale business entities are outside their target group.

From 11 April 1988, deposit and lending interest rates were reduced by about 3 per cent. The preferential agricultural lending rate was reduced from 18 per cent to 16 per cent, thus reducing the gap between this rate and the prime overdraft rate from 2 to 1 per cent. What precipitated this adjustment was the large build-up of deposits at commercial banks in 1987, mainly following buoyant farm incomes from tobacco.

The commercial banks complained that the cost of funds at the high rates of interest was unbearable and that high lending rates were discouraging borrowing. The Reserve Bank, with which a lot of surplus funds had been placed by the commercial banks, found the interest cost that it had to pay on these funds unbearable and decided not to pay interest on most of them. Upon hearing this news, the commercial banks decided not to accept new fixed and short-term deposits from any source or savings deposits from companies, thus creating the possibility of a parallel money market developing in the economy. To avert a possible financial crisis, interest rates were adjusted downwards as stated above.

The present *Post Office Savings Bank* began operating as a government-owned institution in January 1964 when it succeeded a similar institution which had operated before independence. The savings deposits it collects through its hundreds of offices spread all over the country are wholly invested in government obligations.

The Post Office Savings Bank has a larger network of branches and agencies, numbering 257 in 1983; it is open more hours and days per week and interest income on its deposits is exempt from taxation. It enjoys security and safety. It has a lower minimum deposit balance requirement and withdrawal is allowed at any Post Office. However, withdrawals are limited to K20 within three days, larger withdrawals require one or more months' notice. Besides, customers must furnish proof of identity. Since its clientele consists of small savers, it does not have as much money in deposits as each of the commercial banks. Lastly, the fact that it does not lend money to the general public also acts as a disincentive to banking with it.

The Investment and Development Bank (Indebank) provides equity finance as well as medium- and long-term loans for new and existing industries and agricultural ventures. Its resources are share capital and loans; it does not accept deposits. Established on 30 December 1972, its shareholders include four foreign organizations, namely, the Netherlands Development Finance Company, the Commonwealth Development Corporation of the United Kingdom, the German Finance Company for Investments in Developing Countries and the International Finance Corporation (IFC), an affiliate of the World Bank. Through these foreign shareholders, Indebank has considerable access to foreign finance.

The *New Building Society* provides mortgage finance to businesses and individuals. It started operating in March 1964 as a successor and merger of three separate building societies. Its shareholders are the Malawi government, Protea Assurance Company Limited and Lonrho (Malawi) Limited. The New Building Society is open about the same length of time per week as the Post Office Savings Bank, has a low minimum deposit balance requirement and offers several deposit instruments of varying maturities up to 24 months. However, it places restriction on the amount of each savings withdrawal and has a more limited range of branches serving only five urban centres.

Savings and Credit Societies are fairly new, relatively few in number (58), small in size and do not cover the entire country. Moreover, they are considered unsafe (a reaction to the failure of the cooperative movement in the country), are unpopular because many people believe that the Catholic Church, which set some of them up, is trying to convert them, and lack the sound image which would induce the confidence of savers. The low dividends rate of 5 per cent allowed on shares compares most unfavourably with interest rates paid on fixed, investment, short-term and savings deposits. In addition, they do not offer alternative savings deposit instruments.

There are eight *insurance/assurance companies* and four insurance brokers in the country. Life insurance and pension funds provide long-term loans for industrial and commercial buildings. Mercantile Credit Limited finances hire purchase transactions as well as capital leasing activities and block-discounts commercial trade debts.

Finance Corporation of Malawi (FINCOM) provides import confirming and export debt factoring services; it also acts as a foreign buying agent. The *Leasing and Finance Company of Malawi Ltd* (LFC) provides leasing finance for the acquisition of capital equipment of various kinds for agricultural, industrial and commercial enterprises. It also intends to offer hire purchase finance in the near future. LFC is accepting fixed deposits of varying maturities at high rates of interest but is not intending to accept savings deposits.

There are a few organizations which concentrate on providing finance and advice to small-scale businesses owned by Malawians. These do not mobilize domestic savings. One is the *Investment and Development Fund* (Indefund) which was formed in 1981 as an offshoot of Indebank. The other is the *Small Enterprise Development Organization of Malawi* (SEDOM) which started operating in January 1983 with financial assistance from the EEC. A third one, the *Development of Malawian Traders Trust* (DEMATT), does not provide finance but assists Malawian small-scale businesses in acquiring finance and gives them technical and managerial advice. It began operating in December 1979 with financial assistance from USAID.

There is no written information on unorganized financial markets in Malawi. From our personal observations, we do know that households keep savings in the form of currency at home; sometimes the money is given to relatives or neighbours for safekeeping in homes. In either case, the risk of loss through theft or damage is high. Besides, interest income is foregone. Some of the savings of traders and small-scale businesses are also held at home.

Informal savings and credit societies (*chilimba* or *chiperegani*) are also active. Most of these societies are two-person clubs formed between friends who trust each other. They are common among urban proletarians who find them a means of augmenting their low incomes. Often such societies are short-lived. They get wound up if unexpected demands on the incomes of the members make it difficult for them to honour obligations to their partners.

Despite legal constraints, money-lenders *(katapila)* are also active in the economy as evidenced by the large number of letters carried by mass media dealing with the relative merits of lending money at high rates of interest (ranging from 25 to 100 per cent). Lenders do not mobilize savings; they lend out of their own limited resources. No attempt has been made to integrate the activities of organized and unorganized financial markets to ease the financial constraint faced by the latter or as a means of strengthening central bank control over the money supply.

The organizations described above make up the financial market in Malawi. We should note that there is no stock exchange in Malawi. However, certain Malawi securities are quoted outside the country based on special external registers authorized by the Reserve Bank of Malawi in its role as exchange control authority. At present the local securities market consists solely of Malawi government local registered stocks which are traded through the Reserve Bank, which also quote the prices.

6. Conclusions and Recommendations

Financial savings have not been influenced significantly by real rates of interest in Malawi. In practice, because interest rates are controlled, adjusted infrequently and negative in real terms most of the time, interest rate policy has not been of much assistance in attaining the policy objective. This implies that sole reliance should not be placed on real rates of interest as a means of encouraging savings. Besides, interest rate policy is not relevant with regard to mobilization of non-financial savings.

The emphasis on real, rather than nominal, rates of interest is also appropriate. Our study has shown that real interest rates are positively associated with financial savings while the ADB has shown that nominal interest rates are negatively related to savings. But the question is whether real rates of interest can be brought about by upward adjustment of nominal interest rates only. The option of achieving real rates of interest by controlling inflation is one that has not been actively pursued in Malawi. There was, in fact, no active anti-inflation policy until 1987. In the early 1980s, much of the pressure on prices came from switching from short, cheaper transport routes to longer, more expensive ones. Transport routing has now stabilized and, therefore, most of the impulse is coming from increases in transport costs unrelated to switching routes, currency devaluation, price decontrol, periodic upward adjustment in producer prices of smallholder crops, increases in indirect tax rates, and government budget deficit financing by credit from the central bank. To the extent that currency devaluation is necessitated by changes in the exchange rate which are inconsistent with the country's economic position, there is need to review the desirability of the present currency peg or to avoid currency appreciation. But there is also need to review the effectiveness of devaluation as a tool for promoting exports and restraining imports, and to consider non-inflationary incentives for expanding exports and discouraging imports.

With most of the prices which were formerly subject to official control now decontrolled, several firms are freer to make upward adjustments in those prices. Some of the upward adjustments are justified on grounds of cost increases. Others reflect the market power of the firms concerned. In these cases, where there is no market competition, some form of price control should be reintroduced to protect the consumer. When producer prices of smallholder crops are adjusted upwards or indirect tax rates are raised, the impact on consumer prices needs to be considered, together with alternative ways of raising smallholder agricultural production and additional tax revenue.

In the context of Malawi, achieving real deposit rates of interest by whatever means is not enough in itself, unless financial intermediaries are willing to pay those rates on customers' deposit balances. To instil that willingness requires abolishing or reducing interest rate subsidies on credit to estate maize and tobacco growers, where bank lending is concentrated, establishing a more realistic spread between deposit and lending rates, raising the cost of central bank funds to commercial banks, and developing new lending business. Upward adjustments in interest rates must take into account the consequential increase in the cost of funds to financial intermediaries and borrowers and hence their profitability. They must also take into account the implications of high rates of interest for the burden of the public internal debt.

The results of our study and the others reviewed here indicate that aggregate income influences financial savings positively and significantly. Sectoral income also influences sectoral savings positively. These results do suggest that the strategy for increasing savings in Malawi must pay more attention to income variables and ways of increasing incomes. Raising aggregate income requires resolving the foreign exchange constraint and the transport problem, and an improvement in the net barter terms of trade. Raising export income similarly requires resolving the foreign exchange and transport problems, and diversification into non-traditional exports and manufactures.

Our analysis and the analysis of the ADB have shown that net capital inflows complement rather than compete with domestic savings in Malawi. More net capital inflows can thus be expected to encourage rather than discourage domestic savings. But whether increased net capital inflows to the individual sectors would encourage sectoral savings has not been determined by these studies.

Our analysis has also shown that generally there is a negative association between changes in the number of branches of banks and non-banks and real changes in the amount of financial savings, although the association is not significant statistically. Thus, there would appear to be little scope for raising savings by increasing the number of branches and agencies, or by increasing the number of banks and non-banks for that matter.

With respect to the effect of inflation as measured by the GDP deflator, inflation hedges do not seem to discourage financial savings, as shown by the positive association between financial savings and the GDP deflator.

One of the major macro-economic problems facing Malawi today is the large overall balance of payments deficit. The challenge before policy-makers is how to reduce (and, if possible, eliminate) this deficit. The analysis of the macro-economic adjustment problem has shown that cutting the domestic private and public sector deficits would assist in improving the external account. That, in turn, requires that the rate of domestic savings must be raised. If the rate of domestic savings were raised, investment would expand and the rate of economic growth would increase. To the extent that taxable capacity would rise as a result, tax revenue would increase and assist in reducing the public sector deficit.

Financial intermediaries can play an important role in macro-economic adjustment if both the mobilization of savings and the allocation of credit are optimal. In Malawi, because of the factors noted above, mobilization of savings is not optimal. Thus, the country is unable to generate the financial surplus which is a necessary condition for attaining a surplus on the current account of the balance of payments. The low domestic savings mobilization effort, in turn, implies that the country's reliance on foreign capital inflows will increase rather than diminish in the medium term. These inflows may help to improve the balance of payments now, but subsequent repayments of principal and interest will strain the future performance of the external account.

Notes

1. In recent tests of causality between savings, investment and the current account deficit of seven non-African countries, it was found that savings and investment were generally the cause rather than the effect of current account changes (Zaidi, 1985). A positive correlation between improvements in the current account and the fiscal deficit was also found, but the causal results were mixed. Similarly, empirical tests of the direct relationship between the size of the government deficit and the size of the current account deficit in developing countries proved inconclusive (Tahari, 1978).
2. The regression coefficient, which indicated a marginal propensity to save of 0.25, was significant at the 5 per cent level of significance. With a high coefficient of determination of 0.95, the regression equation as a whole was similarly significant. The estimated Durbin–Watson statistic showed that there was no serial correlation in the formulation, implying efficiency in the estimators.
3. The results of our analysis, which used official or World Bank data on real domestic or national savings and on real gross domestic or national product to assess the influence of income on savings, gave negative or insignificant marginal propensities to save.
4. In the non-monetary sector, savings necessarily equal investment because the acts of saving and investment are the same. The factors that influence this type of savings have been noted as being (1) the longevity of physical assets which determines the replacement rate; (2) the types of physical assets that a particular community has need for; (3) local enthusiasm for self-help development projects; (4) the availability of complementary resources in cash or in kind; and (5) the ability of government to finance operating expenses once self-help projects have been completed.
5. From 23 July 1987, commercial banks have been free to set prime lending rates.

References

African Development Bank/Economic Commission for Africa ADB/ECA (1987). *Economic Report on Africa.*
Bhatt, V. V. (1986). 'Improving the financial structure in developing countries', *Finance and Development*, Vol. 23, No. 2, June.
Chipeta, C. (1971). 'Semi-subsistence saving and investment', unpublished paper.
Harawa, R. D. (1981). 'Savings function: review of hypotheses', unpublished B. Soc. Sc. (Hons) dissertation submitted to the Department of Economics, Chancellor College, University of Malawi.
IMF (1983). *IMF Survey*, 10 October.
Malawi Government (1983). *International Conference of Partners in Economic Development: Past Performance and Prospects for 1983–1987.*
Malawi Government (1986). *Economic Report.*
Malawi Government (1987). *Economic Report.*
Malawi Government (1988). *Economic Report.*

Reserve Bank of Malawi (1985). *Financial and Economic Review,* Vol. 17, No. 2.

Sharpley, J. (1986).'Financial instruments and macro management', paper prepared for IDRC Conference, Nairobi, 18–20 March.

Tahari, A. (1978). 'Budget deficits, credit creation and the balance of payments: empirical evidence for Brazil, Philippines, Sri Lanka, Thailand and Venezuela', unpublished paper, October.

USAID (1983). *The Private Sector and the Economic Development of Malawi,* Washington, DC.

World Bank (1984). *Malawi: One of Africa's Success Stories,* Washington, DC.

World Bank (1985). *Malawi Economic Recovery: Resources and Policy Needs – an Economic Memorandum,* Washington, DC.

Zaidi, I. M.(1985). 'Saving, investment, fiscal deficits and the external indebtedness of developing countries', *World Development,* Vol. 13, No.5, May.

8 Trends of Savings in Financial Intermediaries in Zimbabwe

Theresa Moyo

1. The Institutional Background

The history of Zimbabwe's banking and financial system dates back to the 1890s when the country was colonized. Standard Bank was the first financial institution to be established in the country in 1892. It became locally incorporated in 1983. In 1895, Barclays Bank was established, followed by Grindlays in 1953. The Netherlands Bank of South Africa became Rhobank after local incorporation in 1972 and changed its name to the Zimbabwe Banking Corporation (Zimbank). Over the years the banks have developed their own subsidiaries and affiliates in specialized and related fields and established a network of branches and sub-branches to offer integrated financial services to their clients. The other commercial bank, Bank of Credit and Commerce Zimbabwe Ltd (BCCZ) was established in 1981 as a subsidiary to BCC International. The Stock Exchange started in 1896 and the first merchant bank was set up in 1956. Bard Discount House was incorporated in 1959. This was followed by the establishment of the Discount Company of Zimbabwe Ltd., in 1959. The three building societies were established in 1951 and 1954.

Thus, at present, Zimbabwe has five commercial banks, four merchant banks (accepting houses), two discount houses, five registered financial institutions, three building societies, five representative international banks, an Export Credit Insurance corporation, seven major trust companies, a Stock Exchange, three development finance corporations, and an insurance industry comprising 46 direct insurers, nine professional reinsurers and ten brokers.

The five commercial banks offer a range of savings facilities which include demand, savings and time deposits. The merchant banks supply deposit facilities to corporate customers and large account holders. Short- and medium-term financing is offered through acceptance credits and the processing of commercial letters of credit and foreign bills of exchange. The finance houses are not permitted to accept deposits of less than 30 days but accept fixed deposits and negotiable certificates of deposit. Finance houses specialize in hire-purchase and lease-hire. The discount houses primarily service other financial institutions and not the general public. They accept call money from the banks and invest these funds in assets with short maturities.

Building societies offer savings facilities in the form of fixed accounts, savings accounts and building society shares. Their loans are usually granted as mortgages.

In the case of the Post Office Savings Bank (POSB), only savings and fixed deposits can be held. The bank is legally obliged to hold all its assets in the form of approved assets. Credit facilities are not, therefore, offered to clients.

The insurance companies offer the full range of commercial and personal insurance. They comprise the second largest group of financial institutions after the commercial banks. Pension funds, as their name implies, are jointly financed by employers and employees. They either operate as self-administered funds managed by the employers or are administered by insurance companies. The funds provide for the payment of a cash lump sum or a pension on the member's retirement.

Development banks do not mobilize resources directly from the public but are supported by government and international financial institutions such as the World Bank.

Finally, there is the Stock Exchange where securities issued by the government, public enterprises and private companies are quoted.

Under the Reserve Bank of Zimbabwe Act (Chapter 173) the Reserve Bank is charged with all the powers traditionally vested in central banks to control and direct official monetary policy. It directly controls the bank rate and fixes the maximum and minimum interest rates on deposits and lending respectively. In the case of rates on negotiable certificates of deposit and treasury bills, the Reserve Bank has to approach each of the appropriate financial institutions and hear how much they are prepared to offer and at what rate. The legal controls mean that the banks cannot freely choose appropriate interest rates as the market might dictate. This may explain why real interest rates have remained negative.

Insurance companies are regulated under the Insurance Act (Chapter 196). They are required to invest at least 60 per cent of their funds in prescribed government securities. The same provision applies to the Pension and Provident Funds as laid out under the Pension and Provident Funds Act, 1976. In the case of the POSB, virtually all of its investments are in government stock.

Table 8.1 summarizes the size, in terms of assets and liabilities, of the major financial institutions, which grew steadily after 1982. Between the years 1985 and 1986 they increased by 13.5 per cent from $4460 million to $5060.9 million. The four deposit-taking institutions (commercial banks, accepting houses, finance houses and the POSB) experienced an expansion in deposits, which rose by 21.8 per cent in 1985. This fell to 16 per cent in 1986.

A noteworthy feature of Zimbabwe's financial system lies in its location. Historically the operations of financial institutions have been concentrated in the urban and relatively more developed centres to the exclusion of communal areas. Therefore these communal areas have been deprived of financial resources needed for development. Since independence the government has introduced a number of measures, including investment incentives, to relocate into rural areas. Slow progress has been made in this regard. A few of the institutions have now introduced mobile units.

Another significant feature is the structure of ownership and control. Zimbabwe's financial system is predominantly foreign-dominated and privately owned. In the commercial banking field, however, the government holds 62 per cent of Zimbank and 47 per cent of the Bank of Credit and Commerce Zimbabwe. The government also owns 51 per cent of the Zimbabwe Development Bank, 100 per cent of the Development Banks. It has recently taken over the reinsurance business, establishing the Zimbabwe Reinsurance Corporation. The government also wholly owns the POSB. It controls some pension funds, but has no stake in the insurance industry.

The insurance business is still largely dominated by foreign capital of British, Australian and South African origin. As at 31 December 1985, of the 46 direct insurers operating in Zimbabwe, 20 were registered in Zimbabwe, ten in the U.K., ten in South Africa, two in Canada, two in Australia, one in the USA and one in Belgium. Of the nine professional reinsurers, eight were registered in South Africa and only one was Zimbabwean. Of ten broking firms, however, all were Zimbabwean except one, which was British.

In line with their geographical distribution, the lending activities of banks and financial institutions have been confined to the more secure and profitable activities of the commercial sector. They have generally been biased against small-scale peasant agriculture and the emergent small-scale businessman.

Table 8.1   Zimbabwe's financial sector (1986) (Z$m)

		1983	1986
1.	*Commercial banks*		
	Total deposits	1312.1	1931.1
	Loans and advances	832.4	1241.5
	Total assets/liabilities	1500.8	2318.6
	(% of total)	45.2	45.8
2.	*Accepting houses*		
	Deposits	198.4	252.1
	Bills of exchange	87.5	98.7
	Loans and advances	135.1	168.0
	Acceptances	419.0	606.1
	Total assets/liabilities	305.2	404.0
	(% of total)	9.2	8.0
3.	*Discount houses*		
	Money at call	93.1	100.5
	Total assets/liabilities	131.1	124.4
	(% of total)	3.9	2.5
4.	*Finance houses*		
	Deposits	170.5	259.9
	Hire purchase agreements	126.1	188.5
	(% of total)	6.1	6.2
5.	*Post office savings fund*		
	Total deposits	376.9	941.1
	Total assets/liabilities	445.4	1038.8
	(% of total)	13.4	20.5
6.	*Building societies*		
	Total deposits	318.8	495.6
	Share capital	285.6	258.6
	Mortgage advances and loans	475.6	559.8
	Total assets/liabilities	652.0	781.7
	(% of total)	19.6	15.4
	Total assets/liabilities of banking sector	3323.8	5060.9
7.	*Insurance companies*		
	Total assets	1124.6	1934.0
8.	*Pensions and provident funds*		
	Total assets	625.2	965.9

Source: Annual Economic Review of Zimbabwe 1986 (October 1987), pp. 35–6

2. Savings Performance and Trends

Commercial banks

In terms of the volume of deposits, commercial banks are the most important institutions for the mobilization of private savings. Table 8.2 shows the deposits held by the commercial banks from 1975 to 1987. After 1980, deposits in the various categories have almost doubled. Demand deposits was the largest component of total deposits, constituting on average about 50 per cent of the total. The second largest component was the savings accounts. Notice deposits and negotiable certificates of deposits are hardly accessible to individual clients since the minimum investment is Z$50,000. These constituted a small proportion of the total.

As a result of the increase in savings and fixed deposits shown in Table 8.2, commercial banks were able to raise their share of the market from 28.1 per cent in 1980 to 35.8 per cent in 1985. It should be noted, however, that real interest rates on deposits did not improve significantly between 1975 and 1987, and may even have been negative over certain periods (Table 8.3).

Table 8.2   Deposits held by commercial banks, 1975 to January 1987 (Z$m)

Year	Demand deposits	Savings accounts	Negotiated deposit certificates	Fixed deposits	Total
1975	213.6	92.6	22.3	196.4	524.9
1976	228.8	120.5	25.6	198.5	573.4
1977	227.5	147.4	49.7	171.4	596.0
1978	255.8	169.7	32.8	158.0	616.3
1979	296.2	200.7	23.1	152.2	672.2
1980	413.4	260.5	28.9	151.7	854.5
1981	453.0	273.1	88.8	236.3	1051.2
1982	491.0	301.2	104.0	396.0	1265.2
1983	480.7	305.9	115.7	409.6	1311.9
1984	594.3	351.7	96.6	481.1	1523.7
1985	671.3	382.1	130.5	600.1	1764.5
1986	743.0	420.6	176.3	591.2	1931.1
Jan 1987	687.0	410.6	165.6	593.5	1856.7

Source: Reserve Bank of Zimbabwe, *Quarterly Economic and Statistical Review*, Vol. 8 No. 2 (Harare, June 1987)

Table 8.3   Commercial banks' deposit rates

End of year	Commercial banks		
	3 months	12 months	24 months
1975	3.25–4.00	4.00–5.00	5.00–6.00
1976	3.25–3.75	4.00–4.75	5.00–5.75
1977	3.00–3.50	3.75–4.60	4.75–5.50
1978	3.25–3.25	3.90–4.25	5.00–5.25
1979	3.00–3.25	4.00–4.25	5.00–5.15
1980	3.20–3.50	4.00–4.40	5.00–5.25
1981	8.25–14.50	8.25–12.00	9.25–12.50
1982	9.00–10.00	10.20–10.50	10.50–10.80
1983	10.00–14.75	10.85–14.20	10.50–14.20
1984	8.25–9.00	8.75–10.50	9.25–11.00
1985	8.25–9.00	8.75–10.50	9.25–10.75
1986	8.25–9.50	8.75–10.25	9.25–10.75
1987	8.25–9.19	8.75–10.25	9.25–10.50

Source: Reserve Bank of Zimbabwe, *Quarterly Economic and Statistical Review*

In 1981, when interest rates more than doubled, demand deposits rose only marginally from $413.4 million in 1980 to $453 million in 1981. The rise in deposits was similarly marginal in 1983, even though interest rates on deposits had been raised further. If one considers the rate of inflation, real deposit rates were negative and must have provided a disincentive to savings.

A further major constraint on savings mobilization through commercial banks lies in the set of administrative barriers erected by the various banks (Table 8.4). These regulations are a major obstacle to potential clients. It should be remembered that in the POSB, 55.3 per cent of accounts in 1984 held less than $20.

Table 8.4   Administrative barriers/restrictions of savings accounts

Bank	Minimum deposit requirements Z$	Minimum balance Z$	Max no. of transactions per months	Minimum value Z$ per transactions
Barclays	50	50	3	10
BCCZ	10	10	–	–
Grindlays	500	500	4	–
Standard Chartered	40	40	–	–
Zimbank	50	10	–	–

Banks have explained these barriers as a way of discouraging constant withdrawals from savings accounts, which would discourage long-term accumulation and bring the banks high administrative costs.

It is further to be noted that the distribution, geographically, of commercial banks is not helpful to the mobilization of savings in the communal areas. Formal financial institutions are concentrated in and around densely populated urban centres, in commercial farming areas and along the main roads. Some commercial banks have branches in tourist and mining centres. In relation to their population density, the communal lands are short of banking facilities, the exception being the communal lands around Harare, Bulawayo and Mutare. Very few areas in the communal lands are within extended walking distance (5 km) of either a permanent branch or a mobile agency. Several densely populated regions (more than 40 inhabitants per square km) have no financial institution at all (e.g., those north of Bindura and Chriedzi, north-east of Masvingo and Rusape and west of Gweru). If a 50 km catchment area is assumed (a day's journey for those who have to rely on public transport), there are some regions which do not have any access to appropriate formal financial institutions (north-east of Bindura, south of Chippinge, north of Mutare). At some locations there is competition between mobile banking units and permanent POSB branches.

In 1985 the Reserve Bank of Zimbabwe persuaded the commercial banks to introduce mobile banking services at 60 rural locations, mostly District Service Centres. This process moved slowly. Banks have reservations about setting up rural-based mobile agencies from the perspective of cost-effectiveness. When the cost of transport, personnel and the use of premises is considered, mobile agencies are expensive to operate, especially given that they tap negligible deposits.

Building societies

The building societies have played a prominent role in the mobilization of personal savings. Their assets constituted 24.6 per cent of total bank assets in 1980 but this had fallen to 15.4 per cent by 1986. There are three building societies: the Central African Building Society

(CABS), accounting for 57 per cent of total savings with building societies, the Beverley Building Society (23 per cent) and the Founders Building Society (20 per cent).

Table 8.5 shows the trend in savings mobilization by the building societies.

Table 8.5   Savings with building societies (Z$m)

	1976	1977	1978	1979	1980	1981	1982	1983	1984	1985
Share capital										
Permanent	180.582	182.464	191.794	207.076	222.43	255.64	267.85	281.02	232.170	217.774
Fixed	1.525	1.375	1.169	1.156	0.87	0.59	–	–	–	–
Subscription	1.440	1.319	1.213	1.157	1.51	2.40	3.42	4.66	5.718	6.707
Sub total	183.547	185.158	194.176	209.839	224.81	258.63	271.27	285.68	237.888	224.481
Deposits										
Fixed	37.655	59.543	78.624	96.960	119.01	68.10	53.48	43.67	63.638	87.857
Savings	127.230	141.912	162.932	183.712	221.27	232.30	262.87	262.07	280.442	313.646
Sub total	164.885	201.466	241.456	280.672	331.28	300.40	316.35	305.76	344.080	401.503
Total	348.432	386.624	435.632	490.511	556.08	559.03	587.62	591.44	581.968	625.984

Source: Report of the Registrar of Banks and Financial Institutions and Registrar of Building Societies, 31 December 1985

Banking through building societies is more attractive than through the commercial banks as minimum balances and withdrawals from accounts are less restricted. Transactions are free of charge and the deposits earn interest. But building societies have found it difficult to break-even in their savings operations, due to the large number of small accounts. Many clients use their savings accounts as current accounts. Despite the costs incurred, however, in 1985 the societies netted profits before reserves of $6.99 million.

The other problem relates to interest rates and inflation. With high inflation, real returns on savings were negative. In addition, the POSB had a clear competitive edge over the societies and this partly explains the slackened pace of growth in their deposits. An important factor was the introduction of tax-free interest on POSB savings accounts in April 1980. This drained the building societies of resources and led to a 162 per cent increase in deposits with the POSB from December 1980 to June 1985. Recently, however, this has been offset by the introduction of tax-free paid-up permanent shares in the building societies.

Most building society branches are centred in the urban areas. Although savings are deposited with the building societies throughout the country, the granting of mortgages is highly concentrated, both regionally and socially. Branches in Harare alone account for some 69 per cent of the total value of private mortgages while branches in Harare and Bulawayo combined account for 88 per cent. The middle- and higher-income group take priority in mortgage advances.

The Post Office Savings Bank.

The POSB's share of total assets grew from 11.2 per cent in 1980 to 20.5 per cent in 1986. It is a state body which offers a limited range of savings facilities and invests its funds mainly in state securities. The POSB witnessed a massive expansion in deposits (Table 8.6). Total deposits increased fourfold from 1980 to 1987.

This success can be attributed to two factors. One is the relatively high interest rates which the POSB paid to depositors and the other is the fact that the interest is tax-free. Deposits could have risen even beyond the $959.4 million mark had there been no ceiling imposed on deposits. The introduction of tax exemption was accompanied by ceilings on

Table 8.6 Deposits held by the POSB, 1975 to January 1987 (Z$m)

End of	Savings	Fixed	Total
1975	116.7	36.7	153.4
1976	129.2	46.1	175.3
1977	140.8	53.9	194.7
1978	146.1	61.9	208.0
1979	159.2	69.4	228.6
1980	174.9	73.6	248.5
1981	203.2	92.4	295.6
1982	254.8	112.3	367.1
1983	287.2	130.3	417.5
1984	363.1	210.6	573.7
1985	455.1	299.9	755.0
1986	547.5	393.6	941.1
1987 Jan	554.4	405	959.4

Source: Reserve Bank of Zimbabwe, Quarterly Economic and Statistical Review, Vol. 8, No. 2 (Harare, June 1987)

the deposits both of individuals and of corporate account holders. Individuals, for example, are not permitted to deposit more than $100,000 with the POSB and the amount deposited in any one year may not exceed $50,000. The maximum total investment permitted for companies is $45,000, with annual investment limited to $15,000.

The terms of the POSB's deposits are the most favourable among all the institutions. The minimum deposit required for savings accounts is $5, with a minimum balance of $1. The minimum amount per transaction is $2 but there are no restrictions regarding the maximum number of transactions per month.

The working hours of the POSB, and its administrative and operational procedures, are all conducive to savings mobilization. However, the long queues at some urban branches, particularly at month-ends, can put off potential new savers. Another obstacle is the application procedure on joint accounts, which can take up to four weeks. Notwithstanding these factors, it is evident that the POSB is well poised to attract the small saver. As Table 8.7 shows, 55 per cent of all savings accounts are of less than $20, and 91.1 per cent of total savings balances are below $500.

Table 8.7   Savings deposits with the POSB at end of December 1984

Principal less than (Z$)	Number of accounts	%	Value of principal	%
5	164,717	19.6	0.4	0.4
20	301,121	55.3	2.9	1.3
100	182,636	77.0	8.4	4.5
500	118,533	91.1	26.2	14.5
1,000	27,318	94.3	19.1	21.7
5,000	33,509	98.3	73.0	49.4
50,000	13,849	99.9	85.9	82.0
100,000	693	100.0	47.4	100.0
Total	842,375		263.3	

Source: German Development Institute Mobilization: of Personal Savings in Zimbabwe through financial development, Berlin 1986

At the end of 1986, the POSB had approximately 167 offices. This constitutes the densest network of branches of all deposit-taking institutions. Table 8.8 shows the POSB to be the only institution with a large number of branches in the remotest of sparsely populated areas. Of its branches, 65.8 per cent are located at places with fewer than 2,500 inhabitants and only 8.4 per cent in the larger and more prosperous centres.

Table 8.8   Post Office Savings Bank regional distribution of permanent branches and agencies

	Number of inhabitants						
	more than 250,000	50,000 250,000	25,000 50,000	10,000 25,000	2,500 10,000	Less than 2,500	total
Branches of Post Office Savings Bank	14	3	4	9	27	110	167
Proportion of total	8.4	1.8	2.4	5.4	16.2	65.8	100

Finance houses, accepting houses, discount houses and the Reserve Bank of Zimbabwe

Other banking and deposit type institutions such as finance houses, accepting houses and discount houses also play a role in savings mobilization. Accepting houses are sometimes referred to as 'wholesale' banking since they do not take deposits from the individual but from large companies. Discount houses, too, do not take deposits from the public but mop up surplus liquidity from the banking sector, the largest depositors being commercial banks. A characteristic feature of these institutions is that they are located in urban areas. None has established any rural branch and logically this is dictated by the nature of their deposits.

Insurance companies

Insurance companies make a major contribution to savings mobilization and inject substantial funds into the economy.

Like the other institutions, insurance companies are centred in major urban areas. Although they offer the full range of commercial and personal insurance, they are mainly geared to the requirements of industrial, commercial and large-scale farming enterprises and the upper urban strata. People with incomes below $500 per month would find it impossible to pay premiums on policies on a regular monthly basis. To the extent that insurance companies tap the extra savings of the middle- and upper- income groups, they offer a useful avenue of productive investment when the funds could have otherwise been used for consumption purposes.

In 1984 pension fund assets totalled $1,688 million, 55 per cent of which was held by funds administered by insurance companies. Resources totalled some $1,626 million, with personal savings, defined as members' contributions alone, accounting for about $729 million, 30 per cent of which was contributed by self-administered funds, 70 per cent by funds administered by insurance companies.

Plans are under way in Zimbabwe to introduce a national pension scheme. If this materializes, the amount of personal savings mobilized by pension funds is likely to increase in the next few years and, if inflation is curbed, the real value of funds will rise.

Savings clubs and associations

Savings clubs and associations have mushroomed all over the country, particularly in rural areas. This could be attributed to the increased role of the peasant sector in national production and the rise in farm incomes, as well as increased remittances from urban areas after the minimum wage was introduced in 1980. These developments point to the potential of the rural sector in national resource mobilization.

Savings clubs date back to the 1960s when, as part of community development programmes, churches encouraged people to group together to form clubs and credit unions. The movement gained momentum after independence in 1981, encouraged by government ministries (Lands, Agriculture and Rural Settlement, Community Development and Women's Affairs), NGOs and private commercial producers and distributors of agricultural inputs.

Table 8.9   Historical development of the savings club movement

Year	Number of clubs	Membership
1970	30	200
1972	202	7,000
1976	501	20,000
1980	200	4,000
1981 (April)	400	8,000
1981 (Dec)	1,500	30,000
1982 (June)	3,000	60,000
1983 (August)	5,000	125,000
1984 (Estimate)	5,500	140,000

Source: G.A.Smith *'Savings, and the Development of Rural Savings Institution'* (Commonwealth Training Workshop on Rural Credit, Harare, 1984), p. 7

After independence the government formed an umbrella organization, the National Association of Savings and Credit Unions Limited, to unite the savings club movement under the auspices of the Department of Cooperatives.

Women constitute about 70 per cent of the rural population and the majority of savings club members (about 90 per cent) tend to be women. Membership of a club varies from around five to as many as 30 members. Contributions can be as low as 20 cents and this, compared to the banks' minimum of $5 to $50, is more convenient for the small saver. In addition, membership fees are also very manageable, ranging from $0.50 to $1.00.

Most savings clubs hold an account with a financial institution. In a survey of 76 savings clubs, the German Development Institute found that 16 per cent of the clubs had no account, 73 per cent held accounts with the building societies, 14 per cent with the POSB and 3 per cent with commercial banks. The preference for the building societies is largely due to their better deposit terms, longer working hours and easier withdrawal terms. The other advantage is that building societies are more accessible than other institutions since they have a wider network of mobile agencies. The largest deposits are made over June and July when communal farmers receive payment for their grain from the Grain Marketing Board.

Savings clubs use funds to purchase agricultural inputs. Other major uses include payment of school fees and purchase of household items like furniture, utensils, etc.

Participation in such clubs allows members to benefit from bulk buying of agricultural inputs, and so benefit from quantity discounts and transport advantages.

Savings clubs are still relatively unevenly distributed. They are more widespread in the more developed rural areas of Mashonaland region and at rural growth points. Given their nature, savings clubs could prove to be a useful tool for mobilizing resources from rural areas, if their distribution could be more widespread.

3. Monetary Policy and Savings Mobilization

The financial sector in Zimbabwe has always operated in a government-controlled atmosphere, even prior to the attainment of independence. The UDI regime maintained a policy of cheap money and a bank rate of 4.5 per cent from 1960. Investment was not stimulated, however, due to external forces.

With an adverse investment climate, the financial sector found itself with excess liquidity in 1980. So the issue was to find investment opportunities to mop up this liquidity rather than intensifying savings mobilization.

Table 8.10   Zimbabwe: Money market interest rates

End of year	Bank rate	Treasury	Bills Agricultural marketing authority	Call money	3 months Bankers' acceptance
1975	4.5	3.55	4.26	3.00–4.25	4.25
1976	4.5	3.60	4.26	3.00–4.00	4.25
1977	4.5	3.55	4.06	3.00–3.75	4.25
1978	4.5	3.61	3.95	3.00–3.75	4.25
1979	4.5	3.57	3.95	3.00–3.75	4.25
1980	4.5	3.30	3.75	2.80–3.50	4.00
1981	9.0	8.18	8.70	6.50–7.65	9.50
1982	9.0	8.29	8.75	7.75	8.90
1983	9.0	8.66	8.75	8.00–8.75	9.25
1984	9.0	8.40	8.75	8.10	8.75
1985	9.0	8.62	9.25	8.00	8.75
1986	9.0	8.62	9.25	8.00	9.00
1987 Jan	9.0	8.62	9.25	8.00	9.00

	Discount houses Negotiable certificates of deposit			
	3 months	6 months	12 months	24 months
1975	4.15–4.25	4.35–4.50	5.00–5.25	6.80–7.10
1976	4.10–4.35	4.25–4.60	4.65–5.15	5.50–5.75
1977	3.60–3.80	3.75–4.00	4.25–4.50	5.25–5.50
1978	3.60–3.90	4.00–4.25	4.40–4.60	5.00–5.25
1979	3.50–3.80	3.75–4.15	4.60–5.00	5.10–5.55
1980	3.80–4.50	4.05–4.70	4.60–5.20	5.20–6.10
1981	14.00–14.90	14.00–14.60	13.25–14.50	14.00–15.00
1982	9.50–11.00	9.75–10.50	10.00–10.75	10.50–11.25
1983	15.00	14.25–15.00	10.00–10.75	10.50–11.25
1984	9.50–9.75	9.60	–	–
1985	9.30–9.75	9.30–10.00	–	–
1986	9.36–9.50	9.65–9.75	9.75	10.00
1987 Jan	9.20–9.50	9.50	9.75	12.25

Source; RB2 *Quarterly Economic and Statistical review* Vol.8 No.2, June 1987

Table 8.11 Inflation, nominal and real interest rates

Year	Inflation rate (%)	Interest rate Average yearly nominal rate (%)	Interest rate real rate (%)
1976	6.3	3.75	−2.55
1977	6.9	3.50	−3.4
1978	6.3	3.25	3.05
1979	10.4	3.25	−7.15
1980	6.8	3.52	−3.28
1981	13.9	7.46	−6.44
1982	16.6	14.46	−2.14
1983	25.6	12.80	−12.8
1984	25.4	10.30	−15.1
1985	16.2	10.04	− 6.16

Source: Calculated from CSO, Digest of Statistics 1980–86

Table 8.12 Lending rates, deposit rates and real returns on savings (%)

	Inflation rates		Lending rates		
Year	Low income group	High income group	Bank rate	Commercial banks overdraft	Building societies (commercial property mortgages)
1977	10.3	9.5	4.5	7.5	8.5
1978	9.7	6.7	4.5	7.5	8.5
1979	13.8	11.3	4.5	7.5	8.5
1980	5.4	9.2	4.5	7.5	8.5
1981	13.1	14.6	9.0	13.0	14.75
1982	10.7	18.4	9.0	13.0	14.75
1983	23.1	16.4	9.0	13.0	14.75
1984	20.2	12.5	9.0	13.0	14.75
1985	8.5	9.5	9.0	13.0	14.75

	Deposit rates on savings accounts		Real returns		
	POSB	Building societies	Commercial banks	Saver	Investor
1977	3.25	3.5	3.0	−6.4	−1.8
1978	3.25	3.5	3.0	−5.9	−0.7
1979	3.25	3.5	3.0	−9.3	−3.4
1980	3.25	3.5	3.0	−2.0	−1.6
1981	3.25	7.75	7.0	−5.0	−1.4
1982	7.5	7.75	7.0	−2.9	−4.6
1983	7.5	7.75	7.0	−12.7	−2.9
1984	8.5	7.75	7.0	−9.7	−0.4
1985	8.5	7.75	7.5	0.0	3.2

Source: Zimbabwe Reserve Bank, Quarterly Economic and Statistical review (December 1987)

Notes: 1. Inflation rate: low-income urban families related to deposit rates on POSB savings accounts.

2. Inflation rate: high-income urban families related to commercial banks' lending rate on main overdraft.

The thrust of monetary policy after independence was to reduce the growth in money supply to counteract inflation. Interest rate changes, as well as adjustments in liquid asset ratios, cash and required reserve ratios, were geared towards short-run stabilization efforts.

Interest rate policy

During the 1980s the level and structure of interest rates in Zimbabwe was fixed by the government and not by market forces. The government fixed maximum lending rates and minimum deposit rates on relevant types of assets and liabilities of the banks. The interest rate policy was designed to finance the government's considerable borrowing requirements as cheaply as possible.

Interest rates were affected by government policy both directly and indirectly. As a major borrower, the government regulated the rate of interest on its securities. The Reserve Bank of Zimbabwe regulates the rediscount rate (bank rate) and interest rate on deposits and credit. It should be noted, however, that only official rates were controlled in the informal money market. Rates were anything from two to five times the official rates. This arises from the low credit rating of most clients who do not meet the collateral and other requirements of established banks.

During the 1980s, real interest rates in Zimbabwe were negative due to high inflation rates. Table 8.11 shows that over the entire period 1976 to 1985 real rates were negative with 1983 and 1984 as the worst years due to the high rate of inflation. And since the inflation rates are only official estimates, real interest rates could have been even lower. Table 8.12 shows real returns on savings.

The weight of professional opinion seems to support the view that financial savings tend to respond favourably to positive real interest rates. In developing countries, however, the need to raise interest rates to positive levels in order to stimulate financial savings is sometimes obscured by other policy considerations.

4. Concluding Remarks

This chapter has examined trends in the 1980s with regard to domestic resource mobilization, and the specific role which banks and financial institutions in Zimbabwe could play. The goal of savings mobilization should be viewed in the overall macro-economic framework of stimulating growth.

Major constraints on savings are deteriorating incomes, rising inflation and the narrow spread of financial institutions. Although the interest rate factor appears to be insignificant, it could nonetheless prove to be an important factor if real interest rates were made positive. A substantial rise in interest rates could provide an incentive for people to save.

What then are the policy implications? With regard to banks and financial institutions, they are as follows:-

1. A more detailed study of existing banks and their savings potential needs to be undertaken. Such a study should assess the range of financial assets/instruments on offer and their adequacy in terms of the nature of the clients. It should also assess the savings capacity of the different income groups (high, middle and low) as reflected by the types and volume of deposits they hold. In the same way, it should attempt to analyse the determinants of savings in each income group. This could provide a useful input into restructuring banks in such a way that they tap savings, in an optimal manner. Such a study has never been undertaken. However, in its policy documents the government has stated its intention of setting up a commission of inquiry into the banking and financial sector along the same lines as the Tax Commission. If such a commission is set up, it could, among other things, examine the issues raised in this chapter.

2. A feasibility study on expanding bank branches into rural areas should look into the costs and benefits of such an exercise, and explore the most rational pattern of location and distribution of bank branches. In the years following independence, rural incomes have increased and such an exercise should be worthwhile both for bankers and for the rural population.
3. Education programmes in rural areas should incorporate elements of awareness of the benefits of savings and its importance in economic development.
4. The role of savings clubs must be examined more closely and ways of increasing their contribution need to be explored. In the area of leadership, skills and training on such matters as basic bookkeeping and accounts, there is scope for realizing their potential. Other informal arrangements, like credit unions at work places, should also be explored.
5. The structure of interest rates must be reviewed, and sympathetic consideration given to the need for the type of interest-rate policy which could play an important role in the mobilization of domestic savings.

References

Abdi, A. I. (1977). *Commercial Banks and Economic Development*, Praeger, New York.

Bhatt, V. V.(1986). 'Improving the financial structure in developing countries', *Finance and Development*, Vol. 23, No. 2, June.

Chimombe, T. (1981). 'The role of banks and financial institutions in the accumulation and reinvestment of capital in Zimbabwe', unpublished M. Phil. thesis.

Fry, M. J. (1978). 'Money and capital or financial deepening in economic development', *Journal of Money, Credit and Banking*, Vol. 10.

German Development Institute (GDI) (1981). *Mobilization of Personal Savings in Zimbabwe through Financial Development*, Berlin.

Gurley,J. G. and Shaw, E. S. (1955). 'Financial aspects of economic development', *American Economic Review*, Vol. 49.

Houthakker, A. S. (1965). 'On some determinants of savings in developed and underdeveloped countries', in Robinson, E. A. G. (ed.), *Problems in Economic Development*, Macmillan, London.

U Tun Wai (1972). *Financial Intermediaries and National Savings in Developing Countries*, Praeger, New York.

Virmani, A. (1986) 'The determinants of savings in developing countries: theory, policy and research issues', World Bank discussion paper, Report No. IBRD 186.

Zimbabwe Government(1986–90). *Five Year National Development Plan* , Vol. 1.

9 The Mobilization of Rural Savings in Nigeria: Farmers' Attitudes to 'Formal' & 'Informal' Institutions

B. E. Mofunanya

The importance of mobilizing rural household savings has been neglected, not only in the financial policy-making of most developing countries but also in discussions of rural development. Much emphasis has been placed on government, corporate and aggregate savings, with very little comment on agricultural or rural savings. The development literature has tended to concentrate on the absolute poverty or deprivation of the rural population (Chambers, 1983).[1] From this perspective, the potential for mobilizing savings in the rural areas has been greatly underestimated.

The traditional assumption has been that rural households are too poor to save. For most rural households, the directly disposable income allows little margin over immediate consumption needs for savings, and those who do acquire additional income tend to waste it on ostentatious ceremonies or religious extravagances.[2] Partly as a result of this assumption, government policy in less-developed countries prior to 1980 was to promote credit rather than savings. Thus, in many developing countries, national agricultural policies had become increasingly concerned with the formation of credit programmes, ostensibly set up to channel financial resources to the rural poor. Most developing countries have at least one small-farm rural credit programme (Adams, 1978). International agencies, the World Bank and FAO in particular, have been very active in encouraging the construction of special financial intermediaries, and much aid has flowed into developing countries in the past two decades in the form of loans for on-lending through these institutions.

Some of these programmes are aimed at encouraging the use of inputs such as fertilizers, hybrid seeds and improved breeding stock, or investment in machinery and irrigation; others are aimed at providing some financial services to target groups such as members of cooperatives or agricultural and cooperative banks. Some supervised credit agencies have been created to administer these programmes. By 1979, the annual volume of agricultural loans in low-income countries had risen to $30–40 billion (Adams and Graham, 1981). This escalation of agricultural lending activity has been based on the general belief that most poor farmers without access to loans would be unable to adopt new technology or invest productively (Braverman and Guasch, 1986). In part this is a response to the realization that government policies to direct more funds to the agricultural sector in general, or to farmers in particular, have not always been successful.

Fungibility of funds, for instance, means that the use of selective credit controls to direct more funds to the poor farmers may have failed, since research shows that such funds find their way back to the urban sector through indirect channels (von Pischke et al., 1983).

152

Even when such funds reach the farmer there is no guarantee that he will use them to increase farm inputs, as intended by government policy. Rather, they can be used to supplement consumption expenditure.[3] Also, interest rates kept below market rates by government policy lead to credit rationing which discriminates against poor farmers, the very group the government aims to support. 'At low interest rates, credit demand often exceeds the supply of loanable funds. Lending agencies, therefore, select only the borrowers who have excellent credit ratings. In this environment small farmers are often denied regular channels of credit' (Adams, 1973, p. 13). Secondly, savers are not given the incentive of higher returns to increase their supply of savings. Low interest rates also mean that credit programmes cannot be self-supporting but must rely for their existence on the continued willingness of governments and international aid agencies to provide large grants.

The above realization has also led to the recognition, by most African countries, that foreign assistance is unlikely to increase at the rate experienced in the past. Debt servicing problems have reduced the capacity of most countries to raise loans in foreign capital markets. Agricultural development will involve increasing use of capital resources from sources within the countries themselves. In this emphasis on the increasing use of domestic resources to foster rural development, the issue of savings mobilization in rural areas becomes very important.

A. P. Thirlwall (1983) contends that

> In classical theory, saving and investment are one and the same thing, in that all savings finds investment outlets through variations in the rate of interest. Investment and development are led by savings. It is this classical view of development which underlies the phrase 'the mobilization of savings for development' and the policy recommendation of high interest rates to encourage voluntary savings.

There is now an emerging consensus that despite widespread poverty and deprivation in the rural areas of Africa, savings do exist, though in small units per individual, and that policies are needed to mobilize rural savings and direct them to productive investment. Small farmers have been found to be very capable savers, given the opportunity and appropriate rates of return. According to von Pischke (1978), 'the existence of intervals between the realization of income and the act of expenditure is normal and virtually universal. Thus virtually everyone saves.' Adams (1978) showed that substantial potential exists for mobilizing voluntary savings from rural households in developing countries. With information from several African countries, he argues that relatively large savings exist in rural areas when incentive and opportunities to save are present. This is also true of many African countries as DeLancey (1978) showed in his studies of West Africa. There are numerous studies of traditional savings institutions which show them to possess great potential for utilizing mobilized saving for either agricultural investment or community development. (Okorie and Miller, 1976; Bouman, 1976; Massing and Seibel, 1974; Miracle et al., 1980). It is clear from these studies that unexpectedly large amounts of savings are involved in a typical rural environment.

In summary, the purpose of savings mobilization policies should be (1) to gather surplus funds and put them to productive use, and (2) to provide institutions which encourage the habit of saving in order to make rural households self-reliant. In the rural areas of developing countries where incomes are low, these objectives prove difficult to accomplish. This chapter discusses the results of a fieldwork study in Anambra State (Eastern Nigeria). The underlying objective of this work was to suggest lines of inquiry in an appraisal of the effectiveness of existing formal and informal arrangements for mobilizing rural savings in Nigeria.

1. Area of Survey and Research Methodology

The study was carried out in the Anambra State (East) of Nigeria. The survey was restricted to two neighbouring local government areas, Uzo-Unani and Anambra. Farming practice, land ownership, the tenurial arrangements and crops produced were representative of the socio-economic conditions in rural areas across the state. Small farmers in the area are sufficiently similar to others in Nigeria to warrant broader observations and recommendations.

Research was conducted by means of structured questionnaires and personal observations. The aim was to provide insights into the problems of savings mobilization in the area, rather than to test theories. Results were obtained by way of household interviews. A farming unit consisted of a household, a man, his wife or wives and children. The farmers surveyed were predominantly traditional, and dependent on basic inputs involved in a hoe-cutlass technology. They employed little capital and utilized long-established traditional methods of cultivation, including shifting cultivation. The main crops were rice, cassava, yams and maize. The results of the survey are summarized below, in separate sections dealing with attitudes to savings and sources of fund.[4]

2. Attitudes to Saving

Eighty-six per cent of the 150 farming households surveyed had farms of less than one hectare. None of the farming households owned more than five hectares. Generally, farmers have small parcels of land. The holdings were small and were further sub-divided into many plots (around 3–5) scattered in all of the cropping areas. Small farm size is a characteristic feature of Nigerian agriculture. According to Olayide (1980), 'Nigerian agricultural and rural landscape is worked by small-holder farmers who produce not less than 98 per cent of total output of any crop in any given year.'

Those engaged in food production were the older men and women. Adherence to traditional methods and cultural allegiance is stronger in this group. Of food crop farmers, 86 per cent were over 45 years of age. Younger men and women tend to drift away from the farms in search of employment, or other occupations, in townships and cities.

Table 9.1 relates respondents to their highest levels of literacy and education. A high rate of illiteracy was a feature of the surveyed farming households. It is one of the important limiting factors in the use of formal savings facilities. In general, the more educated the farmer, the more aware he is of the wide range of services and facilities provided, both for savings and as sources of credit. In the study area, about 86 per cent of the farmers interviewed had little or no formal education. More than half of them were illiterate.

Table 9.1   Educational background of farmers

Background	No. of farmers	% of total
No formal schooling	72	48
Attended primary school	48	32
Attended secondary school	18	12
Further or higher education	12	8
	150	100

The farmers surveyed had acquired income from both farm and non-farm sources during the survey period (July–September 1987). There were difficulties in getting information from farmers who did not keep records. Some farmers were unwilling to be interviewed and to disclose information about such matters, but the estimates and approximations seem reasonable. About 90 per cent of the farmers stated that they had earned between N500 and N2000 over the preceding 12 months from farming activities. This represented about 60 per cent of total receipts. The remainder of income came from non-farm sources and included earnings from hunting, carpentry and petty trading. Some farmers also received allowances from their children. Others drew on past savings and a few sold or leased non-farm land.

Because farmers kept no records of any kind, and because of their reluctance to disclose detailed information on their financial position, it was not possible to derive quantitive information on individuals' 'saving' and 'borrowing'. Instead, the study concentrated on ascertaining the forms in which savings were kept, the uses to which savings were put and the reasons for rural indebtedness.

The farmers saved both through formal and informal channels, but when asked to denote their favoured form of savings out of current income, more than half of the farmers indicated that they preferred to keep cash at home rather than deposit it with any institution or person, 'formal' or otherwise. Of the 20 per cent of farmers who made use of commercial banks, the majority were farmers with some form of education (for example, retired civil servants), familiar with banking procedures.

Table 9.2   Farmers' preferred method of holding savings

Savings Method	No. of farmers	% of total
Commercial banks	30	20
Post Office Savings Bank	6	4
Co-operative societies	12	8
Cash at home	81	54
Local savings club (*esusu* societies)	0	0
Trusted friend or relative	3	2
	150	100

Whilst commenting on their unwillingness to use the banks, most farmers revealed that they were unaware of the services provided. Banks were regarded as institutions for the relatively well-off, powerful and educated, with little to offer the poorer members of the community struggling to meet subsistence needs. These are the reasons why, even in urban areas, unskilled workers, artisans, traders and other self-employed people appear reluctant to deposit their money in banks. Interest rates were of little relevance. Only a small fraction (8 per cent) of the farmers questioned understood bank procedures and the role that interest rates play. The post office savings bank was similarly dismissed as being too aloof and bureaucratic for the small saver. Interestingly, transport problems involved in transferring savings to banks or post offices did not feature strongly in the farmers' explanation of their unwillingness to use banks. This reflects the more recent spread of branch banking into the commercialized areas of rural Nigeria, with relatively few farmers nowadays having to travel long distances to make use of banking facilities.

Table 9.2 also indicates that only 12 per cent of the surveyed farmers favoured the local savings clubs (or what is now generally known in the development literature as Rotating Savings and Credit Association).[5] *Esusu* clubs are organized among people on a shared basis of trust and confidence. The underlying structure may be the village, an age-grade meeting, a dance or religious group. Usually the club is based in a single location. The reasons why farmers join these associations include social factors and community expectations. The possibility of obtaining a loan and pressures from friends or relatives will also be important. The survey indicated that only 12 per cent of the farmers favoured the *esusu* clubs as a repository for their savings. This is in spite of the fact that over 80 per cent of the respondents belonged to a form of *esusu* club. Many authorities, however, regard such clubs as having a great potential for rural savings mobilization. Aside from their regular contribution to the club (the amount is often a very small proportion of the farmer's income), the majority of farmers surveyed preferred to keep their income at home rather than deposit it with the *esusu* club. The cooperative societies did not play much part at all in mobilizing rural savings because most farmers do not belong to them.

Informal sources of credit assumed greater importance than formal credit sources for agricultural finance in the study area. Most of the farmers had borrowed from friends and relatives or local savings clubs. Others had used, in descending order of importance, banks, government loans, money-lenders and farmers' own cooperative societies. Just over half of the farmers surveyed had used outside finance, as opposed to own resources or savings, to finance capital expenditure in the previous 12 months.

Table 9.3   Sources of credit

Source of funds	No. of farmers	% of total
Self-financing	66	44
Friends and relatives	21	14
Local savings club, i.e., *esusu* clubs and other informal organizations	21	14
Loans from government institutions through supervised scheme	15	10
Banks	12	8
Money-lenders	9	6
Cooperative society	6	4
	150	100

Although it was assumed that the farmers borrowed to finance investment in the farm and in related productive activities, the survey revealed that no firm distinction could be drawn between credit for production and for consumption needs. Sixteen per cent of farmers reported that they had borrowed to finance children's school fees; 18 per cent had borrowed to meet social obligations or to cover necessities such as food and clothing; 10 per cent had borrowed to meet payments on past borrowing. Even some of those who stated that they had borrowed to finance farm investment appeared to have directed their own savings towards consumption needs, when outside funding for the purchase of producer inputs like fertilizer became available. Farmers, therefore, were not using all the money they borrowed for agricultural purposes. And though non-farm uses of borrowed funds are equally important to farmers in the sense that they cannot be dispensed with, non-farm uses of borrowed money often lead to default. Nevertheless, it is important to recognize that the tying of loans to particular production purposes by credit agencies is often a time-wasting exercise since farmers may simply direct their own savings to consumption; in other words, their own cash becomes 'fungible' towards consumption needs.

Table 9.4   Use of funds

Use	No. of farmers	% of total
Farm investment	84	56
Social obligation	6	4
Food and clothes	21	14
Payment of children's school fees	24	16
Repayment of previous loans and other purposes	15	10
	150	100

3. Concluding Remarks

In the areas of Nigeria to which this survey was directed, financial institutions (such as the banks which have been established under the federal government's rural banking scheme), some of them within walking distance of many villages, have not been able to make any significant impact on mobilizing the savings of the small-scale farmers. This is the very group which such banks are meant to serve. Most of the banks' customers are those who derive their livelihood predominantly from trade rather than from farming; some of the customers are well-to-do farmers or public servants such as agricultural extension workers, teachers and other educated members of the community. This is a familiar situation. Direct access to bank offices in rural areas has not resulted in the participation of the poorer farming members of the community.

Non-financial institutions such as rural self-help organizations and credit and savings associations like the *esusu* clubs do, however, encourage and promote the habit of savings. By holding membership in these organizations, farming households do become accustomed to saving small amounts of money on a regular basis, but these are primarily social-orientated organizations. Although there is a growing popular view that these organizations may possess the potential for mobilizing rural savings, no one has assessed just how great or small the potential is. For example, what exactly is the proportion of a farmer's income devoted to such an organization, in the form of an annual or monthly contribution? The amount contributed may, in fact, represent a quite insignificant proportion of total savings.

Secondly, even though most of the farmers surveyed were members of an *esusu* club, it is very doubtful whether the clubs involved could handle large volumes of funds and act as formal deposit takers. They do not possess the managerial skills or the technical expertise necessary for the proper organization of financial transactions. There have been numerous accounts of mismanagement of funds, embezzlement and corruption.[6] It may well be premature to suggest that *esusu* clubs can act as substitutes for banks.

Finally, the volume of 'hoarding' in the area of the survey was larger than may be generally recognized.[7] A tentative suggestion is that the establishment of unit rural banks (as against branch banking), identifiable with a particular community or group of communities, may be a better way of reaching the savings of the rural population.[8] Being a regionally or locally concentrated institution, such a bank would have greater knowledge of the local conditions of the savers and borrowers which constitute its potential market. The advantage of this type of arrangement is that it would make better use of the very scarce expertise in the organization and administration of financial institutions in Africa.

Notes

1. 'The poorer rural people, it is said, must help themselves; but trapped as they are, they often cannot do. The initiative in enabling them better to help themselves, lies with outsiders who have more power and resources and most of them are neither rural nor poor'. Robert Chambers, *Rural Development: Putting the Last First*, (Longman, London, 1983), pp. 2–3.
2. In Africa, for example, this view was widely held by colonial and foreign observers. Lord Lugard wrote in 1922 that, 'In character and temperament, the typical African of this race type is a happy, thriftless, excitable person, lacking in self control, discipline and foresight.' Lord Lugard, *The Dual Mandate in British Tropical Africa* (1922). On a rather different note, W. Arthur Lewis argues that only the profit-making entrepreneurs are significant savers in Third World countries. Indeed, he noted, 'there is very little evidence of savings out of wages, salaries and peasant income', though he does suggest that 'measures needed to realize these savings lie in the provision of a whole range of savings institutions.' W. A.Lewis, *The Theory of Economic Growth* (Allen and Unwin, London, 1955), pp. 226–9.
3. Money is 'fungible' because it can be converted into any good or service in the market. See von Pischke and Adams, 'Fungibility and the design and evaluation of Agricultural Credit Projects', *American Journal of Agricultural Economics*, No. 62 (1980), pp. 719–26. Also, credit is not always productive in the strict sense, because part of it is used for farm consumption, especially in the pre-harvest season. Isolated study of productive credit overlooks this special feature of farms in Africa and Asia. There is no point in insisting that credit be used to increase productivity, since families may starve to death before the harvest. Secondly, a cash loan, whether tied to a particular use or not, becomes pooled with farmers' other liquid assets. The additional cash will have consequences not just for productive inputs but also for other household expenditures. If cash can be borrowed only for productive purposes, it will still be pursued by farmers. The problem need not be different if the loan is made in kind. Credit in kind can be sold or exchanged by the borrower and used to purchase something else. Examples of this can be found in G. M. Scobie and D. L. Franklin, 'The impact of supervised credit programmes on technological change in developing agriculture', *Australian Journal of Agricultural Economics*, Vol. 21, No.1 (1977), pp. 1–12.
4 . This survey was carried out between July and September 1987.
5. Savings and Credit Associations are known by different names, for example, the 'chit funds' in India and Asia, the 'partner systems' in Jamaica, the *djanggi* in Cameroon. In Nigeria the term is *esusu* club. The *esusu* clubs provide for a combined savings and credit arrangement in which a group of people come together, contribute fixed amounts at fixed intervals and assign the total contributed to a member in rotation. Sometimes the fund contributed may be used for the club's social obligations.
6 . See, for instance, the cases used in Anthony I. Nwabughuogu, 'The *Isusu*, an institution for capital formation among the Ngwa Igbo. Its origin and development to 1951', *Africa*, Vol. 54 , No. 4 (1984).
7. Hoarding is a traditional method of saving which takes money out of circulation by accumulating it, rather than spending it or depositing it with any financial intermediary. In rural areas of Africa, the accumulation of cash occurs frequently because farmers are always contemplating specific needs of the future such as a reserve against misfortune, education of their children, marriage or other ceremonial events. Hoarded cash often forms a large proportion of their economic surplus. Any policy for the mobilization of savings must take into account a strong tendency to hoard. During the currency conversion in Nigeria and Uganda, for example, a large amount of cash was reportedly de-hoarded from the rural areas.
8. A major justification for setting up this type of local institution was provided by Bhole (1978) for India. He noted that, 'A decade of the functioning of commercial banks after nationalization has thrown open the limitation of branch banking becoming a major financial intermediary in rural India'. Bhole emphasised that the inherent characteristic of branch banking, transfer of resources from local areas to the city areas, continued to exist even after the public ownership of banks. L. M. Bhole, 'Financial structure for rural development, in retrospect and future prospect', *Indian Economic Journal* (1978), Part 2, p. 6.

References

Adams, D. W. (1973). 'The case for voluntary savings mobilization, why rural capital markets founder', *USAID Spring Review of Small Farmers Credit*, Vol. 19.

Adams, D. W. (1978). 'Small farmer credit programmes and interest rate policies in low-income countries', *Studies in Rural Finance. Department of Agricultural Economics and Rural Sociology*, (Ohio State University, Columbus, Ohio).

Adams, D. W. and Graham, D. H. (1981). 'A critique of traditional agricultural credit projects and policies', *Journal of Development Economics*, No. 8.

Bouman, F.J.A. (1976). 'The *ndangi*, a traditional form of saving and credit in West Cameroon', *Sociologia Ruralis*, Vol. 16, No's 1/2, pp. 103–19.

Bhole, L. M. (1978).'Financial structure for rural development in retrospect and future prospect', *Indian Economic Journal*, Part 2.

Braverman, A. and Guasch, J. L. (1986). 'Rural credit markets and institutions in developing countries. Lessons for policy analysis from practice and modern theory', *World Development*, Vol. 14, Nos. 10/11.

Chambers, R. (1983). *Rural Development, Putting the Last First*, Longman, London.

Delancey, M. V. (1978). 'Savings and credit institutions in rural West Africa, introduction', *Rural Africana*, No. 2 (Fall).

Lewis, W. A. (1955). *The Theory of Economic Growth*, Allen and Unwin, London.

Lord Lugard (1965). *The Dual Mandate in British Tropical Africa* (first edition,1922).

McNamara, R. (1973). *Address to the Board of Governors of the World Bank Group*, IBRD, Washington DC (September).

Massing, A. and Seibel, H. D. (1974). *Traditional Organisations and Economic Development Studies of Indigenous Cooperatives in Liberia*, Praeger, New York.

Miracle, M., Miracle, D. and Cohen, L. (1980). 'Informal savings mobilization in Africa', *Economic Development and Cultural Change*, Vol. 28, No. 4 (July).

Nwagbughuogu, A. I. (1984). 'The *isusu*, an institution for capital formation among the Ngwa Igbo. Its origins and development to 1951', *Africa*, Vol. 54, No. 4.

Okorie, F. and Miller, L. F. (1976). '*Esusu* clubs and their performance in mobilising rural savings and credit', University of Ibadan Technical Report Acts/76, University of Ibadan, Department of Agricultural Economics, Ibadan.

Olayide, S. O. (1980). 'Characteristics, problems and significance of farmers', in *Nigerian Small Farmers, Problems and Prospects in Integrated Rural Development*, Olayemi, J. K. (ed.), Caxton Press, Nigeria.

Scobie, G. M. and Franklin, D. L. (1977). 'The impact of supervised credit programmes on technological change in developing agriculture', *Australian Journal of Agricultural Economics*, Vol. 21, No. 1.

Thirlwall, A. D. (1983). *Growth and Development with Special Reference to Developing Countries*, Macmillan, London (third edition).

von Pischke, J. D. (1978). 'Towards an operational approach to rural savings', *Savings and Development*.

von Pischke, J. D. and Adams, D. W. (1980). 'Fungibility and design and evaluation of agricultural credit projects', *American Journal of Agricultural Economics*, No. 62.

von Pischke, J. D. *et al.*, (eds) (1983). *Rural Financial Markets in Developing Countries. Their Use and Abuse*, World Bank, Baltimore.

10 Savings Determinants & Mobilization in Sub-Saharan Africa: The Case of Côte d'Ivoire

Allechi M'Bet

The central problem in the theory of economic development is to understand the process by which a community which is previously saving and investing 4 or 5 per cent of its national income or less, converts itself into an economy where voluntary saving is running at about 12 to 15 per cent of national income or more. This is the central problem because the central fact of economic development is rapid capital accumulation.

Arthur Lewis (1954).

In underdeveloped countries, the rate of voluntary saving is low, and existing institutions are not very successful in mobilizing such savings as there are. Most people have incomes so low that virtually all current income must be spent to maintain a subsistence level of consumption.

Benjamin Higgins (1968: Chapter 23)

Like many developing countries, for almost a decade Côte d'Ivoire has been going through an unprecedented economic crisis. During the coffee and cocoa boom in the early 1970s, the Ivoirian government launched a variety of ambitious development programmes, financed mostly by public saving through the agricultural marketing board (*Caisse de Stabilisation et de Soutien des Prix Agricoles* – CSSPA), as well as by external borrowing. Given political stability and a convertible currency, Côte d'Ivoire had the ability, throughout the 1970s, to borrow from private sources on commercial terms.

However, since 1979 Côte d'Ivoire has had a balance of payments deficit, forcing the government to reschedule its overseas debt payments. Moreover, interest and amortisation charges are unreasonably heavy and Côte d'Ivoire, once seen as an 'economic miracle', stopped its debt payments in 1987 in the face of continuing decline in commodity prices and a consequent reduction in foreign exchange earnings. In addition, the conditions of international credit are becoming tougher all the time. All this leads to the central issue of raising the level of domestic savings as an alternative or, at least, as a complementary source of capital formation. It is widely recognized that LDCs must make additional efforts to mobilize and achieve effective use of their internal resources.

The issue has become so important that African heads of state and governments adopted in July 1985, at the United Nations, the African Priority Programme for Economic Recovery (APPER) for the period 1986–90, as reported by Frimpong-Ansah (1987). This programme emphasized the adoption of imaginative policies for savings mobilization, if an improvement in the economic condition of Africa is to be achieved along a dynamic self-reliant growth path, as hoped for in the Lagos Plan of Action. Out of the US $128 billion to be injected in new resources into the economy in this period, African countries must contribute at the outset 64.4 per cent of the total amount (or $US82.5 billion) from domestic resources.

The question naturally arises as to how such a sizeable contribution can be raised from people with income barely sufficient for subsistence. This chapter analyses the problems of domestic resource mobilization in Côte d'Ivoire. The principal question to be asked is how far can voluntary domestic savings go towards meeting capital requirements, in situations where the rate of net investment must increase twofold or more as part of the 'minimum effort' needed for economic take-off. It should be mentioned that although domestic resources include a financial and a non-financial component (human capital and natural resources), we will focus only on the mobilization of financial resources.

This chapter is divided into five parts. The first briefly reviews the literature on the role of saving in the process of economic growth and development. The second indentifies the behavioural and economic determinants of financial savings (income, wealth, interest rates, contract terms, tax laws). The third provides an empirical investigation of the determinants of savings in Côte d'Ivoire. The fourth describes the organized (formal) financial and informal financial institutions. Finally, the fifth part summarizes and concludes the chapter.

1. Domestic Resource Mobilization in Economic Development

'Old wine in new bottles'

The central importance of savings rates for capital accumulation and output growth was emphasized in early discussions of economic development. The new economic environment must be taken into account, however, in examining the role of domestic resources in economic growth. Old wine must be put into new institutional 'bottles'.

Many economists have cited capital accumulation as the major factor governing the rate of development. Rostow specified a rise in the rate of productive investment to over 10 per cent of national income as a necessary requirement for a country's economic take-off. As early as 1955, Arthur Lewis contended that 'it is particularly important to stimulate savings amongst the peasants, because of the role that agriculture has to play in economic development'. In 1966 he stressed that 'measures to increase the rate of private savings deserve high priority. . . . The amount saved is a function of the effort put into promoting savings . . . a countrywide network of saving institutions of various kinds must be created . . . and some public agency should concern itself specifically with making savings easy.' Lewis thus went beyond his early concern about the importance of saving to start addressing the issue of how to mobilize potential savings.

To examine the links that exist between savings and economic growth, it is useful to develop a model which formally exposes that relationship. The Harrod–Domar model has the advantage of focusing on the form of the savings function. Since we are interested primarily in the role of savings in economic growth, we study the model in a closed economy. This derived model contains the first three equations of the Harrod–Domar model.

(1) Equilibrium condition on the capital factor market

$$g_K = \frac{S}{K}$$

where K stands for capital stock
and S for national gross savings

g_K may also be defined as:

$$g_K = \frac{dK/dt}{K}$$

that is the growth rate of capital. g_K corresponds to the 'warranted' growth rate of the Harrod–Domar model.

(2) Fixed coefficient production function

$$Y = \frac{K}{k}$$

where Y is Gross National Product
and k the capital output ratio

(3) The population growth rate
This is defined as $g_P = n$

where n is the rate of increase of the population.

This n corresponds to the natural rate of population growth defined by Harrod–Domar. This third equation underlines the importance of population growth in development. In fact, one of the major problems of economic development is one of saving and investing enough to generate an income flow that will grow faster than the population. Rapid population growth will not only increase the ratio of savings and investment needed to guarantee rising per capita incomes, but will also aggravate the difficulty of saving. High fertility can depress private saving in two ways: first by reducing the volume of saving by individual families and, secondly, by increasing the proportion of national income that must accrue to non-savers.

When the government rather than individual entrepreneurs provides a large proportion of national investment, then population affects the level of investment through its impact on the capacity of the government to raise money through taxation. Consequently, the population factor is a major determinant to be included in an analysis of savings behaviour.

The salient feature of this derived model is to allow the presentation of a savings function which posits that the increase in savings per capita depends upon a fraction (l) of the increase of the per capita income. Fei and Paauw characterize this (l) as the per capita marginal saving ratio.

To give a description of the evolution of savings, Harrod–Domar add the following two equations to the previous ones.

(4) $S_{(o)} = s_{(o)} Y_{(o)}$

where $S_{(o)}$ is the saving level in the initial period.
$s_{(o)}$ is the average propensity to save at the initial level of the gross national product.

(5) $\dfrac{dSc}{dt} = \dfrac{zdYc}{dt}$

where Sc is per capita saving
and Yc the gross national product per capita.

According to (5), if (z) is a positive fraction whose value lies between 0 and 1 ($0 < (z) < 1$), then per capita consumption as well as per capita savings increases when the gross national product per capita (Yc) increases. Since our aim is to derive a savings function, one can integrate equation (5) to get such a function, as presented in equation (6).

(6) $Sc = z\,Yc - Yc_{(o)}\,[z - s_{(o)}]$

Rearranging (6) yields:
(6a) $Sc = z\,[Yc - Yc_{(o)}] + s_{(o)}\,Yc_{(o)}$

Equation (6a) postulates that the per capita saving for a given period of time is equal to the increase of the per capita saving caused by the increase in the gross national product plus the initial level of savings per head. The average propensity to save can be derived from equation (6) as follows:

6b) $s = \dfrac{S}{Y} = \dfrac{Sc}{Yc} = \dfrac{z\,[Yc - Yc\,(o)] + s(o)\,Yc\,(o)}{Yc}$

Hence, for the average propensity to increase, we must have $z > s(o) > 0$ when the per capita income increases. To show how the population variable affects the rate of growth of the economy we will compare the rate of growth of the Gross National Product (GNP) with the growth rate of the population.

The model reveals that an increase in the propensity to save per capita will have no effect whatsoever on the economy unless growth in GNP per head occurs at the same time to help generate the necessary savings, since the growth rate of savings is a function of GNP. A high per capita saving ratio (z) leads to an increase of the saving rate only if GNP grows.

One other economist reached a similar conclusion, namely Ragnar Nurske (1953). According to him, the supply of capital is low because of the low level of income which is itself a reflection of low productivity. The insufficient productivity is itself due to lack of capital, resulting in a weak or inadequate capacity to save. We are thus in the 'classical' vicious circle which may be broken by a 'big push'.

The lesson to be learned from the above is that savings is one key element for growth of GNP. Savings permit an increase in the supply of capital which allows, in turn, an increase in production. Nevertheless the model reveals that the population factor, when uncontrolled, can constitute a hindrance to the positive impact of saving on growth. In fact, the closer per capita income is to the subsistence level, the weaker will be the saving per capita.

Beyond the population variable, other factors exist that can hamper the savings generation process. Specifically in developing countries like Côte d'Ivoire, the inadequacy of the banking system, capital flight, demonstration effects and the related conspicuous consumption, are factors which make the mobilization of savings a difficult task to accomplish.

2. Determinants of Saving

Income

In fact, in Keynesian thinking, savings constitute a residual. It is the amount that remains after consumption needs have been met.

A similar definition of savings has been used in most empirical studies. One definition used by the OECD as a residual computed by taking current spending out of current revenues according to the accounting principles of the NAS or National Account System of the United Nations, adopted since 1968 in OECD countries.

Most studies have confirmed the dominant role of income as a determinant of savings, albeit with variations in the concept of income which is used. These studies have used either the Keynesian absolute income hypothesis, or Milton Friedman's permanent income hypothesis. The permanent income hypothesis has the advantage of distinguishing permanent from transitory income. In theory, it is a concept well suited to the circumstances of Côte d'Ivoire (and other African countries) where swings in world prices create a large transitory element in income.

But to be usable in an empirical investigation, the permanent income Friedman defines as long-run income expectations has to be measurable. This is the main hindrance for using the permanent income variable in empirical work, especially in Africa where limitations of the data are well known. Frimpong-Ansah (1987) presents a detailed review of the role of income in savings determination for several African countries.

Taxation is another factor that affects savings. Indeed, only disposable income should be considered, that is income from which taxes have been deducted. Civilization requires that the state plays a certain role in society and tax payers contribute to the payment of services provided by the state. The higher the tax rate, the smaller will be the disposable income. The smaller the disposable income, the more difficult it will be for the individual consumer to meet consumption expenditure and, accordingly, the smaller the chance for savings. Hence taxation should be taken into account in analysing savings behaviour. But it should be pointed out that taxes from private sources represent revenue for the government and, if properly used, can contribute to the welfare of the people of the country.

The interest rate is another determinant of savings that has received attention both in developed countries and in less-developed countries. But empirical investigations in developing countries (Kessler, 1984), sometimes run counter to theoretical analysis. As a reward for accumulating financial assets and postponing current consumption, interest rates influence the willingness to save currently earned income. In this sense, the supply of loanable funds should be positively related to interest rates. The higher the reward, the more individual economic units will tend to save, *ceteris paribus*. Secondly, on the demand side interest rates constitute an element of the cost of capital. The higher the interest rates, and therefore the more costly is borrowed money, the less capital firms will demand. From that viewpoint, the demand for loanable funds should be inversely related to the level of interest rates. Accordingly, interest rates must be set at a level not too high to deter demand for capital, but high enough to draw in the supply of loanable funds. Determining such an equilibrium level of interest rate is a challenge to all economies. In developed countries, with well organized financial markets, interest rates do vary according to market forces and can directly affect the flows of savings and investment. It should be noted that the relevant interest rate is the real interest rate, that is, the nominal rate adjusted to the inflation rate. It is well-known that in LDCs financial markets are not sufficiently well organized to make the link between interest rate and savings a strong channel through which funds can flow. In Côte d'Ivoire, the role of interest rates in savings mobilization is interesting. Côte d'Ivoire belongs to the *Union Monetaire Ouest Africaine* (UMOA) (or West African Monetary Union). This institutional framework has great impact on interest rates. In brief, the UMOA was established in May 1962 between France and seven West African countries, formerly French colonies. UMOA is part of the larger 'Franc Zone' which is characterized by four principles: (1) fixed parity between the currencies of the zone, in particular between the French franc and the franc of the *Communauté Financière Africaine* (CFA F), set at 1 French franc (1FF) = 50 CFA F and unchanged since 1948; (2) freedom of transfer of funds within the zone, without limitation; (3) the pooling of foreign exchange earnings; and (4) a unique exchange rate policy vis-à-vis non-member countries. In addition, France ensures unlimited convertibility of the CFA F into FF through a special account called *compte d'operation*. This *compte d'operation* is the key to the UMOA. It is an account at the French Treasury that holds the foreign exchange reserves of all the member countries and handles the UMOA's foreign exchange transactions. There exists a common central bank in UMOA countries, the *Banque Centrale des États de l'Afrique de l'Ouest* (BCEAO), also established in 1962. BCEAO issues bank notes and implements the same monetary policy for the entire Union. A common monetary unit is used in all member countries.

Concerning interest rate policy, until 1973 the BCEAO pursued a relatively low and stable nominal interest rate. These interest rates were applied uniformly across the entire CFA zone. Average levels of the nominal and of the real rate are presented in Table 10.1.

Table 10.1   Evolution of nominal and real interest rate (period averages)

	Nominal interest rate	Real interest rate
1960–1972	3.50	−1.10
1975–1979	5.50	−8.28
1980–1981	10.00	−1.89
1982–1985	10.50	+6.03
Minimum	3.50	−19.40
Maximum	12.00	+8.64
Mean	6.26	−1.42

Source: Computed by the author. Data from BCEAO, *Notes d'Information*, various issues.

As can be seen from Table 10.1, the BCEAO's rediscount rate in the 1960s was set at 3.5 per cent (and the maximum commercial bank rate, at 7.5 per cent) on the lending side. On the deposit side, the interest rate varies according to size and maturity of the deposit. Thus, deposits up to CFA F 200,000 (about US$700) earned no interest while larger amounts earned interest between 1 per cent and 4.5 per cent only.

This policy of low interest rates has been criticized frequently on two points. First, such a policy is likely to discourage savings. Second, given the free movement of funds within the Franc Zone, especially the inflows and outflows of funds between France and UMOA, the gap between the level of French interest rates and BCEAO's rates has tended to encourage capital outflows. The low-interest policy of the BCEAO has tended to discourage domestic savings and prevented it from conducting an active monetary policy for development.

The inflation rate

Economic theory has it that as the inflation rate increases, the real value of assets declines. In order to avoid such erosion, economic agents tend to increase their real cash balances during periods of inflation. Evidence tends to support the hypothesis that savings rates increase during periods of inflation. Horiaka (1986) argues that the low inflation rate in Japan has led to a level of private savings about 1.7 per centage points below that observed in the USA. In Côte d'Ivoire, as in other inflation-prone African countries, we note the simultaneous growth of the so-called informal financial sector. The development of a parallel or underground saving sector may reflect, in inflationary circumstances, the absence of alternative forms of holding assets. The relationship between savings, especially households savings, and inflation, needs to be investigated to shed more light on this particular issue.

Demographic factors

Following Modigliani's life-cycle savings hypothesis, several empirical studies have introduced the demographic factor in the form of the age structure of populations. Horiaka, (1986), for instance, found that the low ratio of senior citizens to the total labour force in Japan is the most significant factor in the high savings rate achieved in that country. In Côte d'Ivoire comparative data for saving rates by age groups are lacking, so it is not possible to make assessments of this kind. The population structure reveals a pyramid shape with a wide base and narrow top. This indicates a high proportion of youth, not yet working, and a low percentage of aged people. Further research needs to be undertaken on this issue for Côte d'Ivoire, in order to evaluate the impact of the structure of the population on savings, especially on household savings. In this chapter, we include population growth rate, to indicate its impact on savings.

Other factors have been found to influence savings, namely economic and political conditions such as the UMOA institutional framework described earlier. The international economy also affects gross national savings through public savings derived from foreign trade taxes such as import duty and export tax. Another major source of public sector savings is the surplus of the *Caisse de Stabilisation* or Marketing Board. There is no available data on the amount of this surplus, but what is certain is that it fluctuates with the international price levels of cocoa and coffee, and with the variations in the exchange rate, since most export earnings are in foreign currency, especially in the US dollar.

3. Empirical Analysis of Savings Behaviour in Côte d'Ivoire

The famed Pearson Report claimed that 'contrary to the widespread idea which states that poor countries have little to save, they have generated locally most of their capital for investment'. The question to address concerns the nature of such savings in the Ivoirian context, where they come from and to what extent they contribute to capital formation.

As in other countries, such savings are generated by households and by non-financial firms on the one hand and, on the other, by the state through the budget and through the CSSPA.

Empirical investigation begins with an examination of data on savings of households, of public administration, of non-financial firms and of Gross National Savings. Most of the data are collected from *Les comptes de la Nation,* published by the ministry of finance and the economy, and from BCEAO's *Notes d'Information.*

According to the Ivoirian national accounts system (SICN), Gross National Savings include six elements. These are savings stemming from (1) households, (2) non-financial firms, (3) public administration, (4) financial (credit and loans) institutions, (5) private administration and (6) insurance firms.

We can break Gross National Savings down into three broad classes: public savings, non-financial firms' savings and household savings. We examine each briefly in turn.

Public savings

In most francophone African countries, investments in the public sector are financed by the state and by some parastatals. In Côte d'Ivoire, the Marketing Board is also an important source of saving for investment. But the confidentiality that surrounds the CSSPA surplus does not permit an analysis as to how and by how much the board contributes to public savings. Rather, the most important tools for *budgetary* and *monetary* policy are budgetary savings (state budget), especially the *Budget Special d'Investissement et d'Equipement* (or BSIE). This special budget which corresponds to the 'development budget' in an anglophone African country, constitutes the second element in the nation's budget besides the 'Budget General de Fonctionnement' (BGF) or recurrent budget that serves to pay civil servants, and is geared mainly to investment, in all sectors of the economy, with particular emphasis on agriculture.

Besides budgetary savings, there exist monetary savings made by financial institutions, namely, the policy of the Central Bank (BCEAO) to spur public investment. We analyse each component of public savings in turn.

1. *Budgetary savings* consist essentially of taxes, direct as well as indirect. Taxes on income and on wealth (INCOT) and taxes on foreign trade (FTT) are the most prevalent sources of budgetary savings. But foreign trade taxes contribute much more to budgetary savings. This is a typical situation for a developing country. Since colonial times the foreign trade sector (import duty and export tax) has been well organized in Côte d'Ivoire to compensate for the low yield from income tax.

   The percentage share of foreign trade tax (SFTT), has always been above that of income tax (SINT). SFTT also displays wider fluctuations, generated by variations in world prices of the major crops exported, and of manufactured goods imported as a result of exchange rate changes. Given the difficulties encountered in foreign borrowing in recent years, the Ivoirian government has launched a dual programme for generating public revenue. First, the government raised tax rates substantially, in particular value-added tax and stamp duties. Secondly, the government is improving collection procedure. Besides indirect and direct taxes, there exists a provision for forced purchase of assets and bonds, the certificates of the '*Fonds National d'Investissement*'. Similarly, taxes on the '*Benefice industriel et commercial*' (BIC), or commercial and industrial profits, contribute to the generation of public savings.

2. *Monetary savings* constitute the second element of *public savings*, credits of the BCEAO to the Budget or to the other sectors of the economy. The BCEAO, like other central banks throughout the world, has an important role in the development process. The actions of the BCEAO on the Ivoirian economy have two main strands. The first is *the role of BCEAO in the distribution of credits*. This is undertaken through the discount rate, the quantitative control of credit by way of credit ceilings, the qualitative or selective control of credit by way of allocating the limited available credit to sectors with backward and/or forward linkages, and finally through the purchase of shares of some financial institutions established by the state such as the *Banque Nationale pour le Développement Agricole* (BNDA) and the *Credit de Côte d'Ivoire* (CCI)). The second type of action undertaken by the BCEAO concerns *credits granted to the treasury*. Such advances, in conjunction with the rediscount of public assets, amount to 20 per cent of the previous year's fiscal receipts. This level was set some years ago at 10 per cent, then moved to 15 per cent and more recently reached 20 per cent. This demonstrates that monetary savings are growing in importance in Côte d'Ivoire as in other UMOA countries where the BCEAO is becoming more active in financing development over and above its classical role of an issuing institution.

We now turn to private sector savings, beginning with the savings behaviour of non-financial firms.

Non-financial firms savings

By definition, and according to the theory of loanable funds, households are savers (suppliers of capital) and firms are borrowers of funds to be invested. Nevertheless, in Côte d'Ivoire

Table 10.2   Forms of savings (billions CFA F)

	GNS	HOS	NFFS	PADS	GNCF	RESGAP
1960	22.17	8.53	8.09	5.17	19.12	3.04
1961	21.29	5.82	7.14	7.68	24.29	-3.00
1962	18.56	3.79	0.38	13.45	25.23	-6.67
1963	28.85	7.41	3.59	16.65	28.36	0.49
1964	46.92	10.02	12.82	22.84	39.20	7.72
1965	35.30	11.69	8.16	14.60	43.64	-8.33
1966	41.69	13.40	10.71	17.13	47.08	-5.39
1967	40.26	14.93	7.34	17.49	49.81	-9.54
1968	59.92	17.23	17.80	24.45	54.02	5.90
1969	77.43	15.38	28.81	31.03	61.83	15.60
1970	88.36	21.04	29.72	34.65	83.88	4.48
1971	78.65	21.33	32.11	20.56	92.36	-13.70
1972	83.60	22.87	30.43	24.87	94.25	-10.64
1973	108.25	25.30	33.87	44.85	121.96	-13.70
1974	157.36	38.57	39.62	78.87	143.65	-13.71
1975	117.87	38.17	36.81	39.18	183.94	-66.06
1976	221.04	46.73	18.77	153.61	183.94	37.10
1977	390.04	30.90	11.09	336.79	397.63	-7.59
1978	351.04	71.75	56.72	213.30	529.04	-177.62
1979	282.19	81.49	31.18	152.49	526.71	-244.51
1980	200.18	51.01	16.83	116.06	523.60	-323.42
1981	145.96	12.32	169.74	11.44	558.38	-412.42
1982	148.39	53.00	66.43	14.30	538.70	-390.31
1983	131.68	14.50	54.30	47.85	461.80	-330.12
1984	203.69	15.80	75.81	76.38	361.60	-157.91
1985	317.74	17.40	70.56	171.68	339.36	-21.62

Source: Government of Côte d'Ivoire, *Les comptes de la nation,* various issues

GNS = Gross National Savings
HOS = Households Savings
NFFS = Non Financial Firms savings
PADS = Public Administration Savings
GNCF = Gross National Capital Formation
RESGAP = Resource Gap (absolute) or (GNS – GNCF)

Table 10.3   *Saving rates*

	HOSSR	PADSR	NFFSR	GNSR	RESGAPR
1960	6.06	3.68	5.74	15.76	2.16.
1961	3.65	4.82	4.48	13.36	−1.88
1962	2.28	8.09	0.23	11.17	−4.01
1963	3.78	8.49	1.83	14.73	0.25
1964	4.18	9.52	5.35	19.57	3.22
1965	4.88	6.09	3.40	14.73	−3.47
1966	5.19	66.42	4.15	16.16	−2.09
1967	5.41	63.44	2.66	14.60	−3.46
1968	5.27	7.48	5.45	18.35	1.80
1969	4.20	8.48	7.88	21.18	4.26
1970	5.07	8.35	7.16	21.29	1.07
1971	4.85	4.67	7.30	17.88	−3.11
1972	4.84	5.27	6.45	17.71	−2.25
1973	4.46	7.92	5.98	19.12	−2.41
1974	5.22	10.67	5.36	21.29	1.85
1975	4.57	4.69	4.41	14.12	−7.91
1976	4.19	13.78	1.68	19.84	3.33
1977	2.00	21.87	0.72	25.33	− 0.49
1978	4.02	11.96	3.18	19.70	− 9.96
1979	4.19	7.84	1.60	14.51	−12.57
1980	2.37	5.39	0.78	9.31	−15.04
1981	0.53	0.49	7.40	6.37	−17.99
1982	2.13	0.57	2.67	5.97	−15.69
1983	0.55	1.83	2.08	5.03	−12.66
1984	0.54	2.64	2.62	7.06	−5.47
1985	0.74	7.32	3.00	13.54	−0.92
Other Statistics					
Minimum	0.53	0.49	0.22	5.05	
Maximum	6.06	21.87	7.88	25.33	
Mean	3.66	7.11	3.98	15.30	

Source: Government of Côte d'Ivoire, *Les comptes de la nation,* various issues

HOSSR = Household Saving Rate
PADSR = Public Administration Saving Rate
NFFSR = Non Financial Firms Saving Rate
GNSR = Gross National Savings Rate
RESGAPR = Resource Gap Rate

as elsewhere, there do exist savings from firms in the form of retained earnings (mostly profits) for self-financing of activities.

In addition in Côte d'Ivoire, public or semi-public enterprises exist whose role is to finance investment. The *Fonds National d'Investissement* (FNI) and the *Société National de Financement* (SONAFI) are public intermediaries which try to mobilize savings from firms in order to finance investments. The FNI was established by a law of 12 February 1962. Its resources derived from a 10 per cent levy on the financial value of the assets of subscribing firms. In exchange, those who contribute receive certificates or some shares of FNI which will be reimbursed when the firms are making new investments. Weights are attributed to different classes of investment, following an order of need. For example, a weight of two is assigned to the purchase of bonds to SONAFI, a weight of three is assigned to industrial, agricultural or commercial investments, a weight of four for housing and construction, and so on. Accordingly, the FNI levy is not a tax as such, nor a loan, but a form of deposit for future investments. Those certificates of the FNI with two years or more, and not used by the contributing firms, are converted into assets loaned to the state and managed by the *Caisse Autonome d'Amortissement* (CAA), another public institution which manages public debt and public enterprise deposits. These bonds managed by the CAA are interest-bearing at a rate of about 5.5 per cent yearly and free of tax.

Contributing firms to the FNI are, therefore, expected to use their certificates to buy SONAFI bonds created in 1963. These bonds are guaranteed by the financial authorities and bear interest up to 9 per cent. They are income tax free. Hence, investment financed by corporate savings is developing, although slowly. Its full assessment remains difficult due to lack of coherent time series data.

Household savings

Another source of domestic savings is the household sector savings, to which we now turn. When economists and laymen speak of savings rates, they often have in mind the household sector share of savings out of Gross Domestic Product (GNP). We will focus in this section on this aspect of private and voluntary savings in Côte d'Ivoire. Table 10. 2 presents data on the evolution of household savings, along with data on Gross National Savings (GNS), on Public Administration Savings (PADS), on Gross National Capital Formation (GNCF) and on Resource Gap (RESGAP).

Based on the figures in Table 10.2, different saving rates can be computed. These saving rates are indicators of the propensity to save. They are what people generally refer to when speaking about saving rates. Table 10.3 presents savings as a percentage share of GDP.

The rates are revealing and higher than might have been expected given the low level of personal income in Côte d'Ivoire. For example, the Gross National Saving Rate (GNSR) is on average 15.30 per cent of GDP for the study period. According to the study by Rene Lenoir, adviser to the managing director of the Caisse des Depots et Consignations in France, the saving rates by regions of groups of countries are as follows (GNSR as a percentage of GDP):

Table 10.4   Gross national saving rates

Group of Countries	saving rate
I. OECD countries	22.3
II. Other developed countries	19.9
III. Oil exporting developing countries	32.9
IV. Oil importing developing countries	17.9
V. Least developed countries	6.6

Source: Rene Lenoir: Symposium on savings mobilization. Yaounde 10–15 December 1985

Overall, Côte d'Ivoire is close to group IV Gross National Saving Rates. Household saving rates, on the other hand, seem low. For the study period, the Ivoirian household average saving rate is about 3.66 per cent of GDP. It is about 12.6 per cent in the USA, 25.1 per cent in Italy and 25.0 per cent in Japan. The mean values of the households, public, and corporate saving rates show a clear picture. Public sector saving is almost twice the size of household saving as a percentage share of GDP. Ranking savings rates from the highest to the lowest gives the following result: (1) public sector savings; (2) non-financial firms' saving; and (3) household savings. This is an important piece of information when we examine the environmental factors influencing the gross national saving rate.

The determinants of household savings

We will estimate the determinants of households savings using different specifications. A log-linear functional form is used so that the estimated coefficients are elasticities which are useful in the interpretation of the results.

Specification 1

$$\text{Log Hos} = -1.46 + 0.94 \log \text{GDP} - 0.98 \log \text{IRATE}$$
$$(-1.23) \quad (2.62) \quad (-1.29)$$

$R^2 = 0.48 \qquad R^2 \text{ adjusted} = 0.44$

$\text{D.W} = 1.19 \qquad \text{DF} = 33$

t – statistics are in parentheses

The results are revealing. First the intercept is negative. This implies that there exists a minimum level of income above which saving is possible.

Secondly, GDP has the expected positive sign on households savings, and it is statistically significant. The interest rate, defined here as the official discount rate, has a negative but barely significant impact on household savings. Although the adjusted coefficient of determination is only 44 per cent, the message seems clear: the interest rate appears not to be a major determinant of household savings.

Income, on the contrary, is highly important. A 10 per cent increase in income would increase household sector savings by 9.4 per cent. This impact is very significant statistically. This confirms previous studies on the role of interest rate and income on savings generation in BCEAO countries.

Specification 2

To the previous equation we add the demographic factor by way of the population growth rate (DPOP). We obtain the following result.

$$\log \text{Hos} = -2.23 + 0.65 \log \text{GDP} - 0.53 \log \text{IRATE} + 1.40 \log \text{DPOP}$$
$$(-2.06) \quad (1.98) \quad (-0.79) \quad (3.72)$$

$R^2 = 0.67 \qquad R^2 \text{ adjusted} = 0.62$

$\text{D.W} = 1.53 \qquad \text{DF} = 21$

The introduction of the population factor brings some notable changes in the outcome. The intercept becomes more important and is now significant. This implies that if the population growth rate increases, the minimum income level required before savings could be generated also increases. In addition, the impact of income, although still positive and significant, is not as strong as earlier. A 10 per cent increase in income, in this specification, would increase household sector savings by 6.5 per cent. More interesting, the negative and non-significant effect of the interest rate has been confirmed. The negative interest rate–household saving elasticity coefficient is weak and clearly not significant.

The most noticeable result, so far, is the positive and significant impact of the population growth rate on household savings. A 10 per cent increase in DGDP would, it appears, yield a 14 per cent increase in household savings. This impact is very significant. Finally the coefficient of determination adjusted is now 62 per cent, which demonstrates a better explanatory power.

Specification 3

By introducing the income tax variable, and after correcting the serial correlation by the Cochrane-Orcutt iterative technique, we obtained the following results:

$$\log \text{Hos} = -8.16 + 1.97 \log \text{GDP} + 0.16 \log \text{IRATE} - 1.41 \log \text{INCOT}$$
$$\quad\quad (-1.33)\ (1.38) \quad\quad\quad (0.17) \quad\quad\quad\quad (-1.15)$$

$$\quad\quad + 1.59 \log \text{DPOP}$$
$$\quad\quad\quad (3.09)$$

$R^2 = 0.67 \quad\quad R^2 \text{ adjusted} = 0.58$

$\text{D.W} = 1.98 \quad\quad \text{DF} = 19$

The inclusion of income tax brings some changes in the estimated elasticity coefficients and significance. As was expected, income tax has a negative effect on household savings. As income tax increases, disposable income diminishes and therefore savings are reduced. Our results reveal that a 10 per cent increase in income tax would in principle yield a 14 per cent reduction in savings. The effect, however, is not significant statistically. Here, the interest rate has a positive but non-significant impact on savings. Population growth rate maintains its strong positive impact.

Specification 4

To incorporate the effect of the price level into the households' saving behaviour, we made an estimation in real terms, then deflated by the population level to get a picture of the real household saving per capita.

$$\log \text{RHOSC} = -6.58 + 3.44 \log \text{RGDPC} - 0.11 \log \text{INCOTC}$$
$$\quad\quad\quad (-1.76)\ (3.16) \quad\quad\quad\quad (-0.16)$$

$$\quad\quad -1.25 \log \text{IRATE}$$
$$\quad\quad (-3.22)$$

$R^2 = 0.72 \quad\quad R^2 \text{ adjusted} = 0.68$

$\text{D.W} = 2.22 \quad\quad \text{DF} = 21$

Variables used are as follows:

RHOSC :   Real household saving per capita
INCOTC :   Income tax per capita
IRATE :   Nominal interest rate level

The intercept is still negative. Income tax has a negative but non-significant effect. The interest rate has a negative but significant impact.

It appears from the above analysis that household sector savings are determined mostly by income. Increases in the interest rate appear to depress household savings in Côte d'Ivoire, and increases in the rate of income tax have an insignificant impact on savings.

The determinants of gross national savings

To get a broader picture of savings behaviour in the country, we examine the determinants of Gross National Savings (GNS).

To that end, we regressed GNS against Gross Domestic Product, interest rate and the growth rate of population.

$$\log \text{GNS} = -1.70 + 1.09 \log \text{GDP} - 0.64 \log \text{IRATE} + 0.19 \log \text{DPOP}$$
$$\quad\quad\quad (-1.40)\ (3.53)\quad\quad\quad (-1.29)\quad\quad\quad\quad (0.56)$$

$$R^2 = 0.91 \quad\quad R^2 \text{ adjusted} = 0.89$$

$$\text{D.W} = 1.29 \quad \text{DF} = 20$$

The results indicate that the intercept is negative, as in the case of household sector savings. This means that a minimum income level is required before Gross National Savings could be generated. Similarly, income has a strong and positive impact on Gross National Savings. A 10 per cent increase in income leads to a 10.9 per cent increase in GNS. This would imply that, on a national level, economic growth must occur to allow savings generation. Interest rate continues to have a negative impact on savings and the growth rate of the population exerts a positive influence on GNS, although not as significantly as in household sector savings.

4. The Mobilization of Formal and Informal Savings in Côte d'Ivoire

Now that we have identified the variables that determine savings, both at household and national level, we take on the mobilization strategy of such savings. In this section, we attempt to answer three fundamental questions:
1. Do savings exist within the Ivoirian economy?
2. If so, how can they be collected; and if not, how can they be generated?
3. How should savings be invested after their mobilization?

These questions are not new. They have been debated over the years in seminars, colloquia, conferences and symposia. Among these meetings was the 1971 conference in Milan (Italy) on savings mobilization in African countries; the Third International Symposium on Household Savings Mobilization held in Yaounde (Cameroon) on 10–14 December 1984; the colloquium on savings mobilization in Africa held in Cairo on 1–5 June 1985 by the Inter-African Association of Financial Institutions for Development and, more recently, the colloquium held in Yamoussokro, Côte d'Ivoire, 'Savings and its Mobilization in Africa' on 23–25 November 1987, initiated by the international confederation of alumni associations of the *Institut Technique de Banque* (IBT). All of these gatherings have discussed the issue in a general setting. In what follows, we discuss these issues in the Ivoirian context.

In answer to the first fundamental question, most people in the field, including economists and bankers, agree that savings potential does exist in Africa, and this has been confirmed in Côte d'Ivoire. It is estimated at about 15.3 per cent of GDP on average for the period since 1960. Nevertheless, the resource gap shows that more effort is needed to generate savings for a self-reliant economy. Empirical analysis has been based upon data from official sources only. These analyses concern savings generated in the formal or organized sector. In addition to the formal sector, there exists the so-called 'unorganized' financial market, the now widely adopted expression coined by U Tun Wai, in his article of 1957.

Analysis of the structure of formal savings

Here we look briefly at the Ivoirian banking and financial system. This system is controlled by the national branch of the BCEAO. In addition, the *Comité National de Credit* (CNC) ensures the regularity of the credits loaned to various economic agents of the country. The CNC is under the supervision of a council whose members are the Minister of Finance, two representatives of the state to the board of directors of BCEAO and four other members designated by the Ivoirian government. To ensure the legality of all banking operations, there exists a Control Commission for commercial banks and financial institutions, the chairman of which is the president of the *chambre des comptes* of the Supreme Court.

Under those safeguards, the banking networks comprise 40 establishments. These 40 institutions include 4 development banks, 11 commercial banks, 5 branches of foreign commercial banks, 7 bureaux of foreign banks and 14 financial institutions.

The four major commercial banks are (1) the *Société Générale de Banque en Côte d'Ivoire* (SGBCI) with 59 agencies; (2) the *Banque Internationale pour le Commerce et l'Industrie de Côte d'Ivoire* (BICICI) with 55 agencies; (3) the *Société Ivoirienne de Banque* (SIB) with 52 agencies; and (4) the *Banque Internationale pour l'Afrique de l'Ouest Côte d'Ivoire* (BIAOCI) with 37 agencies. All these banks are subsidiaries of French banks. SGBCI is a subsidiary of the *Société Générale France*; BICICI is a subsidiary of the *Banque Nationale de Paris* (BNP); SIB is a subsidiary of the *Credit Lyonnais* and BIAOCI is a subsidiary of BIAO, a bank which has no agency in France itself.

Michel Lelart (1986) remarked correctly that these banking institutions, invented more than one century ago in countries that have become industrialized, have transplanted almost unaltered into developing countries with a different cultural attitude towards money and savings. It is not, therefore, surprising that the formal system is predominantly used by the urban middle class.

Nonetheless, the Ivoirian banking system is composed of 342 permanent or temporary offices, the most developed network in sub-Saharan Africa. Of these, only 26 per cent are in Abidjan, the economic capital of the country. This reflects a real effort to get banking closer to the people, especially in rural areas. Each major city in the administrative setting (Préfecture or Sub-Préfecture) has its own commercial bank agency. Despite that, only a few civil servants and Lebanese traders use the system. What are the reasons? There are many obstacles to the use of the banks as a vehicle for savings in Côte d'Ivoire. Beyond the availability of disposable income, obstacles of a psychological, technical and sociological nature exist.

On the *sociological* side, one should note that investment in the favoured assets of residential housing and the acquisition of prestigious goods such as jewellery (in the south) and cattle (in the north) do not allow middle-income individuals to dispose of sufficient income to make financial savings on a large scale. These savings in kind have been studied by Denis Kessler. Another highly important sociological factor is in the significance of the extended family system. In such a system, solidarity which leads to a redistribution of the little portion of income not allocated to consumption of basic needs is a restraining factor for savings. Extended family pressure may squeeze saving capacity. Very expensive funerals, also a reflection of cultural honour, are common in Côte d'Ivoire as elsewhere in sub-Saharan Africa. These expenditures manifestly reduce savings capacity.

Among *psychological* factors, it should be noted that a lack of trust in the banking system prevails in Côte d'Ivoire. Such trust has been shaken by mismanagement. The failure of banks has occurred due to the violation of standard banking principles. For instance, a savings and loans association type of institution called the *Banque Nationale pour le Credit* (BNEC) recently closed down because of mismanagement. Some customers are still waiting to be reimbursed. This sort of attitude, in an institution towards which many individuals already harbour some suspicion, creates further mistrust among a largely illiterate, rural and highly cautious population. Another psychological barrier for some potential savers is the lack of confidentiality surrounding the banking system, which may expose savers to criticism and jealousy.

Among *technical* difficulties, despite the real effort to get bank offices closer to the population (especially in the countryside) the banking network is still located principally in provincial and regional headquarters. Those rural people who are willing to use it, dislike the cumbersome and time-consuming administrative process. 'Why should I wait so long to get hold of my own money?' is a common complaint.

To make things worse, the high rate of bounced and stolen cheques, has limited the popularization of current accounts. In most big stores in Abidjan, cheques are not accepted unless guaranteed by the bank or issued by expatriates. In the African culture 'money is what you see'. That is the reason why cash is so often used in transactions. This leads to a very high ratio of cash to the total money supply. Such preference for liquidity lowers the money multiplier and thereby restrains the money creation potential of the banking system. And since 'loans make deposits', the preference for cash reduces the value for bank deposits and hence slows down the banking habit.

For the 35 per cent of the Ivoirian population living in urban areas who are potential users of the formal financial system, there is another technical reason for the reluctance to use those institutions. They offer potential savers relatively low returns. Interest rates are subsidized in Côte d'Ivoire as in the rest of the UMOA countries. The purpose of this policy is to keep the cost to investors low. But the application of this policy has clearly reduced the incentive to save in the formal financial institutions. Our empirical analysis reveals a negative (though insignificant) impact of the interest rate on savings. These rates must be liberalized so as to reach a level from which they can positively affect savings.

To all of these drawbacks must be added the inability of formal institutions to deliver credit to small borrowers promptly when needed (funerals, school fees) and without elaborate paperwork. This is the strength of the informal financial sector. In the urban centres, parallel to the organized sector, there exist in Côte d'Ivoire many *tontine*, the most developed form of informal savings institutions.

Among the many authors who have studied such systems, Bouman (1977) called them more generally the 'Rotating Savings and Credit Associations or ROSCAS'. Time and space constraints do not allow us to go into detail on the working of ROSCAS, their size, how much savings they mobilize and their impact on the Ivoirian economy. However, according to a recent survey by Marcomer Gallup International in Senegal, Côte d'Ivoire, Cameroon, Gabon and Congo, about 28.6 per cent of the population in each country take part in a ROSCA, against the 13.2 per cent who hold bank accounts and 13.4 per cent who hold savings accounts.

In Côte d'Ivoire, according to estimates by some experts, ROSCAS savings are as high as CFA F700–800 billion, which is equivalent to the total value of demand deposits in the banking system as a whole. ROSCAS usually do not charge interest. The members are generally of the same ethnic group, of the same neighbourhood or of the same working place. ROSCA members are therefore homogeneous. ROSCAS are based upon trust and solidarity at the village community level. With ROSCAS, savings and credits are directly linked, whereas banks grant loans to 'unknown' individuals and require substantial collateral to protect them against the consequences of lack of information. The idea of collateral is, however, unknown among people of the same ethnic and cultural group in a ROSCA.

The informal financial sector in rural areas

As in other SSA countries, rural Côte d'Ivoire has its specific savings network. We can rank these savings in an increasing order of sophistication.

1. *Customary savings* which consist of individual or family thesaurization of precious metals (gold, jewellery, cattle) which is shown off to others.
2. *Labour savings*, which are chores on a family or whole-village basis. They consist of exchange of services on plantation work: cutting of weeds, harvesting, etc. These exchanges of services allow all peasants to save on labour costs.
3. *Cereal or other roots (yam) savings* realized on a family or village basis.
4. *Monetary family savings* accumulated by the family members under mattresses or in boxes in order to meet unanticipated and urgent events (deaths, weddings, festivals). This form of savings is often exposed to all kinds of risks: fire, destruction by mice, other natural causes.
5. *Savings in ROSCAS*, very informal and flexible associations which are guided nevertheless by very strict codes of conduct, the violations of which lead to an excommunication from all ROSCAS.
6. *Savings clubs*, which are like ROSCAS except that they are open to more people and can steer mutual savings into collective investments.
7. *Cooperative thrift and credit associations*, called *Caisse Rurale d'Épargne et de Prets* (CREP) in Côte d'Ivoire. They are institutions geared to mobilize savings in (4) and (5) and complement the savings club effort in (6) by offering to members individual or collective credit.

In the face of the rigid rules of commercial banks and the various and flexible forms of rural savings institutions, cooperative thrift and credit associations such as CREP appear to be the hope for a rural banking system of the future.

Monetary savings in CREP are determined by characteristics which can be grouped into three types. First, there are *anthropological factors* (privacy, security and credibility); next are the *socio-cultural factors* (availability, access, proximity, confidentiality); and finally *economic factors* (interest-bearing, proportionality, final use, function). The official banking system must take into account these factors if it is to offer services which correspond more effectively to the peasants' desired mode of savings. Among all these characteristics, privacy and security seem very important.

Indeed, peasants distinguish between what they term 'hot money' (*argent chaud*) and 'cold money' (*argent froid*). Hot money is money obtained by hard work, by individual effort which goes with a lot of 'sweating' under the hot sun. Cold money is money of the state, which comes from nowhere and can be spent carelessly. For peasants, hot money must stay hot and immediately usable. A mix with cold money causes hot money to disappear in the form of taxes (state), commissions (banking institutions), or in credit to 'unknown' customers.

New ways and means of savings mobilization

In the face of huge and growing 'underground' savings, the official banking system has made attempts in both rural and urban centres to bring these 'parallel' savings into the organized sector. In this organized sector, we discuss two cases: the new 'products' offered by banks to attract potential savings, and the role of the new Abidjan stock exchange. Jacques Chanard, General Secretary of BIAOCI, once observed that the banking and financial products offered to the public are often limited to straightforward time and deposit accounts. These two items cannot satisfy the various needs of a very heterogeneous group of savers. Recently, the four major commercial banks, SGBCI, BICICI, SIB and BIAOCI, have begun to offer differentiated accounts of the type already in existence in France and in other developed countries. For example, there is the 'plan épargne logement' (PEL) which is a time/deposit account. At maturity, these accounts may be transformed into low-interest housing loans; they are thus a project-specific form of savings in urban areas. But experience has revealed that PEL holders, at maturity, could not get the necessary loans, due to heavy administrative paperwork and red tape. This has discouraged many savers in PEL, including this author. To complement PEL and/or to overcome its rigidity, bankers launched another time deposit account called 'creditmatic'. It is like PEL. The main difference is that, at maturity, the holder automatically gets twice the size of the deposit with no conditions on how the money is to be used.

The role of interest rate

Denis Kessler, of the *Centre d'Étude et de Recherche sur l'Épargne, le Patrimoine et les Inégalités* in France, attributed the weakness of organized savings to the low or subsidized interest rate in most African countries, and especially in UMOA countries. He advised that interest rates must be raised, at the cost of high credit. Low rates favour a few borrowers at the expense of the majority who have no access to credit at all, even at high cost. These low rates create excess demand which generates the parallel market. In fact, Francois Kamajou's study in Cameroon (1980) revealed that the key to credit is not the interest rate but its ready availability. Some desperate borrowers have been willing to pay rates as high as 50 per cent, even 100 per cent or more. 'The fruit must fall where the tree stands'. Another reason for the reluctance of the rural potential savers is that commercial banks collect money in the countryside to grant loans to urban dwellers, whereas ROSCAS use their money where it is collected, implying no rural–urban capital transfers.

The Abidjan Stock Exchange

At the Yamoussokro colloquium, Tanoe Apagny, the President of the *Bourse des Valeurs d'Abidjan* (BVA) (the Abidjan Stock Exchange), clearly stated that the BVA was the best way to mobilize and invest new money in the Ivoirian economy into productive activities. Most loans from banks are not large enough to be invested in intermediate productive instruments. Rather, these loans go into the purchase of durable consumer goods often not manufactured in Côte d'Ivoire. Or they may go simply into the import of food products. In the long term, a change in consumption habits will be necessary. In the meantime, the BVA can use savings more effectively, in our view, than other financial institutions.

The process of creating the BVA began with the Law 74–353 of 24 July and the Decree 74–717 of 27 November, both of the year 1974. These regulate the structure of the financial market and the general organization of the stock exchange. The official opening of the BVA took place on 7 April 1976, with the first quotation session. Since then, the BVA has been part of the Ivoirian financial system. The BVA's major functions are (1) to organize and direct the securities market; (2) to check the regularity of transactions in the interest of security; and (3) to increase national capital formation.

With respect to its organization, the BVA is a commercial public entity with civil status and financial autonomy. It is under the supervision and control of the Minister of Finance. The Stock Exchange Council, the General Manager and Stock Registrar are the main functioning organs. Because of the lack of skilled and financially endowed professionals, and because of the low income of the brokers, the stockbroker function is performed by the four major commercial banks and, as of today, no individual can perform the brokerage function.

At the time of writing (1988) only 24 companies are listed on the stock market. Those companies are selected on the basis of CFA F100 million minimum of own funds and the capacity to put 20 per cent of their capital into the hands of the public on demand. These precautionary steps are taken to avoid any situation of illiquidity. Ivoirian Stock Exchange deals are transacted twice weekly, using the system of bids and calls. To avoid speculative manoeuvrings, only cash transactions are allowed and price variations are controlled from one session to the next one (3 per cent for bonds, 5 per cent for stocks).

The overall value of securities exchanged has increased. By putting more money into stock instead of bonds, economic agents revealed their preference for risky assets. Ivoirians show clearly that orthodox savings accounts are not the best instruments to attract savings. And since the average share price is not too high, most people can afford to buy shares for risky assets. Shareholders are encouraged by the prospect of casting a vote for the board of directors and also by the prospect of monitoring management through reports and balance-sheets. The BVA appears to be an adequate tool to collect and invest savings in productive activities.

In the rural sector, the most innovative organisation remains CREP, the cooperative thrift and credit institution. Taking its first step with the inauguration of Bonoua, by far the most important of all CREPS, the movement was established officially in 1976. The CREPS are intended to take over from the usurers who charged high interest rates in rural areas. It is also intended that CREPS offer small savers the possibility of collectively managing their savings. They aim to mobilize village savings, then to distribute them in the form of loans, allowing the Ivoirian rural population to control its own cooperative thrift organization. The operation has been a success. As of 31 September 1986, the movement had 74 CREPS with about CFA F480 million of assets and more than 3,500 members. But these CREPS have been through rough times, for political reasons. Indeed, the Office National de Promotion Rurale of the Ministry of Agriculture, which oversees the operation of CREP, was dissolved following a governmental reshuffle. CREPS were entrusted to the *Société Mutuelle de Promotion Rurale* (SMPR) of the Ministry of Rural Development which was born out of the Ministry of Agriculture. The SMPR was short-lived and gave birth to the Direction de la Mutualité et de la Cooperation (DMC) of the Ministry of Rural Development. The management of CREP was divided between two ministries. This has made it more difficult to lay down consistent guidelines for CREPS. Civil servants came and went, new faces appeared to the peasants, and all these movements brought mistrust into the minds of cautious rural people. Finally, a link could not be established between CREP and the pre-cooperative organization, which was also present in most villages. Moreover, the National Bank for Agricultural Development (BNDA) which receives the deposits of CREP funds, did not find appropriate financial investments to utilize these funds.

'Overground' savings or capital flight

So far we have dealt with on-ground savings, either organized in urban centres, or unorganized, parallel, 'underground' savings in the rural sector. But there is another phenomenon, a very sensitive one, which authors usually gloss over, consciously or unconsciously. This is the capital flight phenomenon. It may be called the 'overground' savings movement, because such savings usually pass over the national borders to another country, one which is more developed, say to Switzerland. What is capital flight?

According to Khan and Haque (1987), there is no precise definition of capital flight. The concept varies from one author to the next. At one end of the spectrum, all exports of private capital are instances of capital flight, be they short-term, long-term portfolio, share-taking or other investments. Authors use the expression capital flight when the country of origin is poor and where capital, by definition, is needed more than in the country of destination. But if one considers the canons of the free market and of liberal economics, this may be regarded not as capital flight but as a movement of capital in search of a higher reward. At the other end of the spectrum, we have the exit of capital for precautionary motives, based upon political or economic uncertainties in the country of origin. Here we may have a genuine case of 'capital flight' in the sense that these savings are a total loss for the country of origin. Khan and Haque contend that, 'if it were possible to repatriate funds accumulated by national residents, say Ivoirians, to foreign banks (in Switzerland or elsewhere), or at least reduce such phenomenon, LDCs heavily in debt could cope with the decline of foreign borrowings.'

In Côte d'Ivoire, as in other African countries, the phenomenon does exist, but no one knows exactly its magnitude. The managing director of the *Caisse Autonome d'Amortissement* (CAA) indicated at the Yamoussokro colloquium that 'overground' savings constitute one of the drawbacks of savings mobilization. The Ivoirian daily *Fraternité Matin* (September 1985) revealed that 'today we have Ivoirian citizens wealthier than Côte d'Ivoire', and continued, 'Capital flight towards foreign banks, especially Swiss banks, is a disease not unknown to our country. The low reward (interest rate) of bank accounts in our banks is one of the reasons. But, it is about time that the State, without renouncing its liberal options, regulated these abuses. The future of our economy depends upon that.' This quotation crystallizes common sentiments that capital flight hampers the mobilization of savings and must be stemmed, if possible by adopting appropriate fiscal and monetary measures, including lower income tax rates and higher interest rates.

5. Concluding Remarks

In the face of toughening conditions for foreign borrowings, the Ivoirian economy must generate more savings from domestic resources. This chapter reveals that a savings potential does exist in the Ivoirian economy. There are, however, many factors that hamper its mobilization.

Income tax rates must be reduced so as to allow a larger share of disposable income to remain in the hands of households. The role of interest rates is, as yet, uncertain. At the institutional level, more effort needs to be taken to make bank policy sympathetic to Ivoirian socio-cultural habits. ROSCAS and other cooperative thrift associations need further research. We need to explain the factors behind their success if we wish to integrate them into the extensive Ivoirian bank network. Fiscal incentives, the maintenance of bank confidentiality, higher interest rates and sustained economic growth may all be necessary to generate savings in the future and thereby reduce the dependence on foreign capital. The Abidjan Stock Exchange, by investing savings into productive activities, is potentially a very powerful instrument for generating savings from domestic resources.

References

Bedard, G. *et al.* (1983).'Argent "chaud" et argent "froid": la mobilisation de l'épargne rurale par les institutions de type cooperatif et son impact sur le developpement', in *Les Actes de l'Université Cooperative Internationale.*

Bouman, F. (1977). 'Indigeneous savings and credit societies in the third world – any message?', *Conference on Rural Finance Research,* San Diego.

Chambre d'Agriculture de Côte d'Ivoire (1987). 'Les Caisses Rurales d'Épargne et de Prets (CREP) dix ans apres', Colloque sur l'Épargne a Yamoussokro, 23–25 November.

Daubrey, Auguste (1973). 'La mobilization de l'épargne pour le developpement rural en Afrique', *Communication au 2e Congrès du Credit Agricole ,* Milan, September.

Domar, E. (1957). *Essays in the Theory of Economic Growth,* Oxford University Press, New York.

Fei, John and Paauw, Douglas S. (1965). 'Foreign assistance and self help: a reappraisal of development finance', *Review of Economics and Statistics,* August.

Frimpong-Ansah, J. H. (1987). 'Domestic resource mobilization in Africa', consultant's working file, African Development Bank, January.

Gaudran, Jacques (1987). 'Ces milliards qui échappent a l'Afrique', *Jeune Afrique Economie,* No. 101, November.

Harrod, R. F. (1948). *Towards a Dynamic Economics,* Macmillan, London.

Higgins, B. (1968). *Economic Development: Problems, Principles and Policies,* Norton & Company Inc., New York, revised edition.

Hirschman, A. O. (1958). *The Strategy of Economic Development,* Yale University Press, New Haven.

Horiaka, Yuji (1986). 'Pourquoi le taux d'épargne prive est-il si éleve au Japon', *Finances et developpement,* Vol. 23, No. 4 (December).

Kamajou, F.(1980). 'Subsidised interest rates and restricted agricultural credit in LDCs', *Savings and Development,* No. 2.

Kessler, D. (1984). 'Domestic savings and foreign capital flows', *Saving for Development,* New York.

Khan, M. and Haque, N. U. (1987). 'La fuite des capitaux des pays en developpement', *Finances et Developpement,* Vol. 24, No. 1, March.

Laffite, Alain (1987). 'Les tontines dans le developpement auto-centre', *Communaute Africaine,* No. 1.

Lelart, Michel (1986). *L'Épargne Informelle en Afrique,* Centre Africain d'Étude Monetaire, No. 2.

Lenoir, Rene (1985). Symposium on Savings Mobilization, Yaounde, 10–15 December.

Lewis, Arthur (1955). *The Theory of Economic Growth,* Allen and Unwin, London.

Miracle, M. P. *et al.* (1980). 'Informal savings mobilization in Africa', *Economic Development and Cultural Change,* Vol. 28, No. 4, pp. 701–24.

Nurske, Ragnar (1953). *Problems of Capital Formation in Underdeveloped Countries,* Blackwell, Oxford.

U Tun Wai (1957). 'Interest rates outside the organized money markets of underdeveloped countries', *IMF Staff Papers,* Vol. 4.

U Tun Wai and Patrick, Hugh T. (1973). 'Stock and bond issues and capital markets in less developed countries', *IMF Staff Papers,* Vol. 20, pp. 253–317.

11 Mobilizing Savings in Cameroon

Rosemary Nana-Fabu

1. Financing Development in Cameroon

During the 1980s Cameroon was regarded as the paradigm for African development. In 1981, the World Bank reclassified Cameroon from a low-income to a middle-income country with a GNP per capita income of more than $560. Unlike many African countries, Cameroon enjoyed favourable economic growth rates. The GDP average annual growth rate during the period 1980 to 1985 was 8.6 per cent compared with 3.4 per cent for the same period in Nigeria, – 1.7 per cent in Côte d'Ivoire, 3.3 per cent in Senegal, – 0.7 per cent in Ghana and 3.1 per cent in Kenya. Production in Cameroon is relatively diversified and the country earns foreign exchange from a wide array of products, whilst maintaining self-sufficiency in food. Until recently, the revenue obtained from oil exports has meant a surplus in the trade balance and has also contributed to a reasonable level of creditworthiness.

The stagnation in aid flows, however, and the collapse in the price of primary commodities (especially of oil) have now combined to reduce sharply net resource flows. According to a report (December 1986) on the Cameroon economy, in October 1986 the spot market price for Cameroon's Kole crude averaged only $12.95 a barrel, compared with the $27.30 average for the third quarter of 1985. Assuming an overall average price for 1986 of $12.80, oil earnings for the year were projected to be some $950 million less than in 1985, the equivalent of $2.6 million a day. Given such a huge loss of earnings it comes as no surprise that Cameroon experienced a debt crisis. The total outstanding public external debt at the end of 1986 stood at $3.17 billion as compared with $544 million in 1976.

An important factor which exacerbated the problem of indebtedness is Cameroon's membership of the Franc Zone (FZ). By virtue of the equivalency of currencies principle, any modification in the value of the French Franc (FF) *vis-à-vis* other foreign currencies automatically and fully affects the CFA Franc.[1] In order to maintain a fixed exchange rate, the CFA Franc has to be devalued by the same percentage as the FF each time the latter is devalued. This was notably the case in August 1969, October 1981, June 1982 and March 1983. The devaluation *vis-à-vis* the US dollar was 12.3 per cent in 1980, 21 per cent in 1981, 15 per cent in 1982 and 15.8 per cent in 1983 (Guy Martin, 1986). This gives an idea of the significant gains that the African central banks might have realized, had they held most of their resources in US dollars during that period.

An important negative effect of devaluation of the Franc Zone was to increase the amount of capital and interest on the foreign debt of the African countries, denominated in foreign currencies. The more these countries were indebted to strong currency countries, the greater the additional amounts due. It is estimated that 80 to 90 per cent of LDC foreign debts are denominated in US dollars. Other sources estimate that devaluations account for 60 per cent to 70 per cent of the present external indebtedness of the FZ countries. Cameroon is a case in point. Its external debt amounted to $2,487 million in 1980. On the basis of the then prevailing exchange rate ($1 = 4.55FF), Cameroon needed FF11.32 billion (or CFA F565.80 billion) to settle its debt. In January 1983, as a result of the FF devaluation ($1 = 7.43FF), Cameroon owed FF18.48 billion (or CFA F932.92 billion) (UN Statistical Year Book, 1983/4). Thus the same debt had increased from CFA F565.80 billion to CFA F932.92 billion between 1980 and 1983.

This worrisome aspect of the FZ system has had serious implications for the Cameroon economy. Firstly, Cameroon's problem of increasing external indebtedness is to some extent outside the control of the government. Secondly, the fixed exchange rate policy in the FZ system means that Cameroon is compelled to hold most of its foreign exchange reserves in a constantly depreciating currency with consequential net losses. Thirdly, the scope for action is very limited as far as devaluation is concerned. Indeed, recommendations made by the International Monetary Fund (IMF) in this area are very ineffective.

Although Cameroon's current external debt is relatively small compared to other African countries (e.g., Nigeria, $18.348 billion in 1985; Côte d'Ivoire, $8.446 billion in 1985), the effects of the debt should not be underestimated, in particular the debilitating effect it has on overall economic development. The total interest payment on long-term debts alone has increased from $5 million in 1970 to $133 million in 1985. The servicing of external public debt took up about CFA F58,000 million in 1983, representing about 11.9 per cent of export earnings.

These figures are an indication of the extent of the problems facing the economy in the 1980s especially as regards the financing of economic development. The difficulties of financing assume different forms in different sectors of the Cameroonian economy. They stem from a common base: the low capacity of the economy to create income, which, in turn, limits the ability to accumulate capital out of current output. The inadequacy of domestic savings becomes acute when efforts are made to accelerate the growth rate.

During the 20 years from 1966 to 1986, domestic capital formation considerably increased and higher levels of domestic savings were attained. In the same period, gross domestic savings increased from CFA F22.5 billion to CFA F1,232.7 billion (World Bank World Tables 1987, 4th edition). Gross fixed capital formation increased from CFA F24.1 billion in the period 1964/5, to CFA F936.0 billion in 1984. As a percentage of GDP, gross domestic savings stood at 13 per cent in 1965, and 28 per cent in 1986, while gross domestic investment was 13 per cent in 1965 and 25 per cent in 1986. Per capita GNP increased from $340 in 1977 to $910 in 1986. These figures imply that the marginal propensity to save is high.

In spite of considerable increases in domestic savings, the Cameroonian economy has yet to reach a stage of self-sustaining growth, and the investment targets given in the Sixth Five-Year Development Plan require further increases in domestic savings. The aim of the government has been to reduce the inflow of foreign aid in the future. Domestic savings must be increased.[2] This is not an easy task.

The windfall gains from the coffee and cocoa boom from 1975 to 1977, coupled with the discovery of offshore oil, which went into production in 1978, had a favourable impact on the capacity of the Cameroonian economy to save and invest. With the decline in the terms of trade for primary commodities in recent years, one cannot hope for a recurrence of this bounty. In addition, the buoyancy of the Cameroonian economy (from the mid-

1970s to the early 1980s) attracted foreign capital which enhanced the ability of both public and private sectors to create savings. Recent years have seen a marked decline in foreign aid and foreign borrowing.

Social justice, moreover, is the principle advocated in the Sixth Five-Year Development Plan. As more equity is sought by the government in the distribution of income, it is increasingly difficult to raise the marginal propensity to save.[3]

On the other hand, there are some factors, the effects of which are more favourable. In the Sixth Five-Year Development Plan, it is proposed to channel funds into more productive areas. This is a reaction against previous policy, especially in the public sector, where investment was directed towards areas which had low rates of return and created little in the way of a reinvestible surplus. Private sector investments, on the other hand, while frequently showing high profitability, were also characterized by a low social rate of return.

In addition, reforms visualized in the Plan aim to improve the efficiency of financial institutions in both the public and private sectors, thus increasing their capacity to use funds more effectively.

2. Foreign Capital, The Commercial Banking Sector and Domestic Savings

The Cameroon government has aimed to maximize foreign investment and, until recently, foreign investors continued to find the investment climate favourable. In 1980, foreign investors (principally French, British, American, Dutch and West German) accounted for investment of the order of CFA F197 billion, about 50 per cent more investment than in 1979. Net direct investment increased from $16 million in 1970 to $50 million in 1986. (World Development Report, 1988).

One of the mechanisms designated by the government to encourage foreign private investment is the revised liberal investment code, Law No. 84–03 of July 1984, contained in the investment code, and guaranteeing foreign investors the free transfer of profits and income realized from invested capital (Part II, section 97). It provides foreign firms with priority status, exemptions from duties and taxes levied on local purchases and a reduced rate of 5 per cent for import duties and taxes. In addition, the National Investment Corporation (NIC), created in 1964, is responsible for investment projects with foreign partners. The Cameroon Development Bank (CDB) was created solely to promote and encourage investment, by financing investment projects and providing technical assistance and credit to entrepreneurs.

These measures seem to have paid off. In 1980, in the 100 largest enterprises in Cameroon, foreign capital contributed CFA F28.6 billion or 48 per cent of the total capital. (Ndongko, 1986). Cameroonian efforts to attract foreign investment have proved so successful that foreign capital dominates in most industrial sectors. As Table 11.1 indicates, foreign capital is dominant in the food industry (81 per cent) drinks (69 per cent), tobacco (75 per cent), textiles (73 per cent), timber and wood processing (80 per cent) and material processing (76 per cent). An interesting feature in Table 11.1 is the predominance of French interest in activities such as food (72 per cent), tobacco (75 per cent) and metal processing (72 per cent). This illustrates France's predominant role in the Cameroon economy, even after more than two decades of independence.

The high degree of participation of foreign capital in the banking sector in Cameroon serves to highlight the importance of the role commercial banks can play in mobilizing domestic resources. Though they can be major mobilizers of personal savings, in Cameroon unfortunately they tend to concentrate branches in the larger towns, attracting deposits from the urban dwellers, while doing very little to mobilize the savings of country people.

Table 11.1   Sectoral investment participation (1980) (in million CFA Francs)

	Total	Total %	Public %	Private %	Total foreign %	Total French %
Agro-industry	16,185	81	76	5	19	17
Food industries	2,388	19	10	9	81	72
Drinks	5,913	31	11	20	69	49
Tobacco	1,679	25	–	25	75	75
Textile industries	3,890	27	19	8	73	37.5
Leather products	2,370	77	59	18	23	–
Timber processing	5,055	20	19.8	0.2	80	39
Chemical industries	4,520	43	24	19	57	46
Construction materials	3,088	52	51	1	48	17
Metal processing	9,153	24	23	1	76	72
Paper & pulp processing	250	100	–	100	–	–
Gas, electricity & water	5,974	99	99	–	1	1
Total (estimated)	59,556	52	44	8	48	34.5

Source: Ndongko (1986:93)

The banks contend that the management of small savings accounts is not profitable because deposits are small, accounts numerous and the large number of withdrawals costly to handle. Small savers often have difficulty in obtaining loans from commercial banks, even if they have deposits there. It is not surprising that small-scale farmers in Cameroon are generally unable to use banks. Research carried out among employees of the Cameroon Development Corporation (CDC) in 1978 showed that very few of them used banks for saving or credit purposes (DeLancey, 1978). Similarly, in research studies in 1983 among credit union members, only 10 per cent of the interviewees had savings in a bank. DeLancey notes that only civil servants or wage-employed persons whose salaries are paid directly to the bank by the employer, or whose income is regular and large enough to take advantage of certain benefits of the bank, make use of its facilities. This also applies to traders with sizeable incomes who have contact with urban areas, or export crop farmers who receive large lump sum payments at harvest time. They too maintain balances in bank accounts.

The emphasis placed by commercial banks on short-term loans for working capital, or for the financing of trade, means that the community must look elsewhere for medium-term financing, which is mostly limited to long-standing customers, generally well-established firms. Medium-term credit to small- and medium-size enterprises is limited because of the risks and costs involved. Table 11.2 shows that short-term financing by the banking sector accounted for more than 60 per cent of total lending during the period 1980–5. Medium-term financing averaged about 26 per cent. Long-term financing has actually decreased from 2.5 per cent in 1980/1 to 1.2 per cent in 1984/5. Generally, medium-term loans are made in consortial form with the Cameroon Development Bank as the lead bank. This is in order to benefit from the Bank's extraordinary recovery privilege, which is equivalent to the collection right of the government. Commercial banks claim that in order to extend more long-term loans, they need similar recovery procedures for long-term liabilities.

Since the commercial banks have sufficient funds to finance purely orthodox banking activities and obtain satisfactory profits therefrom, they see no reason to broaden the range

Table 11.2   Financing of credits in the Cameroon economy (1980–5) (per cent)

	80–81	81–82	82–83	83–84	84–85
1. BEAC lending (re-financing)	13.2	18.9	20.2	20.3	18.4
2. Commercial bank lending	82.3	76.8	76.1	76.4	78.3
3. BCD lending	4.5	4.3	3.7	3.3	3.3
Total credits to the economy	100	100	100	100	100
Breakdown:					
short-term	69.4	68.9	72.0	72.2	72.0
medium-term	28.1	29.1	26.4	26.4	26.8
long-term	2.5	2.0	1.6	1.4	1.2

Source: The Sixth Five-Year Development Plan of Cameroon (1986-91)

Table 11.3   Savings by peasants: Mbouda branch of Société Camerounaise de Banque

Date	No. of passbook savings accounts	Total (in m. CFA Francs)	Dept.	Population
31/7/82	2,000	237	Bamboutos	198,000
30/6/83	2,300	299	–	–
30/6/84	2,500	300	Mbouda	80,000

Source: Association Professionelle des Banques, Yaounde, Cameroon, 1984

of their savings mobilization activities to attract more savings, particularly in the form of time deposits which would enable them to increase their medium-term and long-term portfolio. This reluctance on the part of the banks to broaden their activities is strengthened by the fact that the banks' main depositor is the public sector. However, things are changing. With the decline in the government's cash flow from oil, in particular during 1986, public sector deposits have been withdrawn, resulting in a liquidity shortage. Banks are now faced with two options, either borrow offshore or set out to mobilize local savings. Small banks find it difficult to borrow offshore because they are tied to Cameroon's fixed interest rate system, which effectively means that only the 'prime names' can get credit this way.

On the other hand, the French banks could alleviate the situation to some extent by taking advantage of the Franc Zone regulations that allow them to draw funds from their parent banks. It should be noted, however, that the advent of the EC's single market in 1992 threatens the continued existence of the Franc Zone. With such uncertainty, most of these banks will need to look again at a policy of mobilizing local savings.

Some commercial banks like the Société Camerounaise de Banque (SCB) are already carrying out successful savings mobilization in the rural as well as the urban sector. The SCB has taken bold steps, not only in extending loans to small- and medium-size enterprises, but also by adopting a system of branch offices in order to extend loans to small farmers and mobilize savings from them. A typical example is that of the Mbouda branch (see Table 11.3). The number of passbook savings accounts increased from 2,000 in July 1982 to 2,500 in June 1984. Similarly, the amount deposited increased from CFA F237 million to CFA F300 million in the same period. SCB's experience with such a system revealed some important characteristics of savings behaviour of these peasant farmers, which are summarized below.

1. Amounts deposited by peasant farmers are likely to remain on deposit for some time. Farmers do not feel the need to withdraw their money frequently, although they are anxious to be assured of the possibility of doing so should the need arise.
2. Adopting the practice of depositing money at the bank is highly susceptible to effective public relations and the influence of personalities. Personal contact between the depositor and the depository is very important. The farmer does not deposit his money with an abstract institution but rather entrusts it to a familiar person.
3. In areas where peasant farmers receive resources from a body like the cooperative union, it is easy to encourage savings by having such resources paid out by a banking institution, which can thus introduce the farmers to the idea of opening accounts.

It could be argued that if commercial banks were to follow in the footsteps of the SCB, then the volume of savings in the country would increase significantly. Such would be the case, however, only if capital flight from the country were to be reduced. As a result of the principles prevailing within the Franc Zone and the policy of low interest rates in Cameroon, inevitably there has been significant capital flight from Cameroon towards France, where the interest rates are much higher.[4] The Cameroon investment code's provision of guarantees for the repatriation of earnings and profits within and outside the Franc Zone has exacerbated the problem.[5] The extent of capital flight from the country over the years is difficult to estimate, but it is the general feeling that as much capital has left the country as has entered it from abroad. If total disbursements of public guaranteed and private non-guaranteed external capital amounted to $481 million in 1986 compared with $40 million in 1970 (World Development Report, 1988), then capital flight could be substantial. In this respect, the economic benefit of foreign private investments in Cameroon is almost completely offset by repatriated earnings and profits.

Capital flight, by siphoning off domestic savings into purchases of foreign assets, can reduce the domestically generated resources available for domestic investment and may leave a country more reliant on foreign capital than it would otherwise have been. It is difficult to determine which private capital outflows are properly to be described as 'flight' and which represent other outflows, such as the accumulation of foreign assets for transactions purposes, by enterprises and banks. Until the onset of the debt crisis, the outflow of private savings was generally returned, often in the form of bank loans to the public sector, and the Cameroon economy consequently suffered little or no net outflow of resources. But circumstances have changed radically with the debt crisis. The private sector continues to attempt to avoid the consequences of 'financial repression' and inefficient domestic financial markets, and the banks that receive private savings are no longer willing to lend money to countries with debt-servicing problems. Consequently, capital flight in a country like Cameroon has real resource transfer implications.

3. Savings Behaviour in Cameroon

In this section we consider an important question for Cameroon: how to channel savings accumulated by households into productive investment. Savings attitudes of households are linked to many variables, including current income, interest rates and socio-demographic characteristics.

Cameroon (classified as a 'middle-income' developing country with a GNP per capita income in 1986 of $910) has an income distribution pattern between the rural and the urban sector which is highly unequal. Minimum monthly wages for the primary sector are well below those of the secondary/tertiary sector. Nevertheless, research carried out on savings propensities amongst rural households in Cameroon does indicate a high savings propensity amongst these groups. For example, J. F. Gadway, in his survey of credit unions in Cameroon in 1986, noted that the 249 rural families that he interviewed had, on average, CFA F295,286 in financial savings. At CFA F350 per dollar, this amounted to an average of $844 per rural household, an astounding figure comparable with the 1984 per capita GNP of $880.

Reliable estimates on savings from the informal financial sector are scarce, but judging from various observations made of savings societies in Cameroon, the indication is that savings in this sector are substantial. According to *The New York Times* (30 November, 1987) some monthly *Njangi* pots are now in excess of $1 million.[6] It comes as no surprise that bankers in Cameroon complain that such savings societies (*Njangis*) draw money out of the banking system. Deposit rates do not exist in these savings societies, and the lending rates, if any at all, are generally low, hence the observation by V. De Lancey (1988) that some enterprising members of these societies are now 'buying' money from rural savings societies at low interest rates and then 'reselling' it in Douala (a large town) at higher interest rates.

Another survey carried out in 1988 on credit unions in Cameroon, whose members consist predominantly of rural households with low incomes, revealed a significant growth rate of savings during the period 1969–85 (DeLancey, 1988). Table 11.4 shows that share savings increased in nominal terms every year, from CFA F21,500 in 1969 to CFA F6,471.59 million in 1985. DeLancey notes that although the percentage increase has slowed over the years, it has never been less than 20 per cent in any year. In view of these findings, and taking into account the low real interest rate structure that prevails in Cameroon, it is difficult to agree with the perception of a simple positive correlation between rates of interest and savings in the Cameroonian context. Variables other than the interest rate structure or interest rate policy influence the savings behaviour of rural households.

Factors such as the existence of acceptable and reliable financial institutions, and the general societal attitudes towards consumption and accumulation of wealth, seem to influence savings behaviour in Cameroon strongly. As regards the former, financial institutions like commercial banks find it unprofitable to operate in rural areas due to low business volume, poor infrastructure, high administrative costs and the difficulty of getting collateral for any advances made. Rural households do not consider the banks as serving their interests and, because they are often situated far from their locality, there is less incentive to open accounts in these institutions. On the other hand, the SCB's success with its Mbouda branch illustrates that with the existence of an acceptable and reliable financial institution, household savings behaviour can be influenced.

Societal attitudes also influence savings behaviour in Cameroon. Attitudes are very susceptible to the changing economic environment. During the long period of economic progress in the country (from independence in 1960 to the early 1980s), personal evaluation, confidence, security and social status depended much on luxury consumption. But the economic situation has changed. Cameroonians are faced with recession. To prevent erosion of their gains, it is perceived necessary to invest productively, through saving. M. Rowlands (1988), observes that in Cameroonian society today, confidence and security depend on the 'massivity of capital accumulation and investment'.

All this means that in assessing household savings behaviour, interest rates are not to be regarded as the single most influential factor. Econometric studies now tend to be supplemented by household surveys of a more sociological nature. In Cameroon, a large proportion of low-income households, especially in the agricultural sector, own their own homes. Such households, lacking access to investments offering rates of interest that would protect them from inflation, often choose property as a form of savings providing a constant return in real terms and protection against inflation.

Table 11.4   Growth of the credit union movement in Cameroon: 1969–85

Date	Membership		Share savings		
	Number	% change	'000s CFA	% change	Average
12/69	5,200	–	21,500	–	4,135
12/70	8,470	62.9	40,700	89.3	4,805
12/71	13,975	65.0	89,005	118.7	6,369
12/72	19,268	37.9	142,861	60.5	7,414
12/73	22,514	16.8	224,124	65.9	9,995
12/74	24,969	10.9	354,969	58.4	14,216
12/75	31,236	25.1	549,732	54.9	17,599
12/76	35,040	12.2	777,432	41.4	22,186
12/77	37,357	6.6	985,941	26.8	26,392
12/78	36,662	(1.9)	1336,080	38.6	37,261
12/79	40,524	10.5	1799,418	31.7	44,404
12/80	41,197	1.7	2338,517	30.0	56,764
12/81	44,778	8.7	2939,424	25.7	65,644
12/82	47,888	6.9	3583,740	21.9	74,836
12/83	50,042	4.5	4307,510	20.2	86,078
12/84	53,016	5.9	5328,310	23.7	100,504
12/85	58,604	10.5	6471,590	21.5	110,429

Source: V. De Lancey (1988: 27)

Socio-demographic characteristics

Education

It is widely argued that illiteracy amongst households, especially rural households in LDCs, is a major constraint on savings. In a narrow context, it could be argued that lack of education leads to little understanding of formal banking procedures. In a wider sense, it could be said that lack of education may hinder the capacity to formulate and carry through rational economic decisions. These arguments have little plausibility in the Cameroonian context. First, some of the most successful indigenous businessmen in Cameroon are not highly educated. Second, until the discovery of offshore oil in 1978, a growing agricultural sector supported the Cameroonian economy. The majority of the labour force in agriculture is only educated to primary level, yet the rural sector is thriving. The study carried out by V. De Lancey in 1975/6, on a total of 228 wage-earning and occasionally employed women on a tea estate in Cameroon, illustrates this point. It was noted that the women were not highly educated: 86 per cent of the waged employees and 53 per cent of the occasionally employed had no education at all. Only 4 per cent of the wage earners and 21 per cent of the occasional workers had completed primary school, while only one of the women, the midwife employed at the clinic, had continued beyond primary school to obtain professional training. In total, this group of women had very little education, but De Lancey's findings revealed a high savings capacity among the group. Third, Rotating Savings Societies (RSS) in Cameroon originated in the rural sector and are run in a very sophisticated manner. S. Haggblade, in his study of these societies, notes that they are 'becoming sophisticated tools for credit distribution with written contracts, collateral requirements and interest rate charges'.

Population

The size of a household, age structure and other demographic characteristics affect household behaviour. But a consensus has yet to be obtained as to whether the above-named variables have a positive or negative effect on household saving behaviour.

As regards household size, Snyder (1974) found that the probability of positive saving for a sample of Sierra Leonean households was unaffected by household size. Large and small households were equally likely to have positive savings. This does not mean that large and small households were saving the same amount. Most probably, larger households save more, but this is difficult to determine because in most studies the savings function is expressed in per capita terms. Household size is not a separate variable.

The age-dependency effect, on the other hand, postulates that rapid population growth raises the ratio of children to working adults and diverts household income from saving towards consumption. Nevertheless, as A. C. Kelly observes, a positive impact of children on saving can result if their presence increases family income more than their impact on consumption. Similar relationships will hold if the bequest motive is strong (e.g., the desire to leave improved land to surviving sons) and if the definition of saving includes human capital such as education. The latter motive is very important in the Cameroonian context, because many surveys carried out on indigenous savings societies reveal education to be one of the principal reasons for saving. For example, in a survey conducted by F. J. Bouman (1976) on 54 members of a Cameroon saving society comprising farmers (60 per cent), artisans (20 per cent), traders (13 per cent) and others (7 per cent), education was shown to be the second most popular motive for saving. Similarly, a baseline survey, carried out in 1983 on eight credit unions in Cameroon, in which loan applications were examined and the purposes of loans tabulated, showed that nearly 31 per cent of all loans taken were for educational purposes, 25 per cent for health, 13 per cent for building, 11 per cent for consumption, 10 per cent for farming and 9 per cent for trade (Table 11.5). These percentages indicate that the largest total sum of money loaned was for education (DeLancey, 1988).

Importance is attached to education in Cameroonian society because education is seen as a form of investment. The amassing of assets in human, rather than physical, form is in response to imperfect capital markets and poorly developed economic and social institutions. In this respect, children may represent a means by which saving can take place. Thus the net impact on savings of this apparent transfer of resources will depend in part on the relative productivity of human rather than physical capital formation.

4. Policies for Mobilizing and Fostering More Effective Allocation of Domestic Savings

Savings behaviour in Cameroon reflects, to a large extent, the inadequacy of financial instruments in the country. It also highlights the fact that an adequate financial structure constitutes an integral element in any growth-orientated stabilization strategy. While adequate monetary control instruments improve monetary policy and promote efficient use of resources, additional structural measures may be required to strengthen the financial sector's role in enhancing the generation and allocation of domestic savings. Such measures include the development of money markets, integration into the formal system of unregulated financial institutions, and improved supervision of the financial institutions and instruments.

The underdeveloped state of the capital market is an important factor affecting the growth of long-term savings and their efficient use in Cameroon. There are no joint stock companies in Cameroon in the real sense of the word. Investment banks or other intermediary institutions are non-existent, or do not operate in ways which would develop the capital market. The lack of public joint stock companies makes it impossible to offer

Table 11.5   Total number and purpose of loans by type of credit union

Type of credit union: small farmers production credit

Purpose of loan	Babanki Tungo	Banten	Ntundip	Tombel Town	Total	%
Education	NA	2	20	4	26	21.3
Trade	NA	2	22	4	28	23.0
Building	NA	6	9	6	21	17.2
Farming	NA	7	10	7	24	19.7
Health	NA	5	16	1	22	18.0
Consumption	NA	0	1	0	1	0.8
Other	NA	0	0	0	0	0.0
Total	NA	22	78	22	122	100.0

Type of credit union: rural

Purpose of Loan	Bangem	Jakiri	Total	%
Education	72	29	100	40.7
Trade	25	23	48	19.5
Building	14	13	27	11.0
Farming	8	19	27	11.0
Health	9	15	24	9.8
Consumption	17	3	20	8.1
Other	0	0	0	0
Total	145	101	246	100.1

Type of credit union: wage earner

Purpose of loan	Mamfe PWD	Tombel CDC	Total	%
Education	37	183	220	28.9
Trade	3	23	26	3.4
Building	11	92	103	13.5
Farming	0	66	66	8.7
Health	4	236	240	31.5
Consumption	9	98	107	14.0
Other	0	0	0	0.0
Total	64	698	762	100.0

Source: V. DeLancey (1988: 35)

shares to the market. This situation helps explain why the household sector continues to direct most of its savings towards traditional outlets, that is housing or real estate.

On the other hand, there are indications that in recent years the propensity of the private sector to invest in industrial activities has been increasing and that businessmen are attempting to meet a steadily growing proportion of these increased investments from sources other than their own capital. Over the past few years, loan funds have gained in importance in the financing of private industrial investments. This suggests that businessmen, instead of forming joint stock companies and attracting the savings of the household sector as participating capital, are following a course of relying heavily on bank credit and foreign resources in order to retain ownership of their enterprises. This can be self-defeating for the Cameroonian government in its efforts to encourage private initiatives. It can also lead to over-concentration in capital markets.

Businessmen and the household sector depend more and more on loan funds. Given such a situation, the tendency for most commercial banks is to raise the rate of interest, in an attempt to screen out untrustworthy borrowers. Cameroon's membership of the Franc Zone, however, indirectly constrains any action taken by commercial banks to raise interest rates. However, studies carried out by Stiglitz and Weiss have shown that raising the rate of interest may increase the average riskiness of the projects a bank is financing. This is because borrowers switch to riskier projects or because safer projects become relatively less attractive and so investors with safe projects do not apply for loans (adverse selection aspect). The result is that the effect on the riskiness of the loans may outweigh the direct gain to the bank from increasing the interest rate.

These problems stem from informational imperfections in the capital market. The informational problem facing most banks in Cameroon is that they do not know how the money they lend is being invested. In order to ease access to credit by small and medium-size enterprises (SMEs), the Bank of Central African States (BEAC) in 1974 made it mandatory for commercial banks to lend a minimum of 20 per cent of their short-term credits to Cameroonian SMEs. However, in most cases these requirements have been met by disguising personal loans and housing loans as SME loans. The result has been high costs and high rates of default. Most importantly, the link between credit and productive capacity is severed.

This has prompted some writers on agricultural credit in LDCs to refer to credit, appropriated by financial institutions and used unproductively by the borrowers, as 'social credit'. In the case of Cameroon, H.F. Illy used this terminology in direct reference to cooperatives which were set up in the mid-1950s in Cameroon as pilot projects to grant credits to farmers, in particular, in reference to CCMs (Cooperatives de Credit Mutuel). A study was conducted on one of these cooperatives which comprised a relatively small group of 38 arabica coffee farmers who had the intention of increasing production. On this occasion, borrowers' requirements were not met by disguising personal and housing loans as being for agricultural production. Instead, the bank yielded to pressures from its customers to distribute loans for the construction of houses. In this case, the loans were 'unproductive' because they were not matched by a higher income from the marketing of cash crops. The use of insecticides dropped by 50 per cent in the same period (H. F. Illy). The result of this was an increase in outstanding debts. In 1958, only 1.2 per cent of debts were outstanding; in 1960 this figure moved to 8.3 per cent; and in 1962 it was 32.5 per cent. This culminated in the termination of the whole project in 1965.

Virtually all the aforementioned shortcomings echo the problems of the financial institutions set up by governments in LDCs. Two fundamental problems can be traced in today's agricultural credit institutions: high costs and high rates of default which are consequential on the intertwining of the agricultural credit and other credit (e.g., for housing) and the fact that the latter type of credit predominates over agricultural credit which could secure the repayment of debt. This confirms empirical research carried out by von Pischke *et al.* (1983), on loan delinquency in agricultural programmes in LDCs. This revealed that loan deliquency rates are not always high on agricultural loans, even when the lenders are state-owned banks with development objectives. Costa Rica is cited as an example of a country where deliquency rates have been found to be lower in agricultural than in non-agricultural loans.

The implication of this finding in the Cameroonian context helps unravel some of the problems that have constantly plagued financial institutions in the country, such as the earlier CCMs and FONADER in the present day.[7] In the case of CCMs, Table 11.6 shows a decline in the production credits from CFA F127 million in 1958/9 to CFA F45 million in 1960/1, while housing credits increased from CFA F14 million in 1958/9 to CFA F69 million in 1960/1. In the case of FONADER, Table 11.7 shows an increase in the share of agricultural credits out of the FONADER budget, from CFA F250 million in 1973/4 to

CFA F2,796 million in 1979/80. In percentage terms, this is not significant, especially if one considers the fact that agriculture is only one of the purposes for which credit is advanced, since FONADER advances credit for other purposes such as personnel, equipment and subventions. As a percentage of the total budget, agricultural credit stands at 10 per cent for the period 1973/4 and 23 per cent for the period 1979/80. A substantial share of the budget went to financing inputs or equipment. Although inputs are considered by economists as a form of credit, their viability is highly dependent on several factors such as timing of supply and the vagaries of the weather. For example, if inputs are not delivered on time, yields are likely to be much lower and the farmer is unlikely to be able to service his loan.

The provision of bad loans is not only a characteristic of specialized farm credit institutions.[8] Commercial banks also exhibit this trait. In recent years, in order to resolve this problem, banks have devised contracts that provide strong incentives not to default, such as contracts in which the availability of credit at a later date depends on the borrower's previous performance. This, however, has the effect of creating what A. Okun calls a 'customer market' whereby particular borrowers are tied to particular lenders. In this respect, there may be classes of borrowers (such as small businesses, small farmers and average households) for whom denial of credit by 'their' bank has the effect of making credit inaccessible.

The problem of accessibility to credit in Cameroon is exacerbated by the fact that, in recent years, the liquidity of the banks has been under severe pressure. The public sector has always been the bank's main depositor. As the government's cash flow from oil has decreased steadily since 1986, it has been forced on several occasions to withdraw deposits lodged with the commercial banks by parastatals, such as the social security fund (Caisse Nationale de Prevoyance Sociale), national produce and marketing board (PMB) and housing association (Credit Foncier). It is estimated that the government in 1986 drew some CFA F60,000 million ($180 million to $210 million) in this way. Because of the liquidity shortage, smaller depositors, unable to have access to credit, would rather deposit their savings in the informal financial sector, particularly in the *Njangis*.

Table 11.6   Purpose of CCM credits, 1958–61

Year	Production credits (CFA F million)	Housing credits (CFA F million)
1958–1959	127	14
1959–1960	55	41
1960–1961	45	69
Total	227	124

Source: Illy (1978: 62)

Table 11. 7   FONADER budget and the share of agricultural credits (1973–80 in CFA F million)

Year	Budget	Agricultural credits	Percentage
1973–1974	2,487	250	10
1974–1975	3,870	910	23.5
1975–1976	4,661	1,289	27.5
1976–1977	6,037	1,819	30
1977–1978	9,218	2,401	26
1978–1979	11,530	2,468	21.4
1979–1980	14,460	2,796	23.9

Source: Ndongko (1985: 130)

Faced with this apparent crisis in the formal financial sector, the Cameroon government can no longer afford to cast aside these indigenous savings societies when formulating policies for mobilizing savings. *Njangis* have evolved in such a way that they are gradually filling in the gap created by commercial or state-owned banks. In the words of S. Haggblade, 'the *Njangis* are potentially a powerful force in terms of mobilizing local financial resources'. He notes that 'these societies are becoming larger and larger in terms of amounts loaned; they are coming more and more to resemble Western-style banks'.

The Sixth Five-Year Development Plan of Cameroon makes no mention of the country's segmented financial structure whereby the informal and the formal financial sectors operate independently of each other in terms of their clientele, mode of operation and interest rates.[9] With agriculture the cornerstone of the economy (contributing 22 per cent of the GDP in 1983/4), and the growing need to mobilize domestic savings (a need expressed by the President of the Republic when he stressed 'the desire to build an economy which is self-propelled and self-directed'), one would expect the Plan to recognize the growing potential of the informal financial sector (in particular that rural savings exist) and that market mechanisms are sometimes more effective than government intervention. The two worlds of financial institutions are juxtaposed; how both can best be utilized in the service of rural development becomes a question of vital concern.

As long as both financial sectors, informal and formal, continue to be rigidly separated, rural finance will be handicapped severely in its contribution to rural development. Linking the informal financial sector to the formal one seems to be the most promising approach, as it utilizes the institutional resources of both sectors.

At the United Nations Symposium on the Mobilization of Personal Savings in Developing Countries, held in Yaounde (Cameroon) in December 1984, it was agreed that an informal financial institution is more cost-effective than a formal financial institution. At the same time, the informal financial institutions leave the demand for large sums for long-term fixed investment unsatisfied. They generally disburse small amounts on a short-term basis. Informal financial institutions are easily accessible and the default rates are exceedingly low. But there is a consensus that they cannot make up for the dense network of modern institutions providing a wide range of financial services. This brings the conclusion that the main means of improving the performance of the non-institutional sector are policies directed to enhancing its links with the institutional financial sector.

One of the most innovative schemes that has emerged from such a linkage is the Loan Savings Scheme. From the experiences in Côte d'Ivoire, Togo, Nigeria and Congo, H. D. Seibel and M. T. Marx (1987) drew up a blueprint for the 'ideal' linkage:
1. The informal financial institution chooses an appropriate legal form.
2. It enters into a business relationship with a bank.
3. Liabilities of the association *vis-à-vis* the bank are regulated by the status and legal norms.
4. The association deposits its savings with the bank.
5. It obtains group loans for on-lending to its members.
6. The amount of credit is determined by the association's savings with the bank according to rules laid down in a loan savings scheme.
7. The association's savings serve as collateral with the bank.

The fundamental principle behind the Loan Savings Scheme is that loans are tied to savings, a relationship which provides incentives for continuing savings and for regular reimbursements. In recent years in Cameroon, there have been a few pilot projects, in rural areas especially, based on a similar scheme. In these cases, the linkage is between cooperatives and agricultural marketing boards, in which the 'check-off system' is practised whereby members of a cooperative may request that a certain amount of salary be deducted automatically each month and added to share savings. This linkage tends to be very strong in areas where both institutions are housed in the same building. A case in point is that in Jakiri, a rural town in Cameroon, where credit union members may take production loans against future sale of their export crop to the cooperative. At the end of the season, when the crop is sold, repayment of the loan is made by the cooperative to the credit union. In this case, it is a simple matter to request that savings be increased automatically by similar deductions. The main attraction of this linkage system lies in its flexibility, because it can be incorporated easily in a linkage between savings societies and banks or even credit unions and cooperatives. The results have been very encouraging. When total savings were calculated by V. DeLancey in 1983, for each member of either a credit union or a control group, it was found that credit union members had significantly greater savings than the control group members: 43 per cent of credit union members had savings of over CFA F100,000 ($300), whereas only 31 per cent of the control group did. Furthermore, while only 17 per cent of credit union members had CFA F25,000 or less in savings, 52 per cent of the control group did.

This encouraging result makes it all the more important that Cameroon should vigorously promote such schemes. It is a major step in the process of eliminating the dualistic nature of financial markets in the country. The implication of such schemes is that they could end up 'formalizing' or 'upgrading' the informal sector. Already, there has been one such case in Cameroon whereby a group of Cameroonian businessmen, in 1975, formalized their saving society by making it an official, chartered bank, financed with 95 per cent Cameroonian capital. What is even more interesting is the fact that it was the self-generated evolution of these rural savings societies, and not government intervention, that resulted in the formation of this bank, known as the Banque Unie de Credit. S. Haggblade notes that 'what the government has attempted to do in the rural sector, mould savings societies into accredited, chartered institutions, is coming to pass in the cities of its own accord'. This goes to show that if the government encourages schemes like the Loan Savings Scheme, there is a possibility of this leading to an evolutionary link-up, especially between the big savings societies and the institutional banking system. The Loan Savings Scheme could serve as a catalyst to this process.

Interest rate reform

Policies on the level and structure of interest rates have implications for monetary control and for savings mobilization and allocation. While the International Monetary Fund (IMF) programmes typically focus on the level of interest rates which reflect market conditions, reform of the interest rate structure increasingly receives more attention, because such reforms could help improve the allocation of credit.

Unfortunately, in the case of Cameroon, any action on interest rates is constrained by its membership of the Franc Zone. Interest rate policies are crucial to savings, investment and economic development. The uniform lending rate imposed by the two central banks (BCEAO and BEAC) ignores the diversity of economies of member countries in terms of size, markets, resources and overall level of economic development.[10] Although the cost of money is the same in every country in the Franc Zone, the rate of return on investment is bound to vary from one country to the next.

It should be noted, however, that although the discount rates are uniform, each country can, in principle, determine its final lending and deposit rates and apply preferential interest charges on important economic activities. In practice, the scope for interest rate differentials is limited. It is difficult to have an effective, independent interest rate policy in each country because of the potential for capital mobility within the Franc Zone. Moreover, adjustment to changes in international interest rates is prolonged due to necessary negotiations among all members. A case in point is that of Côte d'Ivoire where the lagging of the CFA rate behind the French rate contributed to undesirable early remittances of large expatriate salaries. In 1981, Côte d'Ivoire pushed for higher rates at the central bank (BCEAO) but was obliged by the Zone regulations to enforce the lower rate set by the Central Bank. In this respect, successful adjustment would require a faster and more flexible process of agreement on changes within the Zone once the necessity for the change becomes obvious.

6. Concluding Remarks

Cameroon has yet to reach the level of domestic savings required to permit necessary investment for rapid development. In addition to this basic difficulty, there are others arising from inefficient use of funds and unsatisfactory operation of financial institutions.

The insufficiency of savings can be ameliorated by a policy of ensuring that capital markets operate efficiently. This is what the Sixth Five-Year Development Plan of Cameroon strives to achieve. The plan recognizes that domestic savings must rise sufficiently rapidly to cover increased investment and also to compensate for the negative effects of declining foreign assistance.

It is difficult to increase saving capacity of the business sector, but there is some potential there. It is possible, however, that the savings of the informal financial sector can be raised significantly and can be channelled effectively into productive activities, with the co-operation of the formal financial sector.

There are, however, important shortcomings in the finance mechanism and in the institutions which channel savings into investment in Cameroon. Efforts to improve the efficiency of these institutions can have a very high rate of return and can make a significant contribution to solving the problems of financing development in Cameroon.

The point should not be overlooked that successful economic stabilization and development policies in Cameroon will depend, to a large extent, on the reforms carried out in the Franc Zone system.

Notes

1. The Franc Zone (FZ) is a monetary cooperation arrangement set up between France and her former colonies in West and Central Africa following the latter's independence in the early 1960s. The FZ system includes (1) France; (2) seven West African member states (Benin, Burkina Faso, Côte d'Ivoire, Mali, Niger, Senegal and Togo); (3) five Central African countries regrouped within the Bank of Central African States (BEAC) (Cameroon, Central African Republic, Chad, Congo and Gabon); and (4) The Federal Islamic Republic of Comoros which became a FZ member through the monetary cooperation agreement concluded with France on 23 November 1979.

   Since the African states' independence, the value of the CFA franc has remained fixed at 0.02 French francs (FF). Proponents of the FZ system are of the opinion that, in relation to the FF, the CFA franc enjoys the benefits of equivalency of currencies, freedom of transfers and unlimited transfers. The CFA franc is also argued to enjoy the benefit of free convertibility with the FF through the operations account mechanisms.

2. Under the Sixth Five-Year Development Plan, investment is projected to represent 21.5 per cent of the GDP in 1990/1, an average annual growth rate of 4.1 per cent. Gross savings will represent 23.37 per cent of GDP in the same period, an annual growth rate of 6.8 per cent.

3. According to the Sixth Plan, the target of an annual growth rate of 6.7 per cent for the GDP will bring about a similar growth in the gross available income which, having reached CFA F2,553,200 million in 1982/3, will increase to CFA F4,281,900 million in 1990/1.

4. Because of Cameroon's membership of the Franc Zone, capital movements between Cameroon and France, Monaco, and Operations Account countries are free of exchange control. Depending on family status, the transfer of 20 per cent to 50 per cent of the salary of a foreigner working in Cameroon is permitted upon

presentation of the appropriate pay voucher, provided that the transfer takes place within one month of the pay period concerned. Resident and non-resident travellers to countries of the French Franc area may, subject to prior declaration, take out any amount in bank notes issued by the BEAC.

5. According to Section 9 (2), foreign investors have the right to freely transfer to their countries of residence, profits 'in the currency in which they constituted the investment'.

6. *Njangi* is a rotating credit association defined as 'an association formed upon a core of participants who agree to regular contributions to a fund which is given in whole or in part to each member in rotation' (Ardener, 1964). An example of a simple *Njangi* is one with 12 members who meet once a month. At each meeting everyone pays a fixed amount, say CFA F1000, in dues to a total pool of CFA F12,000. At the January meeting, one member takes home the entire pool to spend as he sees fit. In each succeeding month, a different member takes the pool. By the end of the rotation in December, each member will have had one turn to collect the pool and, over the cycle, each member will have repaid these 12,000 CFA francs in the form of his 12 monthly payments.

7. FONADER (The National Fund for Rural Development) is a public establishment which was set up in 1973. It was reorganized in 1977 into a financing and credit establishment. It is expected to contribute to rural development particularly through agricultural credit. Its objectives were defined as follows: the distribution of agricultural credits; the financial management of specific funds placed at its disposal by the state or domestic and foreign financing bodies; the grant, if need be, of guarantees to loans accorded by commercial banks to certain intervention bodies in rural areas; the provision, with the Cameroon Development Bank and commercial banks, of joint financing for rural development.

8. Specialised Farm Credit Institutions are defined as government institutions or credit programmes which offer farmers loans but no other significant financial services. Many developing countries have such institutions and, among these, certain common problems consistently appear. These problems are seen in their faltering financial performance and limitations in their ability to provide an expanding array of services to an expanding number of clients.

9. Formal financial institutions include commercial banks, development banks, savings and credit banks, cooperative banks and cooperative credit unions or rural banks. Informal financial institutions include a variety of rotating and non-rotating savings and credit associations, which are indigenous financial self-help organizations, and individual financial brokers, among them deposit collectors and money-lenders.

Each of the two sectors has its particular strengths: formal financial institutions excel in modernity, in access to national and international refinancing and other supporting institutions, none of which applies to the informal institutions. Informal financial institutions excel in accessibility, popular participation, organized flexibility, local adaptability, situational appropriateness and socio-cultural integration at local or regional levels, none of which applies to formal financial institutions.

10. The BEAC holds 65 per cent of the foreign exchange reserves of member countries which are deposited in the operation account with the French Treasury through which the Bank's foreign exchange operations are conducted. In addition, in the case of foreign exchange shortfall, FZ members can draw on their operation account in unlimited amounts although subject to progressive interest charges up to the Bank of France rediscount rate and subject to monetary policies required by the Central Bank in order to counteract the imbalance.

References

Adams, D. W. (1978). 'Mobilizing household savings through rural financial markets', *Economic Development and Cultural Change*, Vol. 26, No. 3 (April).

Adams, D. W. (1981). 'Rural financial markets and income distribution in low-income countries', *Savings and Development*, Vol. 5.

Belassa, B. (1988). 'The lessons of East Asian development: an overview', *Economic Development and Cultural Change*, Vol. 36, No. 3 supplement, S273–S290 (April).

Blinda, A. S. and Stiglitz, J. E. (1983). 'Money, credit constraints and economic activity', *The American Economic Review*, Vol. 73, No. 2 (May).

Bouman, F. J. A. (1976). 'The *Djangi*, a traditional form of saving and credit in West Cameroon', *Sociologia Ruralis*, Vol. 16, Nos. 1/2.

DeLancey, V. (1977). 'Credit for the Common Man in Cameroon', *Journal of Modern African Studies*, Vol. 15.

DeLancey, V. (1978). 'Women at the Cameroon Development Corporation: how their money works', *Rural Africana*, New Series, No. 2.

DeLancey, V. (1988). 'The impact of the credit union movement on the production and accumulation in the agricultural sector of Cameroon', in *The Political Economy of Cameroon*, African Studies Centre, Leiden (1–4 June).

Gadway, J. F. (1986). 'The Cameroon Credit Union Development Project: 1986 baseline data survey' (17 March).

Haggblade, S. (1978). 'Africanization from below: the evolution of Cameroon savings societies into Western-style banks', *Rural Africana*, New Series, No. 2 (September).

Harlander, H. and Mezger, D. (1971) *Development Banking in Africa: Seven Case Studies*, Munchen, Germany.

Illy, Hans F. (1978). 'How to build in the germs of failure: credit cooperatives in French Cameroon', *Rural Africana*, No. 2.

Jackobeit, C. (1985). 'The CFA Franc Zone after 1975: burden or benefit for the African members?', *Afrika Spectrum*, Vol. 85, No. 3.

Kelly, A. C. (1988). 'Population pressures, saving and investment in the Third World: some puzzles', *Economic Development and Cultural Change*, Vol. 36, No. 3 (April).

Kharas, H. J. and Levinsohn, J. (1988). 'LDC saving rates and debt crises', *World Development*, Vol. 16, No. 7.

Martin, Guy (1986). 'The Franc Zone, underdevelopment and dependency in francophone Africa', *Third World Quarterly*, Vol. 8, No. 1 (January).

Miller, L. F. (1977). *Agricultural Credit and Finance in Africa*, Rockefeller Foundation, US.

Ministry of Planning and Regional Development (Cameroon) (1986). *The Sixth Five-Year Economic, Social and Cultural Development Plan (1986-1991)*, Cameroon (14 August).

Ndongko, W. A. (1977). 'The financing of economic development in Cameroon', *Africa Development*, Vol. 11, No. 3 (July–September).

Ndongko, W. A.(1985). *Economic Management in Cameroon: Policies and Performance*, Institute of Human Sciences, Cameroon.

Ndongko, W. A. (1986). 'The political economy of development in the Cameroon: relations between the state, indigenous business and foreign investors', in Schatzberg, M. G. and Zartman, I. W., (eds), *The Political Economy of Cameroon*.

Ro, Y. K. *et al.* (1981). 'Income instability and consumption-savings in South Korean farm households, 1965–70', *World Development*, Vol. 9.

Rowlands, M. (1988). 'The material culture of success: households and consumption in Bamenda', in *The Political Economy of Cameroon: Historical Perspectives*, Leiden (1–4 June).

Schiavo-Camp, S. *et al.* (1983). *The Tortoise Walk: Public Policy and Private Activity in the Economic Development of Cameroon*, AID Evaluation Special Study, No. 10 (March).

Seibel, H. D. (1986). 'Rural finance in Africa: the role of informal and formal financial institutions', *Development and Cooperation* (June).

Seibel, H. D. and Marx, M. T. (1987). *Dual Financial Markets in Africa: Case Studies in Linkages between Informal and Formal Financial Institutions*, Saarbrucken, 1987.

Snyder, D. W. (1974). 'Econometric studies of household saving behaviour in developing countries: a survey', *The Journal of Development Studies*, Vol. 10, No. 2 (January).

Villanueva, D. (1988). 'Issues in financial sector reform', *Finance and Development* (March).

von Pischke, J. D. (1979). 'Towards an operational approach to savings for rural developers', *Development Digest*, Vol. 27, No. 2 (April).

von Pischke, J. D. (1980). 'Pitfalls of specialized farm credit institutions in low-income countries', *Development Digest*, Vol. 18, No. 3 (July).

von Pischke, J. D.(1983). 'Selected successful experiences in agricultural credit and rural finance in Africa', *Savings and Development*.

Weiss, A. and Stiglitz, J. E. (1981). 'Credit rationing in markets with imperfect information', *American Economic Review*, Vol. 71, No. 3 (June).

World Bank (1987). *World Tables*, 4th Edition, Oxford.

World Bank (1988). *World Development Report*, Oxford.

Bibliography

Books and Journals

Abdel-Khalek, G. (1987). 'Egypt', World Institute for Development, Economic Research, Country Study No. 9, Helsinki.

Abdi, A. I. (1977). *Commercial Banks and Economic Development; The Experience of Eastern Africa*, Praeger, New York and London.

Adams, D. W. (1973). 'The case for voluntary savings mobilization; why rural capital markets flounder', *USAID Spring Review of Small Farmer Credit*, Vol.19.

— (1978). 'Mobilizing household savings through rural financial markets', *Economic Development and Cultural Change*, Vol. 26, No. 3 (April), pp. 547–60.

— (1981). 'Rural financial markets and income distribution in low income countries', *Savings and Development*, Vol. 5, pp. 105–13.

Aggrey-Mensah, W. (1982). 'Rural banks as instruments for mobilizing savings: a case study in Ghana', Second International Symposium on the Mobilization of Personal Savings in Developing Countries, Kuala Lumpur, Malaysia.

Agu, C. (1988). 'Interest rate policy in Nigeria and attendant distortions', *Savings and Development*, Vol. 12.

Akaah, I., Dadzie, K. and Dunson, B. (1987). 'Formal financial institutions as savings mobilizing conduits in LDCs: an empirical assessment based on the bank savings behaviour of Ghanaian farm households', *Savings and Development*, No. 2, pp. 115–36.

Baker, J. C., Abraham, J. A. and D'Mello, J. (1986). 'The bank/business relationship in a developing country: the Kenyan experience', *Foreign Trade Review*, Vol. 21, No. 2, pp. 123–34.

Balassa, B. (1988). 'The lessons of East Asian development: an overview', *Economic Development and Cultural Change*, Vol. 36, No. 3 (April), supplement, pp. S273–S290.

Baltensperger, E. (1972). 'Cost of banking activities – interactions between risks and operating costs', *Journal of Money, Credit and Banking*, Vol. 4 (August), pp. 595–611.

Bardhan, P. (1988). 'Alternative approaches to development economics', in Chenery, H and Srinivasan, T., (eds), *Handbook of Development Economics*, Vol. 1, Oxford, North-Holland, Amsterdam.

Bascom, W. R. (1952). 'The *Esusu*: a credit institution of the Yoruba', *Journal of the Royal Anthropological Institute*, Vol. 82, Part 1, pp. 63–70.

Bedard, G. *et al.* (1983). 'Argent "Chaud" et argent "Froid", la mobilisation de l'éspargne rurale par les institutions de type cooperatif et son impact sur le developpement', *Actes de L'Université Cooperative Internationale*.

Bell, C. (1988). 'Credit markets and interlinked transactions', in Chenery, H. and Srinivasan, T., (eds), *Handbook of Development Economics*, Vol. 1, Oxford, North-Holland, Amsterdam.

Benston, G. J. (1972). 'Economies of scale of financial institutions', *Journal of Money, Credit and Banking*, Vol. 4 (May), pp. 312–41.

Bhatia, R. J. and Khatkhate, D. R. (1975). 'Financial intermediation, savings mobilization and entrepreneurial development: the African experience', *IMF Staff Papers*, Vol. 22 (March), pp. 132–58.

Bhatt, V. V. (1986). 'Improving the financial structure in developing countries', *Finance and Development*, Vol. 23, No. 2 (June), pp. 20–2.

— and Meerman, J. (1978). 'Resource mobilization in developing countries: financial institutions and policies', *World Development*, Vol. 6, No.1.

Blinda, A. S. and Stiglitz, J. E. (1983). 'Money, credit and constraints and economic activity', *The American Economic Review*, Vol. 73, No. 2 (May), pp. 297–302.

Bottomley, A. (1975). 'Interest rate determination in underdeveloped rural areas', *American Journal of Agricultural Economics*, Vol. 54.

Bouman, F. J. A. (1976). 'The *ndjangi*, a traditional form of saving and credit in West Cameroon', *Sociologia Ruralis*, Vol. 16, Nos 1/2, pp. 103–19.

Bouman, F. J. A. and Houtman, R. (1988). 'Pawnbroking as an instrument of rural banking in the Third World', *Economic Development and Cultural Change*, Vol. 37, No. 1 (October), pp. 69–89.

Chalmers, R. (1972). *History of Currency in the British Colonies* (reprint), Vineyard Press, Colchester, Chapter 18.

Chandavarkar, A. G. (1971). *The Nature and Effects of Gold Hoarding in Underdeveloped Economies*, Oxford University Press, Oxford.

Chandavarkar, A. and Anand, G. (1977). 'Monetization of developing economies', *IMF Staff Papers*, Vol. 24, No. 3 (November), pp. 665–721.

Chenery, H. and Srinivasan, T. (1988). *Handbook of Development Economics*, Vol. 1, Oxford, North-Holland, Amsterdam.

Chenery, H. B. and Carter, N. G. (1973). 'Foreign assistance and development performance', *American Economic Review*, Vol. 63, No. 2, pp. 459–69.

Chimombe, T. (1981). 'The role of banks and financial institutions in the accumulation and reinvestment of capital in Zimbabwe,' unpublished M.Phil.

Clunies–Ross, A. (1989). 'Stabilization targets and instruments in developing countries', *Journal of Economic Studies*, Vol. 15, No. 2, pp. 1–74.

DeLancey, M. V. (1977). 'Credit for the Common Man in Cameroon', *Journal of Modern African Studies*, Vol. 15.

— (1978). 'Savings and credit institutions in rural West Africa'. Introduction: *Rural Africana*, New Series, No. 2. pp. 1–7.

— (1978). 'Women at the Cameroon Development Corporation: how their money works', *Rural Africana*, New Series, No. 2. pp. 9–33.

Dornbusch, R. (1982). 'Stabilization policies in developing countries: what have we learned?' *World Development*, Vol. 10, pp. 701–708.

Egger, P. (1986). 'Banking for the rural poor: lessons from some innovative saving and credit schemes', *International Labour Review*, Vol. 125, No. 4, pp. 447–62.

El–Nil, Y. S. (1986). 'Some important aspects of the structures and role of interest rates in Africa', *Association of African Central Banks Financial Journal*, Vol. 7, No. 1, pp. 1–71.

Fei, J. C. H. and Paauw, D. S. (1965).'Foreign assistance and self–help: a reappraisal of development finance', *Review of Economics and Statistics*, Vol. 47, No.3 (August), pp. 251–67.

Firth, R. (1964). 'Capital, savings and credit in peasant societies: a viewpoint from economic anthropology', in Firth, R. and Yamey, B. S., (eds), *Capital, Saving and Credit in Peasant Societies: Studies from Asia, Oceania, the Carribean and the Middle Americas*, Allen and Unwin, London.

Frimpong–Ansah, J. H. (1981). 'Monetary policy and development: The African experience', in *Monetary Theory and Policy in Africa*, African Centre for Monetary Studies, Dakar.

Fry, M. (1980). 'Saving, investment, growth and the cost of financial repression', *World Development*, Vol. 8, pp. 317–27.

— (1978). 'Money and capital or financial deepening in economic development', *Journal of Money, Credit and Banking*, November 1978, Vol. 10, No. 4, pp. 464–75.

Galbis, V. (1977). 'Financial intermediation in economic growth in less developed countries: a theoretical approach', *Journal of Development Studies*, Vol. 13, No. 2 (January), pp. 58–72.

Galletti, R., Baldwin, D. K. S. and Dina, I. O. (1956). *Nigerian Cocoa Farmers: An Economic Survey of Yoruba Cocoa Farming Families*, Oxford University Press for the Nigerian Cocoa Marketing Board.

Garlick, P. (1971). *African Traders and Economic Development in Ghana*, Clarendon Press, Oxford.

Gaudran, J. (1987). 'Ces milliards qui échappent a L'Afrique', *Jeune Afrique Economie*, No. 101 (November).

Gershenberg, I. (1972). 'Banking in Uganda since independence', *Economic Development and Cultural Change*, Vol. 20, No. 3 (April), pp. 504–23.

Ghatak, S. (1981). *Monetary Economics in Developing Countries*, Macmillan Press, London.

Giovannini, A. (1983). 'The interest elasticity of savings in developing countries: the existing evidence', *World Development*, Vol. 2, pp. 601–7.

— (1985). 'Saving and real interest rate in LDCs', *Journal of Development Economics*, Vol. 18, pp. 197–217.

Griffin, K. (1970). 'Foreign capital, domestic savings and economic development', *Oxford Institute of Economics and Statistics*, Vol. 32, No. 2 (May), pp. 99–112.

Gupta, K. L. (1970). 'Personal saving in developing nations: further evidence', *Economic Record*, Vol. 46, pp. 243–9.

— (1984). *Finance and Economic Growth in Developing Countries*, Croom Helm, London.

Haggblade, S. (1978). 'Africanization from below: the evolution of Cameroon savings societies into Western–style banks', *Rural Africana*, New Series, No. 2, pp. 35–55.

Harrod, R. F. (1948). *Towards a Dynamic Economics, Some Recent Developments of Economic Theory and their Application to Policy*, Macmillan, London.

Hart, K. (1970). 'Small-scale entrepreneurs in Ghana and developing planning', *Journal of Development Studies*, Vol. 6, No. 4 (July), pp. 104–20.

Haswell, M. R. (1963). *The Changing Pattern of Economic Activity in a Gambian Village*, HMSO, London.

Heller, P. (1975). 'A model of public fiscal behaviour in developing countries: aid, investment and taxation', *American Economic Review*, Vol. 65, pp. 368–79.

Hickok, S. and Gray, C. S. (1981). 'Capital market controls and credit rationing in Mali and Senegal', *Journal of Modern African Studies*, Vol. 19, No. 1 (March), pp. 57–74.

Higgins B. (1968). *Economic Development: Problems, Principles and Policies*, revised edition, Constable, London.

Hill, P. (1970). *Studies in Rural Capitalism in West Africa*, Cambridge University Press, London.

Hirschman A.O. (1958). *The Strategy of Economic Development*, Yale University Press, New Haven, London.

Hodgman, D. (1972). 'Selective credit controls', *Journal of Money, Credit and Banking* (May), pp. 342–59.

Hopkins, A. G. (1970). 'The creation of a colonial monetary system: the origins of the West African Currency Board', *African Historical Studies*, Vol. 3, No. 1.

Horioka, C. (1986). 'Pourquoi le taux d'éspargne prive est'il si éleve au Japon?', *Finances et Developpement*, Vol. 23, No. 4 (December), pp. 22–5.

Houthakker, A. S. (1965). 'On some determinants of savings in developed and under–developed countries', in Robinson, E. A. G., (ed.), *Problems in Economic Development*, Macmillan, London.

Hunt, D. (1972). 'The agricultural cooperative credit scheme', *East African Journal of Rural Development*, Nos. 1 & 2.

Ingham, B. M. (1981). *Tropical Exports and Economic Development*, Macmillan, London.

– (1987). 'Shaping Opinion on Development Policy in Africa. The Lewis and Seers and Ross Reports of the 1950s', *Manchester Papers on Development*, November.

Jacobeit, C. (1985). 'The CFA Franc Zone after 1975: burden or benefit for the African members?', *Africa Spectrum*, Vol. 85, No. 3, pp. 257–72.

Johnson, O. E. G. (1974). 'Credit controls as an instrument of development policy in the light of economic theory', *Journal of Money, Credit and Banking* (February), pp. 85–99.

Johnson, P. (1985). *Saving and Spending, The Working Class Economy in Britain, 1870–1939*, Clarendon Press, Oxford.

Johnston, J. (1984). *Econometric Methods*, McGraw Hill, London.

Kamajou, F. (1980). 'Subsidized interest rates and restricted agricultural credit in LDCs', *Savings and Development*, No. 2.

Kelly, A. C. (1988). 'Population pressures, saving and investment in the Third World: some puzzles', *Economic Development and Cultural Change*, Vol. 36, No.3 (April), pp.449–64.

Kharas, H. J. and Levinsohn, J. (1988). 'LDC saving rates and debt crises', *World Development*, Vol. 16, No. 7 (July), pp. 779–86.

Killick, T. (1981). *Policy Economics: A Textbook of Applied Economics on Developing Countries*, Heinemann Educational Books, London.

Leff, N. and Sato, K. (1980). 'Macroeconomic adjustment in developing countries: instability, short–run growth and external dependency', *Review of Economics and Statistics*, Vol. 62, pp. 170–9.

— (1975). 'A simultaneous equation model of savings in developing countries', *Journal of Political Economy*, Vol. 83, pp. 1217–28.

Leite, S.P. and Makonnen, D. (1986). 'Saving and interest rates in the BCEAO countries: an empirical analysis', *Savings and Development*, Vol. 10, pp. 219–32.

Levy, V. (1988). 'Aid and growth in sub–Saharan Africa: the recent experience', *European Economic Review*, Vol. 32 pp. 1777–95.

Lewis, W. A. (1944). *Machinery for Economic Planning in the Colonies*, Public Records Office, London.

— (1954). *Economic Development with Unlimited Supplies of Labour*, Manchester School of Economics and Social Studies (May).

— (1955). *The Theory of Economic Growth*, Allen and Unwin, London.

Martin, G. (1986). 'The Franc Zone, underdevelopment and dependency in francophone Africa', *Third World Quarterly*, Vol. 8, No. 1 (January), pp. 205–35.

Mauri, A. (1983). 'The potential for savings and financial innovation in Africa', *Savings and Development*, Vol. 4, pp. 319–37.

Mbat, D.O. (1985). 'Savings habit of rural households in Cross River State – an exploratory study', *Savings and Development*, Vol. 9, No. 4 , pp. 469–83.

McKinnon, R. (1973). *Money and Capital in Economic Development*, Brookings Institute, Washington DC.

Meltzer, A. H. (1967). 'Major issues in the regulation of financial institutions', *Journal of Political Economy*, Supplement, Vol. 75, No. 4 (August), Part II, pp. 482–501.

Miksell, R.F. and Zinser, J. (1974). 'The nature of saving function in developing countries: a survey of theoretical and empirical literature', *Journal of Economic Literature*.

Miracle, M., Miracle, D. and Cohen, L. (1980). 'Informal savings mobilization in Africa', *Economic Development and Cultural Change*, Vol. 28, No. 4 (July), pp. 701–24.

Mitchell, J. C. and Barnes, J. A. (1950). *The Lamba Village: Report of a Social Survey*, University of Cape Town, School of African Studies, New Series, No. 24, Cape Town.

Moshin, K. and Nadeem, U.H. (1987). 'La fuite des capitaux des pays en développement', *Finances et Développement*, Vol. 24, No. 1 (March).

Mosley, P., Hudson, J. and Horrell, S. (1987). 'Aid, the public sector and the market in less developed countries', *Economic Journal*, Vol. 97, pp. 616–41.

Musokotwane, S. (1985). 'Financial institutions and economic development in Zambia', Ph D dissertation, University of Constance.

Ndongko, W. A. (1977). 'The financing of economic development in Cameroon', *Africa Development*, Vol. 11, No. 3 (July–September), pp. 60–76.

— (1985). *Economic Management in Cameroon: Policies and Performance*, Institute of Human Sciences, Yaounde, Cameroon.

— (1986). 'The political economy of development in Cameroon: relations between the state, indigenous business, and foreign investors', in Schatzberg, M. G. and Zartman, I. W., eds, *The Political Economy of Cameroon*, Praeger, New York.

Nurkse, R. (1967). *Problems of Capital Formation in Underdeveloped Countries*, Oxford University Press, New York.

Nwabughuogu, A. I. (1984). 'The *isusu*: an institution for capital formation among the Ngwa Igbo: its origin and development to 1951', *Africa*, Vol. 54, No. 4, pp. 46–58.

Ofonagoro, W. I. (1979). 'From traditional to British currency in Southern Nigeria: analysis of a currency revolution, 1880–1948', *Journal of Economic History*, Vol. 39, No. 3 (September), pp. 623–54.

Okhawa, K., Ranis, G. and Meissner, L. (1985). *Japan and the Developing Countries: A Comparative Analysis*, Blackwell, Oxford.

Okorie, A. (1988). 'Rural banking in Nigeria: lessons from other developing countries', *Agricultural Administration and Extension*, Vol. 28, No. 2, pp. 147–60.

Olayemi, J. K. (1980). 'Food crop production by small farmers in Nigeria', in *Nigerian Small Farmers: Problems and Prospects in Integrated Rural Development*, Caxton Press W/A Ltd., University of Ibadan, Centre for Agricultural and Rural Development.

Papanek, G. L. (1972). 'The effect of aid and other resource transfers on savings and growth in less developed countries', *Economic Journal*, No. 327 (September), pp. 935–50.

Patrick, H. T. (1966). 'Financial development and economic growth in developing countries', *Economic Development and Cultural Change*, Vol. 24, No. 2, pp. 174–89.

Ro, Y. K. *et al.* (1981). 'Income instability and consumption–savings in South Korean farm households, 1965–1970', *World Development*, Vol. 9, No. 2 (February), pp. 183–92.

Rostow, W. W. (1971). *The Stages of Economic Growth: A Non-Communist Manifesto*, second edition, Cambridge University Press, London.

Saleem, S. T. (1987). 'On the determination of interest rates in rural credit markets: a case study from the Sudan', *Cambridge Journal of Economics*, Vol. 11, No. 2, pp. 165–72.

Schiavo–Camp, S. *et al.* (1983). *The Tortoise Walk: Public Policy and Private Activity in the Economic Development of Cameroon*, AID Evaluation Special Study, No. 10, March.

Seibel, H. D. (1986). 'Rural finance in Africa: the role of informal and formal financial institutions', *Development and Cooperation* (June), pp.12–14.

Seibel, H. D. and Marx, M. T. (1987). *Dual Financial Markets in Africa: Case Studies in Linkages between Informal and Formal Financial Institutions*, Saarbrucken.

Seidman, A. (1986). *Money, Banking and Public Finance in Africa*, Zed Books, London.

Shaw, E. (1973). *Financial Deepening in Economic Development*, Oxford University Press, Oxford.

Sideri, S. (1984). 'Savings mobilization in rural areas and the process of economic development', *Savings and Development*, Vol. 8, No. 3, pp. 207–16.

Snyder, D.W. (1974). 'Econometric studies of household saving behaviour in developing countries: a survey', *The Journal of Development Studies*, Vol. 10, No. 2 (January), pp. 139–53.

Stiglitz, J. (1987). 'The causes and consequences of the dependence of quality on prices', *Journal of Economic Literature*, Vol. 25, pp. 1–47.

Stiglitz, J and Weiss, A. (1981). 'Credit rationing in markets with imperfect information', *American Economic Review*, Vol. 71, No. 3 (June), pp. 393–410.

Suckling, J. (1975). 'Foreign investment and domestic savings in the Republic of South Africa, 1957–72', *South African Journal of Economics*, Vol. 43, pp. 315–21.

Taylor, L. (1983). *Structuralist Macroeconomics: Applicable Models for the Third World*, Basic Books, New York.

— (1988). *Varieties of Stabilization Experience*, Clarendon Press, Oxford.

Thingalaya, N. K. (1979). 'Mobilizing small savings in India', *Development Digest*, Vol. 17, No. 2 (April), pp. 24–34.

Tobin, J. (1984). 'On the efficiency of the financial system', *Lloyds Bank Review*, No. 153 (July), pp. 1–15.

Turok, B. (1981). 'Control in the parastatal sector of Zambia', *Journal of Modern African Studies*, Vol. 19, No. 3 (September), pp. 421–46.

Umo, J.U. (1981). 'Empirical tests of some savings hypotheses for African countries', *Financial Journal*, Vol. 2, ACMS, Dakar.

van Wijnbergen, S. (1982). 'Stagflationary effects of monetary stabilization policies – a quantitative analysis of South Korea', *Journal of Development Economics*, Vol. 10, No. 2, pp. 133–69.

— (1983). 'Interest rate management in LDCs', *Journal of Monetary Economics*, Vol. 13, pp. 433–52.

Villanueva, D. (1988). 'Issues in financial sector reform', *Finance and Development*, Vol. 25, No. 1 (March), pp. 14–17.

Virmani, A. (1986). 'The determinants of savings in developing countries: theory, policy and research issues', *World Bank Discussion Paper*, Report No. DRD 186.

von Pischke, J D. (1983). 'Selected successful experiences in agricultural credit and rural finance in Africa', *Savings and Development*, Vol. 7, No. 1, pp. 21–44.

— (1979). 'Towards an operational approach to savings for rural developers', *Development Digest*, Vol. 17, No. 2 (April), pp. 3–11.

— (1980). 'Pitfalls of specialized farm credit institutions in low–income countries', *Development Digest*, Vol. 18, No. 3 (July), pp. 79–91.

von Pischke, J. D., Adams, D. W. and Donald, G. (1983). *Rural Financial Markets in Developing Countries. Their Use and Abuse*, World Bank, Baltimore.

Wai, U. Tun (1957). 'Interest rates outside the organized money markets of underdeveloped countries', *IMF Staff Papers*, November.

Wai, U. Tun and Hughes, P. T. (1973). 'Stock and bond issues and capital markets in less developed countries', *IMF Staff Papers*, Vol. 20. pp. 253–317.

Warren, J. (1977). 'Savings and the financing of investment in Ghana', in Newlyn, W. T., (ed.), *Financing of Economic Development*, Clarendon Press, Oxford.

Williamson, J. (1983). *The Open Economy and the World Economy, A Textbook in International Economics*, Basic Books, New York.

Williamson, J. G. (1968). 'Personal saving in developing nations: an intertemporal cross section from Asia', *Economic Record*, Vol. 44, pp. 194–210.

Woo, S. (1985). 'Financial development and economic growth: international evidence', *Economic Development and Cultural Change*, Vol. 34, pp. 333–46.

Yao, F. (1986). 'Capital markets and resource mobilization in Africa', *Association of African Central Banks Financial Journal*, Vol. 7, No. 2, pp. 52–83.

Zaidi, I. M. (1985). 'Saving, investment, fiscal deficits and the external indebtedness of developing countries', *World Development* , Vol. 13, No. 5 (May), pp. 573–88.

Discussion Papers, Reports and Official Publications

ADB (1987). *Domestic Resource Mobilization in Africa*, Abidjan, January.

ADB/ECA (1987). *Economic Report on Africa, 1987*, Abidjan and Addis Ababa, March.

ADB/ECA (1987). *Economic Report on Africa*.

Aggrey–Mensah, W. (1982). 'Rural banks as instruments for mobilizing savings: a case study of Ghana', *Second International Symposium on the Mobilization of Personal Savings in Developing Countries*, Kuala Lumpur, Malaysia.

Auguste, D. (1973) 'La mobilization de l'ésparne pour le developpement rural en Afrique', *Communication au Deuxieme Congrès du Credit Agricole*, Milan, September.

Bouman, F. J. A. (1977). 'Indigenous savings and credit societies in the Third World – any messages?', Conference on Rural Finance Research, San Diego.

Buiter, W. (1988). 'Some thoughts on the role of fiscal policy in stabilization and structural adjustment in developing countries', London School of Economics, Centre of Labour Economics, Paper No. 321.

CEAC (1946). *Agricultural Credit in the Colonies*, Report of the Finance Sub-Committee, Colonial Office (46) 74.

Chambre d'Agriculture de Côte d'Ivoire (1987). 'Les caisses rurales d'épargne et de prets dix ans après', Colloque sur L'Épargne à Yamoussokro, 23–25 November.

Chartered Institute of Bankers, Uganda (1988). Summary Report on Financing of the Economic Recovery Programme of Uganda.

FAO (1986). 'Savings mobilization for agricultural and rural development in Africa', paper presented at the *Third International Symposium on the Mobilization of Personal Savings in Developing Countries*, held at Yaounde, Cameroon, 10–24 December 1984, United Nations.

Frimpong-Ansah, J. H. (1987). 'Professor Sir W. Arthur Lewis – a patriarch of development economics', Salford University Discussion Papers in Economics, No. 87–8.

— (1988). 'Some problems of managing and financing of economic development in Africa. An overview' (ADB/ACMS Symposium, Kinshasa, November 1987), Salford University Discussion Papers in Economics, No. 88–3.

German Development Institute (GDI) (1981). *Mobilization of Personal Savings in Zimbabwe through Financial Development*, Berlin.

Green, R. H. (1981). '*Magendo* in the political economy of Uganda: pathology, parallel system or dominant mode of production?', University of Sussex, Institute of Development Studies, Discussion Paper No. 164, August.

IBRD (1985). 'Uganda's Progress Towards Recovery and Prospects for Development', June..

IDRC (1986). 'Financial savings, government spending for production activities and macro-economic adjustment in Malawi', by Chipeta, Kaluma, Khonyongwa and Mkandawire, Macro-economic Workshop, Harare, November.

Lancaster, D. and Williamson, J. (1986). *African Debt and Financing*, Institute for International Economics, Special Report No. 5, Washington DC.

Muser, A. (1986). 'Mobilization of personal savings through self–help promotion Institutions', paper presented at the *Third International Symposium on the Mobilization of Personal Savings in Developing Countries*, held at Yaounde, Cameroon, 10–14 December 1984, United Nations.

OAU/ECA (1986) 'Africa's submission to the UN', Special Session on the Critical Economic Situation in Africa, 27–31 May, 13th Special Session, Agenda Item 6.

Quaidoo Report (1957). Report of the Committee on Agricultural Indebtedness, Government Printer, Accra.

Salami, K. A. (1986). 'Analysis of the role and operation of formal agricultural lending institutions in Ghana', research paper, Institute of European Finance, University of North Wales.

Seibel, H. D. and Marx, M. (1986). 'Mobilization of personal savings through cooperative societies or indigenous savings and credit associations: case studies from Nigeria', paper presented at the *Third International Symposium on the Mobilization of Personal Savings in Developing Countries*, held at Yaounde, Cameroon, 10–14 December 1984, United Nations.

UNCTAD (1987). *Trade and Development Report, 1987*, United Nations.

UNICEF (1986). *The State of the World's Children*, Oxford University Press, New York, Oxford.

World Bank (1988). *World Development Report 1988*, Oxford University Press, New York, Oxford.

The African Centre
for Economic Policy Research
(ACEPOR)

Preamble

Despite the widely acknowledged economic potentials of the African continent, it continues to trail behind the rest of the world in development. Economic gains that were made during the first decade of political independence seem to be receding on all fronts. Indeed, most predictive studies of Africa's structures tend to reach some pessimistic conclusions about its fortune in both the medium and long terms.

One of the reasons why development efforts and policies have stalled can be traced to the limited knowledge of the complexities of African economies. Africa remains perhaps the most under-researched continent. The consequence is that some of the policies and programmes that have worked in certain environments may fail to repeat their success in the African context. There is therefore an urgent need for an African-led economic research focus to strengthen indigenous research capability as well as complement the policy initiatives from outside the region.

The African Centre for Economic Policy Research (ACEPOR) is aimed at creating a centre of excellence in economic research scholarship for filling part of this gap.

Objectives

ACEPOR's objectives include the following:
1. Identify areas of priority in economic policy needs and set up appropriate machinery for carrying out such research.
2. Disseminate research findings through technical and non-technical publications and news media to the African policy community, private sector and international organizations.
3. Bring together, at appropriate intervals, African experts, scholars, policy-makers and experienced persons of wisdom, African and non-African, to exchange ideas on African development problems through symposia, seminars and conferences.
4. Carry out a continent-wide survey of economic policy studies from time to time with a view to drawing the attention of the African policy community to some significant findings.
5. Publish ACEPOR and other relevant research findings through ACEPOR bulletins, journals and books.

6. Carry out an entrepreneurial search for funds to sponsor both specific and paid mission-oriented researches in Africa, and for their publication.
7. Encourage African and non-African experts and scholars to sustain research interest in African economic issues through collaborative individual, institutional and multi-disciplinary efforts.
8. Undertake all appropriate actions to promote any or a combination of the above objectives.

Organizational Structure

ACEPOR adopts a simple organizational structure that emphasizes flexibility and cost-effectiveness. It is therefore structured with the following functional elements:

1. *A Board of Governors* made up of eminent Africans and non-Africans with distinguished records of contribution to African thought and development. The Chairman of the Board is a person with a demonstrated deep and sincere commitment to African economic scholarship and its functional application.
2. *A Director* who serves as the executive head of the Centre on a full-time basis.
3. *A Registrar and supporting staff* dealing with finance, a computer library, conferences and publications.
4. *Programme Directors (Honorary)* who are eminent economists in relevant areas where the Centre decides to focus research attention. Their number varies with the size of the research agenda at any given period. Programme Directors are not resident officers of the Centre and serve for two years, with renewal.
5. *A Senior Fellow and Fellows*, selected from distinguished African social scientists in the academic and policy communities. Fellows form an ACEPOR network, are designated by particular research agendas and are expected to contribute to research and publication in their respective subjects in order to retain membership of the Centre. Senior Fellows should be eminent members appointed to carry out specific research projects for ACEPOR or retired Programme Directors with distinguished records of contribution.

Location and Affiliations

ACEPOR's operating headquarters should be located in sub-Saharan Africa. To the extent that its financial resources will permit, it will maintain working relations with as many African and non-African centres of excellence as possible.

Funding

ACEPOR is a private (non-government) charity organization and depends on:
Grants, donations and endowments from the following sources for its programmes:
    African governments, pan-African and regional institutions,
    Private sector organizations and individual donors,
    Multilateral institutions and agencies,
    Non-governmental organizations,
    Non-African governmental organizations,
    Fellowship fees, and
Internal fund-generating activities through prudent management of its resources, sales of publications, and research contracts on subjects related to the Centre's agenda.

Programme Focus

The broad areas under which specific topics of applied research concern will be identified include:
1. The Economics of African Development
2. Macro-economic and Public Policy Management
3. Micro-economic Studies
4. Trade and Exchange Policies
5. Human Resource Management
6. Political Economy

Founding Fellows

The following Africans and non-Africans were present at the Workshop on Capacity Building in Sub-Saharan Africa in Dakar, 3–5 November 1986, at which the idea of the Centre was first endorsed, and at the Symposium on Capacity Building in Nairobi, 1–3 August 1988, when the above statutes were approved. The list also includes others who have contributed to the development of the idea of the Centre:

Dr E. Y. Ablo, World Bank Mission, Kampala, Uganda
Professor O. Aboyade, PAI Associates International, Ibadan
Alhaji A. Ahmed, Governor, Central Bank of Nigeria
Dr K. Alipui, Minister of Finance, Republic of Togo
Dr Henry Akuoko-Frimpong, Ghana Institute of Management (GIMPA)
Professor George Benneh, University of Ghana
*Dr J. H. Frimpong-Ansah, African Policy Research Company, Accra
Dr James Funna, former Governor, Bank of Sierra Leone
Professor K. Gyekye, University of Ghana
*Professor Olukenle Iyanda, University of Lagos
Professor Tony Killick, Overseas Development Institute, London
Professor Anne Krueger, Duke University
Professor S. O. Kwasa, Moi University
Dr M. W. Makramalla, Economic Commission for Africa
Dr Allechi M'Bet, National University of Côte d'Ivoire
*Professor Alfred C. Mondjanagni, Pan-African Development Institute, Douala
*Dr Essam Montasser, IDEP, United Nations, Dakar
Mrs Theresa Moyo, University of Zimbabwe
Dr K. J. Moyana, Governor, Reserve Bank of Zimbabwe
Mr Harris Mule, Public Policy Consultant, Nairobi
Dr Andrew Mullei, African Centre for Monetary Studies
Dr S. Musokotwane, University of Zambia
*Dr Patrick Ncube, National Commission for Development Planning, Lusaka
Mr Phillip Ndegwa, former Governor, Central Bank of Kenya
Dr Alassane D. Ouattara, Central Bank of West African States, Dakar
Dr Philip Quarcoo, IDEP, United Nations, Dakar
*Dr D. Rwegasira, African Development Bank, Abidjan
Dr Joseph Semboja, University of Dar es Salaam
Dr Germina Ssemogerere, Makerere University
Dr John Stremlau, Rockefeller Foundation, New York
*Dr A. B. Taylor, International Monetary Fund, Washington DC
Dr Mamoudou Toure, International Monetary Fund, Washington DC
Dr S. Tekle-Tsadik, IDEP, United Nations, Dakar
Professor J. Umo, University of Lagos
Dr Dunstan Wai, World Bank, Washington DC

* Members of Coordinating Committee

Index